Romantic Poetry and the Fragmentary Imperative

Romantic Poetry
and the
Fragmentary Imperative

Schlegel, Byron, Joyce, Blanchot

Christopher A. Strathman

State University of New York Press

Published by
State University of New York Press, Albany

© 2006 State University of New York

For information, address State University of New York Press,
194 Washington Avenue, Suite 305, Albany, NY 12210-2384

Production by Judith Block
Marketing by Anne M. Valentine

Library of Congress Cataloging-in-Publication Data

Strathman, Christopher A.
  Romantic poetry and the fragmentary imperative : Schlegel, Byron, Joyce,
Blanchot / Christopher A. Strathman.
    p. cm.
  Includes bibliographical references and index.
  ISBN 0-7914-6457-1 (alk. paper)—ISBN 0-7914-6458-x (pbk. : alk. paper)
    1. European poetry—19th century—History and criticism.
2.   European poetry—18th century—History and criticism.
3. Romanticism—Europe.   4. Schlegel, Friedrich von, 1772-1829—
Knowledge—Literature.   5. Blanchot, Maurice.   I. Title.

PN1261.S72 2005
809.1'9145—dc22   2004054169

10 9 8 7 6 5 4 3 2 1

For Lyle and Bernie Strathman

Contents

It is a widely held belief that modern literature is characterized by a doubling-back that enables it to designate itself; this self-reference supposedly allows it both to interiorize to the extreme (to state nothing but itself) and to manifest itself in the shimmering sign of its distant existence. In fact, the event that gave rise to what we call "literature" in the strict sense is only superficially an interiorization; it is far more a question of a passage to the "outside": language escapes the mode of being of discourse—in other words, the dynasty of representation—and literary speech develops from itself, forming a network in which each point is distinct, distant from even its closest neighbors, and has a position in relation to every other point in a space that simultaneously holds and separates them all. Literature is not language approaching itself until it reaches the point of its fiery manifestation; it is, rather, language getting as far away from itself as possible. And if, in this setting "outside of itself," it unveils its own being, the sudden clarity reveals not a folding-back but a gap, not a turning back of signs upon themselves but a dispersion. The "subject" of literature (what speaks in it and what it speaks about) is less language in its positivity than the void language takes as its space when it articulates itself in the nakedness of "I speak."

—Michel Foucault

Acknowledgments

It is a pleasure to acknowledge those who have read parts, or the whole, of this book over the years. I am especially grateful to Jerry Bruns, Greg Kucich, Al Neiman, Steve Watson, Ewa Ziarek, and Krzysztof Ziarek, who guided this project in its earliest stages at Notre Dame. Andy Auge, Chris Fox, Steve Fredman, Aaron Halstead, Dan Hoolsema, John Matthias, and Jay Walton offered encouragement, support, and timely advice. My colleagues at Baylor, particularly my friends in the English department and in the Baylor interdisciplinary core course, have exhibited patience and kindness at every turn. Wallace Daniel, Dean of the College of Arts and Sciences, supported my work in the form of two summer sabbaticals. Stephen Prickett renewed my faith in irony and the fragment, while Kevin Hart graciously allowed me to see his Blanchot book in manuscript.

Part of chapter 2 first appeared as "Schlegel's Ironic Hermeneutics," in *Arachné: An Interdisciplinary Journal of Language and Literature*, Vol. 2, No. 1 (1995): 77–104. As a Golda Meir Postdoctoral Fellow at the Hebrew University of Jerusalem, I read part of chapter 3 for an English Department Staff Seminar. I am grateful to Lois Bar-Yaacov, Larry Besserman, Andrew Burrows, Natasha Krilova, John Landau, Daphne Leighton, Judy Levy, Shlomit Steinberg, Leona Toker, and especially Elizabeth Freund for making my year in the Holy Land an unforgettable experience. Ralph Berry and Bruce Krajewski read an early draft of the book and offered excellent advice. The readers at SUNY Press offered valuable suggestions, and Judith Block, Katy Leonard, Anne Valentine, and James Peltz guided the book through production with otherworldly patience. Finally, I owe my family, especially my parents, more than I can say. I dedicate the book to them with love and gratitude.

Setting Out: Toward Irony, the Fragment, and the Fragmentary Work

Could a historiographer drive on his history, as a muleteer drives on his mule,—straight forward;—for instance, from *Rome* all the way to *Loretto*, without ever once turning his head aside either to the right hand or to the left,—he might venture to foretell you to an hour when he should get to his journey's end;—but the thing is, morally speaking, impossible: For, if he is a man of the least spirit, he will have fifty deviations from a straight line to make with this or that party as he goes along, which he can no ways avoid. He will have views and prospects to himself perpetually soliciting his eye, which he can no more help standing still to look at than he can fly. . . .

—Laurence Sterne

The purpose of this book is to inquire into a conception of poetry that emerges with special clarity and force during the second half of the eighteenth century. This conception comes into particularly clear view in the 1790s in both German literary theory and English literary practice, although such a distinction between theory and practice is problematic as romantic theory is very much informed by early modern European, especially English, practice.[1] As it happens, this conception finds its most compelling articulation in Friedrich Schlegel's notion of "romantic poetry [*romantische Poesie*]," his call for a new and highly self-conscious literary work that embodies the fractured, decentered consciousness of ancient philosophical dialogue.[2] Historically, this conception originates in the loosening of medieval Christendom's grip on European culture and the emergence of vernacular literatures, especially ones written in Romance languages, out from under the rock of a comparatively monolithic cultural paradigm. In fact, there is perhaps no single work more influential for the formulation of Schlegel's conception of romantic poetry than Laurence Sterne's late-eighteenth century shaggy dog of a novel, *The Life and Opinions of Tristram Shandy, Gentleman* (1759–67), a text that repeatedly dissolves clear-cut distinctions between Latin and the vernacular, high and low styles of English, and religious and secular discursive registers.[3] The critic Richard Lanham has gone so far as to describe Sterne as "a profound philosopher in—and of—the comic mode," while *Tristram Shandy* has inspired poets and novelists from Byron and Carlyle to Flaubert and Mallarmé to Joyce and Beckett.[4] One reason for the book's lasting appeal is that it effectively dismantles traditional Aristotelian poetics, which hinges upon a distinction between form and content, with a display of linguistic anarchy that underwrites one of the premises of this book: that one can read *Tristram Shandy* as a point of origin for what Schlegel calls romantic poetry, or "the romantic genre [*Dichtart*]" (*KA* 2:183; *LF* 175).

Romantic poetry in this sense is a hybrid genre that moves unpredictably back and forth between theory and practice; it exhibits both philosophical and literary, narrative and lyrical dimensions, and it contains both transparent and opaquely self-critical moments. In *The Literary Absolute*, their influential study of German romantic literary theory, Philippe Lacoue-Labarthe and Jean-Luc Nancy articulate this tension in a useful way by describing the dialectical relationship between the fragmentary work and the fragment per se:

> This fragmentary essence of the dialogue has at least one consequence (among several others that we cannot explore here), namely that dialogue, similar in this to the fragment, does not properly constitute a genre. This is why the dialogue, like the fragment, turns out to be one of the privileged sites for taking up the question of genre as such.[5]

At issue here is the genealogy of a supergenre (a genre squared or raised exponentially to the next highest power) predicated on a rethinking of poetry, which has its origins in the novel's displacement of the epic and the simultaneous recognition of the tremendous generic potential inherent in novelistic dialogue. The question of modern poetry, particularly the novel and its relationship to ancient epic and tragic poetry, is a question that is pursued in detail by several eminent theorists, including György Lukács, Mikhail Bakhtin, and Julia Kristeva.[6] And yet it is not simply a question of how to think about the novel.

What is at stake in such a conception of romantic poetry is the status of the old quarrel between philosophy and poetry, which Socrates, in Plato's *Republic*, already regards as ancient. In fact, romantic poetry can be understood as a rethinking of Socratic dialogue based on the assumption that Plato is a quasi-philosophical poet concerned with arriving at the genre most appropriate for (or adequate to) thinking.[7] It is equally a rethinking starting with the thought that modern poetry, or literature, should acknowledge an intimate relationship between philosophy and poetry, a relationship that nevertheless remains unfulfilled. "The whole history of modern poetry," Schlegel says in *Critical Fragment* 115, "is a running commentary on the following brief philosophical text: all art should become science and all science art; poetry and philosophy should be made one" (*KA* 2:161; *LF* 157). At the same time, Schlegel cautions in *Critical Fragment* 103: "many a work of art whose coherence is never questioned is, as the artist knows quite well himself, not a complete work but a fragment, or one or more fragments, a mass, a plan" (*KA* 2:159; *LF* 155). The romantic work thus navigates a precarious passage between knowledge and skepticism, system and fragment, narrative and lyric, and history and language without collapsing into the form of either one or the other. The aim is not so much to reach a settlement as to make one's way to the limits of the opposition itself—and perhaps go beyond it—in response to the claim of what remains unthought in thinking. At its most forceful and most provocative, the fragmentary work of romantic poetry opens onto the domain of ethics and questions literature's relation to moral life.

In his own way, Sterne follows the example of Socrates, and reintroduces the possibility that there is a way out of the endgame of goal-oriented thinking, a passage to the outside, as it were. Consider the following passage from the author's preface to *Tristram Shandy*, in which Sterne speaks directly to the terms of the quarrel. "I now enter directly upon the point," he writes:

> ———Here stands *wit*,———and there stands *judgment*, close beside it, just like the two knobbs I'm speaking of, upon the back of this self same chair on which I'm sitting.
> ———You see, they are the highest and most ornamental parts of its *frame*,———as wit and judgment are of *ours*,———and like them too, indubitably both made and fitted to go together, in order as we say in all such cases of duplicated embellishments,———*to answer one another*. (*TS* 163)

Like the chair, constructed in such a way as to balance two opposing knobbs, signifying wit and judgment (or, as the romantics interpret it, irony), the romantic work operates by way of a signal tension between a bold intuitive leap and the subsequent questioning that inevitably follows. The romantic work accomplishes its design by opening a rift between narrative exposition and lyrical digression, working less to imitate the external appearance of the world than to embody the dramatic event of the world's innermost, revealing and concealing, play.

Sterne goes on to insist that wit and judgment, far from being self-indulgent diversions of the overcritical mind:

> are the most needful,—the most priz'd,—the most calamitous to be without, and consequently the hardest to come at,—for all these reasons put together, there is not a mortal amongst us . . . does not wish and stedfastly resolve in his own mind, to be, or to be thought at least master of the one or the other, and indeed of both of them, if the thing seems any way feasible, or likely to be brought to pass. (*TS* 164)

Sterne makes it abundantly clear that human life, as well as the life of the work of art, depends upon one simultaneously following these two paths. But what Sterne's preface also points to, what marks its dismantling of such commonplace notions as balance between and antithesis of wit and judgment, is the suggestion that such opposing forces persistently generate more questions than anyone can ever possibly hope to answer, and that "if he is a man of the least spirit, [the writer or interpreter] will have fifty deviations from a straight line to make with this or that party as he goes along, which he can no ways avoid" (*TS* 32).

The exigency or imperative of a work of this sort stems from this two-handed state of affairs. Such a dialogue originates in the desire to mediate between wit and judgment (or irony), ancient and modern, classical and romantic, and traditional and experimental. That is, the fragmentary work of romantic poetry also speaks to legitimate concerns about the narrative structure of myth and history. The interesting thing, however, is that the opposition between wit and irony, unlike the opposition between wit and judgment, is never quite symmetrical; rather, it exhibits a remainder that leaves one exposed to that which calls for further thought. As a consequence of this asymmetry between wit and irony, romantic poetry can be figured as a kind of reciprocal interplay between two modes of discourse that have the capacity to generate new progeny. Schlegel's novel *Lucinde* is predicated on this idea: "A great future beckons me to rush deeper into infinity: every idea opens its womb and brings forth innumerable new births" (*KA* 5:10; *LF* 46–47). "The genre of the fragment," observe Lacoue-Labarthe and Nancy, "is the genre of generation" (*LA* 49). It may be that this is what distinguishes the romantic from the post-romantic fragment, as Maurice Blanchot thinks of it. For Blanchot, "fragmentary writing [*l'écriture fragmentaire*]" is not so much a form of generation as it is a form of endurance, survival, way-making, or, as I prefer to think of it, passage.[8] In any case, the twin dimension of the work places the reader under an obligation to answer the call to make a beginning out of the work and, furthermore, to keep moving. It is an invitation to traverse the world with the humility of a desert thinker or an exile rather than a debater (who, after all, desires to win) or an officially anointed poet laureate. What is interesting about this exigency, desire, or will is that it does not originate from inside the subject but from somewhere outside, from the world itself, or from whatever it is that supports the world and allows it to come into being. It is as if this desire or demand issues from the world as a desire to be understood or acknowledged. One might call this, using Lacoue-Labarthe and Nancy's words (appropriated from Blanchot), "the fragmentary exigency" or, as I prefer, "the fragmentary imperative [*l'exigence fragmentaire*]" (*LA* 39).

The fragmentary imperative underwrites much of what usually counts as romanticism. If it initiates romanticism's obsession with fragments and ruins, however, it also exceeds such a concern to anticipate some of the most compelling writing of the twentieth century, especially as these works are explicitly grounded on the exigency of the fragment or fragmentary writing. In fact, Blanchot makes it possible to read romanticism as mediating an inverted or backward-looking Socratic dialogue to the nineteenth and twentieth centuries. "It could be said," Lacoue-Labarthe and Nancy argue, "that this is precisely what the romantics envisage as the very essence of literature: the union, in satire (another name for mixture) or in the novel (or even in Platonic dialogue), of poetry and philosophy, the confusion of all the genres arbitrarily delimited by ancient poetics, the interpenetration of the ancient and the modern, etc." (*LA* 91). But the Socrates whose dialogue is in question here is the ironic, fragmentary, many-sided Socrates of the *Symposium* rather than the conceptual, systematic, hyperrational Socrates of the more philosophical dialogues. It is the Socrates who carries inside himself the rhetorical example of Homer's Odysseus, a wily, skillful, persistent, clever man of many turns, and a forceful reminder of an even more ancient, pre-Socratic way of life.[9] In any case, in keeping with this more rhetorical and less philosophical form of life, the romantics rethink dialogue as a genre-beyond-genre, or, better, a genre-without-genre, a genre composed of bits and pieces of all of the other genres but somehow more (and less) than merely the sum of these parts. "All the classical poetical genres," Schlegel writes in *Critical Fragment* 60, "have become ridiculous in their rigid purity" (*KA* 2:154; *LF* 150). Just so. The romantics open poetics to the possibility of being more than the classification of the genres and at the same time situate it along a fault line between poetry and philosophy; this line exposes philosophical narrative to the threat of the revolution of poetic language in a way that calls into question philosophy's own way of knowing.

Not the product of a poetics in the Aristotelian sense, romantic poetry owes more to Socrates (refracted through the figure of Odysseus) than to the idea of tragedy as the imitation of a human action of a certain magnitude. In fact, it is profoundly non-Aristotelian, calling into question the primacy of plot over character and especially language. "As the 'classical' description of [literary practice]," Robert Langbaum long ago noted, "Aristotle's *Poetics* has much to teach us about modern literature, just because it so illuminatingly *does not apply*."[10] If Langbaum overstates his case, he also makes an important point. Rather than looking to Aristotelian metaphysics for its bearings, romantic poetry looks back through Plato and Socrates to pre-Socratic writing, the tragic chorus, and Homer, while at the same time looking forward to Nietzsche, Heidegger, and the twentieth-century avant-garde. Moreover, the Schlegel brothers' invention of the opposition between Apollonian and Dionysian impulses anticipates not only Nietzsche's discussion of tragedy in *The Birth of Tragedy from the Spirit of Music* but also Heidegger's reflections on the work-being of art in his lectures published as "The Origin of the Work of Art":

> In setting up a world and setting forth the earth, the work is an instigation of this striving. This does not happen so that the work should at the same time settle and put an end to the conflict in an insipid agreement, but so that the strife may remain a strife. Setting up a world and setting forth the earth, the work accomplishes this striving. The work-being of the work consists in the fighting of the battle between world and earth.[11]

Like the origin of the work of art in the interminable strife of earth and world, romantic poetry exhibits both a worldly and earthly dimension. Its wit opens the possibility of a world of understanding while its ironic judgment withdraws this possibility before it can be cognitively grasped and subsumed within the order of knowledge.

One can think of Sterne's novel as setting to work an ongoing strife between moments of self-disclosure and self-concealment. Sterne's work balances itself precisely, if precariously, between nothing, or non-being, and being; it struggles to facilitate the emergence of the one from out of the other. Possibly no other nothing in western culture resonates so deeply as the nothing that opens Sterne's great novel.[12] The question the novel sets for itself is both prescient and profound: how to make a beginning out of nothing? As Tristram knows, however, beginnings are delicate matters and one should "duly consider how much depends upon what [one is] doing [before one attempts such a thing]" (*TS* 5). Accordingly, conversation swirls around the expectation of the birth of the hero of the story, Tristram himself. The book begins with the comedy of the hero's ill-timed conception:

> *Pray, my dear*, quoth my mother, *have you not forgot to wind up the clock?*——*Good G—!* cried my father, making an exclamation, but taking care to moderate his voice at the same time,——*Did ever woman, since the creation of the world, interrupt a man with such a silly question?* Pray, what was your father saying?——Nothing. (*TS* 6)

This passage is telling. It is charged not only with Mrs. Shandy's interruption of her husband but also with Tristram's own self-interruption. Such continuous self-interruption is a responsibility for—responsiveness to—the exigencies of the subject matter in question—to thought itself. As a result, such fragmentary work remains perpetually unfinished, incomplete, unsettling, and a challenge to the limits of philosophical ways of knowing. At the same time it is thoughtful work that continues working at the limits of rationality by virtue of its worklessness or *désoeuvrement*.

For Blanchot, incompletion as worklessness indicates that the working of the work of art is not exhausted in the achievement of an end or a goal but drifts outside the economy of means and ends to remain unfinished, or better, unsettled. This unsettling dimension of the fragmentary work is the aspect of the work that refuses to be exhausted by the logic of metaphysical dualism. Instead, such work demonstrates that (as Blanchot reminds us in *The Infinite Conversation*), "at whatever time, one must be ready to set out, because to go out [*sortir*] (to step outside [*aller au dehors*]) is the exigency from which one cannot escape if one wants to maintain the possibility of a just relation."[13] Here one senses that Blanchot is responding to Plato's insistence in the *Republic* that the political requirements of the just regime necessarily call poetry into question; for his part, Blanchot turns the tables on Plato and makes the fragmentary imperative foundational for justice. Here, too, the peculiarly ethical edge of the fragmentary work clearly announces itself: in the exigency of stepping outside the opposition of philosophy and poetry. The idea of making a beginning, of setting out or stepping outside (oneself or one's assumptions), borders on the ethical; it opens onto unregulated ethical regions of life; it opens up one's capacity for stepping outside one's own world view in response to the claim of an other.

Irony: Deconstructive, Romantic, and Otherwise

Many of the issues at stake here can be traced to one of the watershed texts in the history of studies in romanticism, Paul de Man's "The Rhetoric of Temporality."[14] Now, as is well known, this essay constitutes de Man's attempt to demystify the language of presence established by Coleridge in his definition of the symbol in *The Statesman's Manual* by insisting on the radical discontinuity between words, things, and meanings. "This is a structure shared," de Man argues:

> by irony and allegory in that, in both cases, the relationship between word and meaning is discontinuous, involving an extraneous principle that determines the point and manner in which the relationship is articulated. (209)

What de Man tries to do, using rhetorical figures such as metonymy and synecdoche, is extend the disjunctiveness of irony and allegory so that it might apply to literary language generally. "But this important structural aspect [the discontinuity between word and meaning]," contends de Man, "may well be a description of figural language in general" (209). Thus de Man replaces the continuity of word and meaning, which characterizes the symbol, with the discontinuity of irony and allegory. Moreover, de Man creates an opening for an investigation such as this one, when in the second half of the essay he turns to the problem of figurative language and begins to speculate on its connection to a specific genre, in this case, the novel.

> The tie between irony and the novel seems to be so strong that one feels tempted to follow Lukács in making the novel into the equivalent, in the history of literary genres, of irony itself. . . . [Nonetheless,] the

correlation between irony and the novel is far from simple. Even the superficial and empirical observation of literary history reveals this complexity. The growth of theoretical insight into irony around 1800 bears a by no means obvious relationship to the growth of the nineteenth-century novel. . . . It could be argued that the greatest ironists of the nineteenth century generally are not novelists: they often tend toward novelistic forms and devices—one thinks of Kierkegaard, Hoffmann, Mallarmé, or Nietzsche—but they show a prevalent tendency toward aphoristic, rapid, and brief texts (which are incompatible with the duration that is the basis of the novel), as if there were something in the nature of irony that did not allow for sustained movements. (210–11)

Here de Man opens a window onto the question of the genre of romanticism or romantic poetry without choosing to climb through it. Instead, he develops a theory of poetic discourse as rhetoric (in Nietzsche's sense) which will dominate his later career. But de Man's reflection on the difficulty of identifying irony with a genre bears directly on the origin of what Schlegel calls romantic poetry. Already present in de Man's speculations is the ambiguity of the generic form of the romantic work: its tendency to refuse settlement in either a purely narrative or lyrical literary space and to shuttle back and forth between autobiographical indulgence in English-speaking writers and more theoretically motivated self-effacement in Danish-, French-, and German-speaking writers. So de Man identifies something remarkable about the wit and irony of romantic poetry that puzzles him from the outset: its characteristic back-and-forth or reciprocal interplay between theory and practice.

The critical debate during the 1980s between Anne Mellor and Jerome McGann emerged in part as a dispute concerning their different responses to de Man, to this essay in particular and, more generally, to de Man's project as a whole. Though both Mellor and McGann question de Man's method, their views on what might count as an alternative initially remained far, even worlds, apart. Mellor initiated the exchange by opening her controversial study, *English Romantic Irony*, with remarks explicitly critical of de Man.[15] In her book, Mellor argues that de Man focuses too exclusively on the destructive energies of romantic-era discourse at the expense of its creative energies. By contrast, she insists on a balance:

In this sense, the romantic ironist must be sharply distinguished from modern deconstructors. A radical demystifier like Paul de Man subjects all linguistic discourse to skeptical analysis and rejects poetic symbolism . . .

In so doing, de Man arbitrarily privileges one form of literary discourse, the allegorical, over another, the symbolic. In other words, modern deconstructors choose to perform only one half of the romantic-ironic operation, that of skeptical analysis and determination of the limits of human language and consciousness. But the authentic romantic ironist is as filled with enthusiasm as with skepticism. He is as much a romantic as an ironist. (5)

As an alternative, Mellor proposes the paradigm of English romantic irony, both a philosophical world-view and an informing literary mode of consciousness. Mellor claims that, unlike the downward spiral that results from the temporal predicament of ironic consciousness, English romantic irony acknowledges a more open-ended and flexible dimension of romantic-era writing. Basing her study on a paradigm derived from Schlegel, and also somewhat from Hume, Mellor counters de Man's emphasis on the destructive power of irony by offering a discussion of its more creative, liberating, and enabling energies. In doing so, Mellor makes large claims for the romantic-ironic way of knowing; she describes it as "a mode of consciousness or a way of thinking about the world that finds a corresponding literary mode [in English romantic irony]" (24). Moreover, romantic-ironic consciousness represents a way of thinking that "can potentially free individuals and even cultures from totalitarian modes of thought and behavior" (188).

Unwilling to let this go unchallenged, McGann took strong exception to Mellor's paradigm of English romantic irony.[16] In some pointed remarks in *The Romantic Ideology* McGann reads Mellor's model as a recuperation of the humanistic framework famously articulated by M. H. Abrams. Mellor's interpretation of ironic romanticism, as McGann sees it, represents "a significant alteration of Abrams' position rather than an alternative to it. At the heart of both lies an emphasis upon the creative process of Romanticism, both in its forms and dominant themes" (22). For McGann, Mellor refuses to acknowledge the dark side of romanticism, the more agonizing and troubling side of irony addressed by Søren Kierkegaard. "Mellor secularizes [Abrams'] model," McGann argues,

by introducing the elements of Romantic skepticism, but she does so only to the point where such skepticism does not 'turn from celebration to desperation.' No agonies are allowed into her romantic world which is, like Abrams', a good and happy place: a place of enthusiasm, creative process, and something ever more about to be. (27)

Although McGann himself remained wary of Kierkegaardian irony, his criticism of Mellor nonetheless rings true: in her eagerness to identify a more positive dimension to romantic-era writing and move beyond the impasse of deconstruction, Mellor neglects the dark side of romantic skepticism.

Upon further reflection it becomes clear that the critical object of McGann's criticism is really de Man and, ultimately, Nietzsche, especially his critique of hide-bound historicism in the essay, "On the Advantage and Disadvantage of History for Life." Viewed in such a light, McGann's point of entry into the conversation becomes easier to understand, if no less strident and uncompromising. Moreover, he is adamant about reinforcing the importance not just of history, but more precisely, of historical difference. "Works of the past are relevant in the present," McGann writes, "precisely because of this difference [between the past and present]" (2). "[T]he past and its works," McGann adds,

> should be studied by a critical mind in the full range of their pastness—
> in their differences and their alienations (both contemporary and histor-
> ical). To foster such a view of past works of art can only serve to increase
> our admiration for their special achievements and our sympathy for
> what they created within the limits which constrained them—as it were,
> for their grace under pressure. (2)

However, it is hard to know what kind of sympathy McGann is talking about here, as he claims to study works of the past with "a critical mind in the full range of their pastness." My sense is that it's closer to a mourner's condolences than the sympathy or *Einfühlung* of authentic historical understanding. This is why McGann's historical method looks more like a continuation of Nietzschean suspicion than a rejection of it. From a distance, the interpreter may speak about the past but should not be effected, or effectively situated by it in Gadamer's sense of historically-effected consciousness.[17] This is, as Gadamer puts it, "the consciousness effected in the course of history and determined by history, and the very consciousness of being thus effected and determined" (*TM* xxxiv). McGann seems to be of one mind with Gadamer on the question of the historicality of understanding, but what McGann misses (and Gadamer wants to explore more fully) is precisely the truth-value of the disagreement, or discrepancy, between the present and the past. That is, historical difference need not be appropriated and used as grounds for critique so much as articulated in order to acquire a better, more balanced, understanding.

Marjorie Levinson, more or less following McGann, pursues the question of the relationship between language and history in *The Romantic Fragment Poem*. In this book, she produces a series of readings in which romantic fragment poems are situated within historical contexts of their production and reception. Levinson argues that by focusing on the romantic fragment poem she aims to advance

> a corrective to the concealed and insidious formalism which reifies the conceptual aura surrounding literary works and installs that hypostasis as the essence, cause, or meaning of the work. . . . More simply, the exercise is to pry apart the poem's special maneuvers and projections from the totalizing constructs in which criticism, in great good faith and obedient to the rhetoric of the poetry, has framed them.[18]

Levinson argues that an insidious formalism frames romantic era writing within the false terms of idealistic humanism. This kind of criticism, Levinson says, is "downright appropriative" (11). She writes, furthermore, that "[w]hat sustained commentary there is [on "the Romantic fragment poem"] can best be described as *expressive-essentialist, or zeitgeist* critique" (8, emphasis mine). As her examples of this kind of critique, she offers book length studies by Thomas McFarland and Edward Bostetter. "The former develops the fragment as a vehicle for the symbolization of a cultural theme," according to Levinson, "while the latter represents it as an unfortunate and extrinsically induced deformation of structural intention. The work's unfinishedness is, on the one hand, presented as the source of its poetry, meaning, and value and, on the other, as inimical to the work's formal and conceptual realization" (13). According to Levinson, what is missing from both is (a) an awareness of the material conditions obtaining at the time of the writing of these works and the production of the books or journals in which they first appeared, and (b) an appreciation of the reception history of the particular works under discussion.

McFarland, in the book Levinson mentions, *Romanticism and the Forms of Ruin*, finds himself, like Mellor and McGann, responding to de Man's reading of romantic period poetic rhetoric. Rather than engaging in critique, however, McFarland emphasizes what he calls the diasparactive awareness of romantic-era discursive forms, particularly in Wordsworth and Coleridge.[19] He couches his own readings of poems by Wordsworth and Coleridge in a sense that Heidegger's thought affords a more effective overall framework or horizon for thinking about these sorts of fragmented modalities:

> Incompleteness, fragmentation, and ruin—the diasparactive triad—are at the very center of life. The phenomenological analysis of existence reveals this with special clarity. Heidegger's twin conceptions of *Geworfenheit* (the sense of being hurled into reality, broken off) and *Verfallen* (the sense within life of its continuing ruin) are ineradicable criteria of existence. In truth, the largest contention of this book can be rendered by Heidegger's formulation that 'in existence there is a permanent incompleteness (*ständige 'Unganzheit'*), which cannot be evaded.' (5)

To the extent that he follows Heidegger's lead in rethinking the role of the aesthetic in raising the question of truth, McFarland is certainly not indulging in expressive-essentialist criticism, as these are precisely the middle-class aesthetic values Heidegger rejects, for example, in his lectures, "The Origin of the Work of Art." McFarland presses this thought, observing: "The cultural iconology of Wordsworth and Coleridge is mirrored in that of Romanticism itself. Incompleteness, fragmentation, and ruin—*ständige Unganzheit*—not only receive special emphasis in Romanticism but also in a certain perspective seem actually to define that phenomenon" (7).

Allow me to take up once more de Man's essay, "The Rhetoric of Temporality," for it is here that some of the most promising hints as to the meaning of the irony of the fragmentary work of romantic poetry surface. In a brilliant rhetorical move, de Man turns from Schlegel to Baudelaire in his discussion of irony and ironic consciousness; from this turn, everything else he has to say about irony arguably follows.

> Thus freed from the necessity of respecting historical chronology, we can take Baudelaire's text, "*De l'essence du rire*" ["On the Essence of Laughter,"] as a starting point. Among the various examples of [laughter-provoking] ridicule cited and analyzed, it is the simplest situation of all that best reveals the predominant traits of an ironic consciousness: the spectacle of a man tripping and falling into the street. (211)

Here de Man draws attention to the notion of "*dédoublement* as the characteristic that sets apart a reflective activity" and notes the "reflective disjunction" of ironic consciousness that then follows (212–13). But what de Man deems most important for his critical discussion, and what he will never allow the reader to forget, is that irony is a special sort of existential or ontological falling. "More important still," de Man writes:

> in Baudelaire's description the division of the subject into a multiple consciousness takes place in immediate connection with a fall. The element of falling introduces the specifically comical and ironic ingredient. At the moment that the artistic or philosophical, that is, the language-determined, man laughs at himself falling, he is laughing at a mistaken, mystified assumption he was making about himself. . . . As a being that stands upright . . . man comes to believe that he dominates nature, just as he can, at times, dominate others or watch others dominate him. This is, of course, a major mystification. The Fall, in the literal as well as the theological sense, reminds him of the purely instrumental, reified character of his relationship to nature (213–14).

de Man constructs a remarkable context within which to review the question of the central importance of irony and the fragment for modern literature. It is a passage that demands to be studied more closely, but for now let us attend to de Man's use of the trope of falling to describe ironic or fragmentary consciousness. Such a consciousness is characterized by its inevitable slippage, by virtue of its dependence upon language and its exposure to temporality, into a state of inauthenticity.

What is most striking about McFarland's invocation of Heidegger is the light it sheds on de Man's understanding of Heidegger's conception of *verfallen* or, literally, decay, ruin, decline or dilapidation, a difficult-to-translate concept found throughout his philosophical work, *Being and Time*.[20] On the surface, it means simply to fall or to be falling. This is evidently how de Man understands it: even to an extreme, as though one is forever falling down the empty elevator shaft of temporality. But what complicates things is that there is already a German word for falling: *fallen*. Macquarrie and Robinson include several footnotes in their translation that are instructive. First, they observe that "[t]hough we shall usually translate [*verfallen*] simply as 'fall', it has the connotation of deteriorating, collapsing, or falling down. Neither our 'fall back upon' nor our 'falls prey to' is quite right: but 'fall upon' and 'fall on to', which are more literal, would be misleading for '*an . . . zu verfallen*'; and though 'falls to the lot of' and 'devolves upon' would do well for '*verfällt*' with the dative and other contexts, they will not do so well here" (*BT* 42 n.2). Second, in a note to Heidegger's discussion of "a kind of Being which we interpret as falling," Macquarrie and Robinson confess that "[w]hile we shall ordinarily reserve the word 'falling' for '*Verfallen*' . . . in this sentence it represents first '*Verfallen*' and then '*Fallen*', the usual German word for 'falling'. '*Fallen*' and '*Verfallen*' are by no means strictly synonymous; the latter generally has the further connotation of 'decay' or 'deterioration', though Heidegger will take pains to point out that in his own usage it 'does not express any negative evaluation' " (*BT* 172 n1). A third note, in connection with Heidegger's discussion of *verfallen* and *geworfenheit* also seems germane to the discussion: "While we follow English idioms by translating '*an die "Welt"* ' as 'into the "world" ' in contexts such as this, the preposition 'into' is hardly the correct one. The idea is rather that of falling at the world or collapsing against it" (*BT* 220 n1). Finally, a note in connection with Heidegger's discussion of Hegel's conception of time: "Through this section it will be convenient to translate Hegel's verb 'fallen' by 'fall', though elsewhere we have largely pre-empted this for Heidegger's '*verfallen*' " (*BT* 480 n1). Taken together, these notes suggest there is considerable connotative latitude, or play, in the word *verfallen* that de Man's usage in "The Rhetoric of Temporality" collapses into a single "fall." Moreover, *verfallen* finally suggests more of an ontological or existential mood that obtains in general, rather than a discrete or specific event which might result in a fall. *Verfallen* is, understood this way, a sort of ontological context or horizon for existence.

By contrast, Joan Stambaugh renders *verfallen* as both falling prey and entanglement. In an endnote to her translation of *Being and Time*, she observes, "*Verfallen*, is, so to speak, a kind of "movement" that does not get anywhere" (*JS* 403). This suggests, rather than a literal falling down, a kind of way-making that prefigures and is much more consistent with Heidegger's usage in the later writings on language and poetry to describe a kind of thinking that is "on the way [*unterweg*]." What kind of progress is this? de Man reads it consistently in a negative or unfavorable way, as slipping or falling—even though Heidegger insists explicitly that *verfallen* "does not express any negative value judgment" (*SZ* 174; *JS* 164). Reading McFarland's introductory commentary with de Man's essay in mind, one senses that de Man reads (or thinks with) Heidegger too much in English or, perhaps better to say, forecloses his understanding of *verfallen* on a single meaning of the word (which one is tempted to call *fallen*) and thereby restricts its connotative resonances within Heidegger's original text.[21] The German word *verfallen* doesn't so much indicate falling as fragmentation, dilapidation, ruination or decay, which McFarland rightly picks up on in his introduction, translating it as "the sense within life of its continuing ruin." This "sense within life of its continuing ruin," like Blake's invisible worm, remains in the work to be thought through.

Here one might usefully invoke Walter Benjamin's writings on art, technology, language and history to mediate between de Man and McGann and to build on McFarland's account of the forms of ruin within romanticism. A happy coincidence is that Benjamin's writings became deeply important to de Man at exactly the time of his writing of "The Rhetoric of Temporality." Particularly in his early study, *The Origins of German Tragic Drama*, Benjamin develops the apparatus of allegory and the critique of the symbolic de Man later borrows for use in his well-known essay. In this astonishing work, Benjamin investigates the mourning-play as the forerunner of romantic era fragmentation and ruin: "It is not possible to conceive of a starker opposite to the artistic symbol . . . than this amorphous fragment which is seen in the form of allegorical script. In it the baroque reveals itself to be the sovereign opposite of classicism, as which hitherto, only romanticism has been acknowledged. . . . Both, romanticism as much as baroque, are concerned not so much with providing a corrective to classicism, as to art itself."[22] At the same time, Benjamin understands the mourning-play not as a weakening or corruption of, but as an inventive modernist break from, classical Greek tragedy.

Additionally, in the "Theses on the Philosophy of History," written during the late 1930s but only published posthumously, Benjamin gestures toward a notion of history which accommodates features of both McGann's and Levinson's views without succumbing to their assumptions concerning historical progress—the idea, for example, that we need to shake off a romantic ideology in favor of a new and improved ideological present. In the "Theses," Benjamin unceremoniously criticizes this naive faith in historical progress: "The concept of the historical progress of mankind cannot be sundered from the concept of its progression through a homogenous, empty time. A critique of the concept of such a progression must be the basis of any criticism of the concept of progress itself."[23] Heidegger's discussion of temporality in *Being and Time* is an obvious point of reference here; a neo-Marxist notion of historical progress, that is, getting ourselves beyond the false ideologies of the past, is only possible within a naive understanding of the concept of time. In any case, the epigraph from the very next fragmentary thesis comes from Karl Kraus which, turning history on its ear, reads, "Origin is the goal." "History," Benjamin writes, "is the subject of a structure whose site is not homogenous,

empty time, but time filled by the presence of the now [*Jetztzeit*]"
(261). Furthermore:

> to Robespierre ancient Rome was a past charged with the times of the
> now, which he blasted out of the continuum of history. The French Rev-
> olution viewed itself as Rome reincarnate. It evoked ancient Rome the
> way fashion evokes costumes of the past. Fashion has a flair for the top-
> ical, no matter where it stirs in the thickets of long ago; it is a tiger's leap
> into the past. This jump, however, takes place in the arena where the rul-
> ing class gives the commands. The same leap in the open air of history is
> the dialectical one, which is how Marx understood the revolution. (261)

One would like to know the extent to which Benjamin's idea of a tiger's
leap parallels Heidegger's notion of the origin of the work of art. It's an
intriguing possibility. The work of art unsettles the past and originates
something new. It finds a new origin or opening in the past by means
of the work of the work of art. Geoffrey Hartman's recent essay on
Benjamin, "Walter Benjamin in Hope," underlines this more complex
dimension in Benjamin's view of history: "[Benjamin]," Hartman says,
"refuses to place hope exclusively in the future, or to proceed as if the
past were transcended—nothing but inert, ruined choirs. He talks less
of faith or love than of that more revolutionary virtue, hope, which refuses to leave even the dead undisturbed. Like Scholem, who restored
the neglected Kabbalah to high profile, the true historical thinker addresses the past—or has the past address us, like the dead at Ther-
mopylae from whom Demosthenes kindles an eloquent adjuration."[24]
Here I follow Hartman in reading Benjamin as a thinker who refuses
to proceed as if the past were transcended, as if the past had nothing
more to teach us than the fatuous lesson of the superior perspective of
the present.

As it turns out, McGann comes round to a version of this idea. The
epigraph from his subsequent book, *The Beauty of Inflections*, is borrowed from Benjamin's "Theses on the Philosophy of History," and it
presumably takes a step beyond a more or less naive historical materialism. Moreover, in one of the most interesting essays on the question of
literary history to appear in recent years, "History, Herstory, Theirstory,
Ourstory," McGann specifically addresses the problematic intersection
of irony and historical understanding.[25] In this remarkable piece,
McGann steps back from critique to acknowledge poetry's capacity to
unsettle material, historical determinations of truth and meaning. In a
provocative shift, McGann situates poetry's work against the rhetorical
or contextual power traditionally ascribed to hermeneutics but more

recently appropriated by historical materialism: "These poetical orders," McGann writes:

> increase one's sense of the incommensurability of facts, events, and the
> networks of such things. . . . Poetry, in this view of the matter, does not
> work to extend one's explanatory control over complex human materials
> (an operation which, as we know, purchases its control by delimiting the
> field of view); rather, poetry's function is to "open the doors of percep-
> tion," and thereby to reestablish incommensurability as the framework
> of everything we do and know. In this sense poetry is a criticism of our
> standard forms of criticism. (201–02)

McGann acknowledges poetry's unsettling force with respect to its historical contexts or material conditions, and he identifies poetry with a
self-critical impulse that places it firmly alongside the kind of writing
that the romantics describe. More to the point, such a description of poetry comes remarkably close to Blanchot's articulation of what he calls
the worklessness [*désoeuvrement*] of the work or art. For Blanchot, this
means that the work of art refuses assimilation into the world of cause
and effect, means and ends, and remains other with respect to the productive logic of labor and discourse. This sense of the work as an unsettling overture asks to be read in at least three overlapping senses: (1) as
an introductory but unfinished sketch in which a work first appears; (2)
as an opening marking the fascinating threshold of the in-between; and
(3) as an obligation issued on behalf of what remains for thinking. In
other words, Blanchot is attempting to mediate between the well-
known fragmentary work of the romantics and the impossible claim of
the Other traced by Lévinas over the course of his reassessment of the
Greek philosophical impulse in the light of Jewish scriptural tradition.[26]

The Essential Ambiguity of the Fragmentary Work

Philippe Lacoue-Labarthe and Jean-Luc Nancy go a long way toward
mediating continental thought for English-speaking readers of romantic poetry; their use of Heidegger, Benjamin and Blanchot to articulate an argument concerning the German romantic theory of literature
offers the promise of a more generic way of reading romantic-era
texts in the wake of the huge influence Derrida, de Man, and Foucault had on literary study. In a sense, it opens up the possibility of
thinking about romanticism as de Man thought of it, but without his
commitment to Nietzsche's rhetoric of signs.[27] Lacoue-Labarthe and

Nancy step back from Nietzsche's understanding of rhetoric as a system of signs in order to maintain that:

> romanticism implies something new, the *production* of something entirely new. The romantics never really succeed in naming this something: they speak of poetry, of the work, of the novel, or . . . of romanticism. In the end, they decide to call it—all things considered—*literature*. . . . They, in any case, will approach it explicitly as a new *genre*, beyond the divisions of classical (or modern) poetics and capable of resolving the inherent ("generic") divisions of the written thing. Beyond divisions and all de-finition, this *genre* is thus programmed in romanticism as *the* genre of *literature*: the genericity, so to speak, and the generativity of literature, grasping and producing themselves in an entirely new, infinitely new Work. The *absolute*, therefore, of literature. (*LA* 11)

Lacoue-Labarthe and Nancy insist that the fragmentary exigency represents something different from the instrumentality of Aristotelian poetics, something new on the literary-cultural horizon—namely, the invention of a new kind of writing, call it literature, or literature-as-such (literature as self-determined, apart from what philosophers would like to make [of] it). Recall that romanticism, according to Lacoue-Labarthe and Nancy:

> inaugurates another "model" of the "work." Or rather, to be more precise, it sets the work to work in a different mode. This does not mean that romanticism is the "literary" moment, aspect, or register of "philosophical" idealism, or that the inverse would be correct. The difference in the setting-to-work—or, as one could just as well say, the difference in *operation*—between Schelling and the [romantics] . . . does not amount to the difference between the philosophical and the literary. Rather, it makes this difference possible. It is itself the internal difference that, in this moment of *crisis*, affects the thought of the "work" in general (moral, political, or religious as well as artistic or theoretical). (*LA* 39)

Romanticism thus alters the very mode of being of the work of art, its very identity, one might even say. That is, it doesn't just reflect (i.e., mimetically) the difference between philosophy and poetry, but rather, "it makes this difference [in the setting-to-work between philosophy and poetry] possible." At stake in the work is no longer the work's reflection of the world it represents but rather the very nature of representation, the nature of the work of art, itself.[28]

Lacoue-Labarthe and Nancy's influential reading of the fragmentary work of *romantische Poesie* builds decisively on Blanchot's critical work on the early German romantics and on Nietzsche, and on fragmentary writing generally. In fact, Blanchot's critical conversations with Bataille, Lévinas, and others get to the heart of what this study is about: the question of whether romantic poetry and fragmentary writing retreat into some kind of transhistorical linguistic idealism, or whether by contrast, their linguistic density is better understood to offer a kind of passage (or, even more explicitly, *pas*-sage) outside the dualism of self and other and into an unsettled and unsettling region Blanchot by turns calls the outside or the neutral. For Blanchot, this neutral zone is precisely a space that remains undetermined by the oppositions of self and other, philosophy and poetry, identity and difference, male and female, idealism and materialism, and conservative and radical. It is a space of non-self-identical exteriority where what counts for thinking is less the capacity for making apodictic judgments, either for or against, than the requirement to keep oneself open and moving on. One can think of the outside or the neutral as an unmapped region beyond the grasp of traditional metaphysics opened, or just indicated, by romantic poetry and its not-so-distant cousin, fragmentary writing. The attraction of the region of the neutral is in maintaining the possibility of another kind of relation, a not yet determined relation or a relation to be determined later, a relation without relation that hints at forms of subjectivity other than those determined by what has so often been construed as the opposition between subject and object.

Consider once more de Man's insistence on the relentless falling structure of ironic consciousness. By contrast, Blanchot finds in early German romanticism, and in the fragmentary imperative generally, something very different, something more akin to what the mythic poet Orpheus experienced standing on a precarious ledge between the contiguous realms of being and non-being as he watched his beloved Eurydice slowly move away from him back down into the darkness of the underworld. In the essay, "The Athenaeum," Blanchot writes about early German romantics as though they are the long lost children of Orpheus:

> One can indeed say that in these texts we find expressed the non-romantic essence of romanticism, as well as all the principal questions that the night of language will contribute to producing in the light of day: that to write is to make (of) speech (a) work, but that this work [*oeuvre*] is an unworking [*désoeuvrement*]; that to speak poetically is to make possible a non-transitive speech whose task is not to say things

(not to disappear in what it signifies), but to say (itself) in letting (it-self) say, yet without taking itself as the new object of this language without object . . . (*EI* 524; *IC* 357)

Blanchot describes a work that is also an unworking or workless work; a work that speaks but then withdraws itself from the world leaving only a trace of its truth behind in what has been said. Such a description throws our attention back onto the "I" of the poet who speaks. Blanchot writes:

> The "I" of the poet, finally, is what alone is important: no longer the poetic work, but poetic activity, always superior to the real work, and only creative when it knows itself able to evoke and at the same time to revoke the work in the sovereign play of irony. As a result, poetry will be taken over not only by life, but even by biography: hence the desire to live romantically and to make even one's character poetic—that character called "romantic," which, moreover, is extremely alluring inasmuch as character is precisely what is lacking in that it is nothing other than the impossibility of being anything determined, fixed, or sure. (*EI* 524; *IC* 357)

Blanchot, like de Man, is concerned with working toward an under-standing of the role of language within the modern, fragmentary work of art, and also the question of subjectivity vis-à-vis this connection be-tween language and work. As Blanchot notes, for romanticism the infi-nitely productive subjectivity of the poet is what now matters: "no longer the poetic work, but poetic activity, always superior to the real work, and only creative when it knows itself able to evoke and at the same time to revoke the work in the sovereign play of irony."

But, unlike de Man, who construes romantic-era discourse in terms of falling within the horizon of temporality, Blanchot construes the movement of romantic-era writing laterally or horizontally, as way-making or traversal. In "Wittgenstein's Problem," Blanchot focuses on just this aspect of poetic discourse, calling it "the enigma of language as it is written, the paradox of a direct speech . . . bent by the essential de-tour, the perversion of writing" (*EI* 487; *IC* 332). That is, what the frag-mentary exigency suggests is not so much vertigo or slippage into an abyss of inauthentic existence, as an irregular and unpredictable hori-zontal traversal from one place to another. Blanchot elaborates:

> For in its passage from description to explanation and then, within this explanation, to a narrative account that, though scarcely begun, opens

[*s'ouvre*] so as to give rise to a new enigma that must in turn be described and then in its turn explained (something that cannot be done without the enigma of a new narrative account), Roussel's work—through this series of intervals perpetually opening out one from another in a coldly concerted, and for this reason all the more vertiginous, manner—represents the infinite navigation from one language to another; a movement in which there momentarily appears in outline, and then endlessly dissipates, the affirmation of the Other [*Autre*] that is no longer the inexpressible depth but the play of manoeuvers or mechanisms destined to avert it. (*EI* 496; *IC* 338)

What Blanchot sees in Roussel's writing resembles the discursive structure of *Tristram Shandy*, with its apparently infinite appetite for interruption. Jean-Luc Nancy affirms this thought:

Neither a pure genesis nor a pure event, *Witz* is continually born and reborn like its hero, Tristram Shandy, whose identity is the identity of a *Witz*: although born from the normal generative process, Tristram owes his birth to an accident—his mother disturbing his father at the crucial moment by reminding him to wind the clock.[29]

The question of genre has been reframed within modernity as the question of narrative disclosure versus lyrical concealment, wit versus irony, philosophy versus poetry. It marks an attempt to recover something of the sprit of both the *Odyssey* and the *Symposium*.

In a way, it is the lesson of *Witz*; the uncontrolled and uncontrollable birth, the jumbling of genres, or of what one is tempted to call *the Western genre*, literature and philosophy, neither literature nor philosophy, literature or philosophy. In short, literary dissolution—where "literary" means the domain of letters, or writing in general. (255)

One can think of the exigency of the fragmentary work as a claim the work exerts on us which calls us outside the simple opposition between poetry and philosophy, art and criticism, seriousness and playfulness, and on to what remains for thinking.

Blanchot, again in his essay on "The Athenaeum," points the reader to a key difference between the romantic and postmodern versions of the fragmentary work of art: in a word, Nietzsche. In the closing paragraph of this essay, Blanchot reflects on the shortcomings of the romantic kind of fragment written by the Schlegel circle:

In truth, and particularly in the case of Friedrich Schlegel, the fragment often seems a means for complacently abandoning oneself to the self rather than an attempt to elaborate a more rigorous mode of writing. Then to write fragmentarily is simply to welcome one's own disorder, to close up upon one's own self in a contented isolation, and thus to refuse the opening that the fragmentary exigency represents: an exigency that does not exclude totality, but goes beyond it. . . . It remains nonetheless true that literature, beginning to become manifest to itself through the romantic declaration, will from now on bear in itself this question of discontinuity or difference as a question of form—a question and a task German romanticism, and in particular that of The Athenaeum, not only sensed but already clearly proposed—before consigning them to Nietzsche and, beyond Nietzsche, to the future. (*EI* 527; *IC* 359)

Blanchot acknowledges the inadvertent character of so much irony and fragmentation within what we have come to call romanticism, the result of a failure of nerve or will, one is tempted to argue, as opposed to the more rigorous practice of writing prescribed by the Nietzschean or postromantic fragment. It is as though, for Blanchot, writing, in order to be what he calls fragmentary writing, must be purified of the excessive self-awareness or -consciousness that inhabits romantic poetry; the subject or the ego must be obliterated or burned off so that the writing of the fragment, as fragmentary writing, can begin. To write. To work through what remains unthought in thinking.[30]

The Fragmentary Imperative as a Double Imperative

As I have already intimated, for Schlegel, the exemplary instance of this kind of fragmentary work is Sterne's *Tristram Shandy*. Sterne's "ceaselessly interrupted and deferred story," as one critic puts it, "begins with an interrupted act of coitus, setting the scene for the coexistence of creativity and interruption that characterizes the whole novel."[31] In a moment almost typical of the work, from volume I, chapter 4, the narrator turns aside to implore someone (who?) to "Shut the door."

> To such, however, as do not choose to go so far back into these things, I can give no better advice, than that they skip over the remaining part of this Chapter, for I declare before hand, 'tis wrote only for the curious and inquisitive.
> ————————————Shut the door————————————

I was begot in the night, betwixt the first *Sunday* and the first *Monday* in
the month of *March*, in the year of our Lord one thousand seven hundred and eighteen. I am positive I was—But how I came to be so very
particular in my account of a thing which happened before I was born, is
owing to another small anecdote known only in our own family, but now
made public for the better clearing up this point. (*TS* 8)

Who exactly does the narrator ask to "Shut the door"? And, more important, what kind of an appeal is this? It's hard to say, exactly. But the
tension in the book between the need to tell one's story to another person and the almost absurd inevitability of comic interruption is one of
the main plot lines, to call it that, of the book. Sterne is obviously no
longer working with plot and character in the traditional sense; but, in
what sense is he working with these conventions?

One way to think of *Tristram Shandy* is to view it as Sterne's idiosyn-
cratic interpretation of Socratic dialogue, his version of what it is like to
give birth to, or serve as midwife during the birthing of, the truth in
beauty. A brief look at Plato's *Symposium* reinforces such an impression.
In the dialogue, Socrates and some friends gather at Agathon's house and
decide to discuss the nature of love. Following several extraordinary
speeches, Socrates recounts an experience he had with the prophetess
Diotima in which she convinced him of the truth of the view he now
holds. The prophetess told him that "'Love is the desire of generation
[and production] in the beautiful, both with relation to the body and the
soul'" (206b). "'For the mortal nature,' she insists, 'seeks, so far as it is
able, to become deathless and eternal. But it can only accomplish this
desire by generation, which for ever leaves another new in place of the
old'" (207d). Obviously Diotima has just defined philosophy. However,
as soon as Socrates finishes his speech, Alcibiades enters in a drunken
stupor bringing the party back to earth with a tale of unrequited love—
for Socrates! As David O'Connor points out, the *Symposium* is charged
with the interplay of divine and human loves, delight and grief, and
everyday speech and the speech of the heart.[32] It is also an allegory of
the unsettling relationship between philosophy and poetry. *Tristram
Shandy*, too, revels in the intersection of the sacred and the profane, the
sublime and the ridiculous, philosophy and poetry, and very much in
the spirit of the *Symposium* serves as a tribute to the consequences of a
single, poorly timed interruption.

This interpretation Bakhtin has put to ingenious use; for Bakhtin,
the novel is marked not so much by its capacity for storytelling as by

its insertion of the spirit of Socratic dialogue into its discourse. In fact one might take Bakhtin's locution of "novelistic discourse" as a loose translation of *romantische Poesie*. In any case, as Jean-Luc Nancy says, speaking of wit:

> We about to examine a subject that has been virtually neglected in the history of literature and philosophy, a subject that up to this point has never really been given its due in either of these histories, namely Wit, or in German, the language to which it belongs (while English literature, from Sterne to Joyce, is its favorite playing field), *Witz*. *Witz* is barely, or only tangentially, a part of literature: it is neither genre nor style, nor even a figure of rhetoric. Nor does it belong to philosophy, being neither concept, nor judgment, nor argument. It could nonetheless play all these roles, but in a derisive manner. (248)

This insight more or less lays out the parameters of the present study. On Sterne's and the German romantics' view, the truth of what is at stake does not emerge from an isolated reflection on a world of objects but from the encounter between wit and irony, philosophy and poetry. In this sense, there is an internal connection between what Schlegel calls Socratic irony and romantic poetry: romantic poetry can be understood as Socratic irony translated into the idiom of modern art. For Schlegel, this need for encounter, or commerce, between philosophy and poetry characterizes Plato's dialogues. Schlegel's favorite is the *Symposium*, with its concluding (though by no means conclusive) exchange between Socrates and Alcibiades and its movement into the torpor of the early morning-after—Plato's version, perhaps, of Blanchot's outside or neutral. The dialogue concludes in a space of exhaustion or indifference, with everyone except Socrates and one or two listeners having drifted off to sleep.

What is fascinating about Schlegel's view of dialogue, however, is the extent to which he reads it through the lens of parody, farce, irony, and satire; as though dialogue is inherently serio-comical or generically unstable. This is an important point and one that bears repeated emphasis: "This fragmentary essence of dialogue," Lacoue-Labarthe and Nancy write, "has at least one consequence (among several others that we cannot explore here), namely that the dialogue, similar in this to the fragment, does not properly speaking belong to a genre. This is why the dialogue, like the fragment, turns out to be one of the privileged sites for taking up the question of genre as such" (*LA* 85). The romantic kind of poetry, far from being determinable as another genre, or even the genre of genres, refuses Aristotle's efforts to determine poetry against the standard of tragedy and opens onto a more unsettled and unsettling region that waits at the limits of the opposition between tragedy and comedy, philosophy and poetry. In *The Infinite Conversation*, Blanchot articulates his hope for such a passage:

> And is there poetry because the one who would have seen being (the absence of being through the mortifying gaze of Orpheus) will also, when he speaks, be able to hold onto its presence, or simply make remembrance of it, or keep open through poetic speech the hope for what opens on the hither side of speech, hidden and revealed in it, exposed and set down by it? (*EI* 53; *IC* 38)

The aim of this book is to sketch a genealogy of fragmentary work from romanticism to Joyce and, with important qualifications, Blanchot. What complicates this task is that the fragmentary work seems at times to exhibit the narrative expansiveness of the epic or novel, while at other times it exemplifies the lyrical brevity of the aphorism or fragment. Here one has only to consider the radically different senses in which Blake's *The Marriage of Heaven and Hell* and *Songs of Innocence and of Experience*, Wordsworth and Coleridge's *Lyrical Ballads*, Novalis', Schleiermacher's, and the Schlegels' contributions to the *Athenäum*, and Coleridge's *Biographia Literaria*, Wordsworth's *Prelude*, Byron's *Childe Harold's Pilgrimage* and *Don Juan*, Percy Shelley's *Prometheus Unbound* and *The Triumph of Life*, Mary Shelley's *Frankenstein*, or, indeed, Keats' two *Hyperion* poems can be said to be fragmentary works. Or consider, for example, the differing senses of the fragmentary embodied in Joyce's *Ulysses* or *Finnegans Wake*, on the one hand, and Beckett's *How It Is* or Wittgenstein's *Philosophical Investigations* or Blanchot's *The Step (Not) Beyond* and *The Writing of the Disaster*, on the other. One construes this state of affairs as demonstrating the tension between (after the example of Nietzsche) narrative and lyrical dimensions of the fragmentary work. One might begin to think of this back-and-forth movement of romantic poetry as a reflection of the romantic-era consciousness of a deep-seated tension between self-indulgence and self-effacement, summarized in Keats's description of the poet as being simultaneously everything and nothing. With this difficulty in mind, I wish to keep this question—the question of the worklessness of the work—open by addressing ways in which the fragmentary exigency inhabits both the more expansive work of Byron and Joyce, and the more strictly aphoristic work of Schlegel and Blanchot. This suggests that there remains both a decidedly worldly and earthly dimension to the fragmentary work of romantic poetry. Efforts to collapse this tension into a single aesthetic or poetic tend to do violence to the variability and complexity of the modern work of art.

Such interpretations of dialogue raise provocative questions concerning the nature of the modern work of art. For example, what role does *Tristram Shandy* play in reviving, for German romantics, the idea (embedded within Plato's dialogues) of the fragmentary work of dialogue? To what extent does Byron's *Don Juan* exemplify this kind of work within the context of British romanticism? In what sense does Joyce's *Ulysses* constitute a modernist fulfillment of it? How does *Finnegans Wake* gesture beyond it toward what Blanchot (following Nietzsche) calls fragmentary writing? Finally, where does the fragmentary exigency leave us? These are some of the questions addressed in this study of the emergence of the fragmentary imperative from the fragmentary work.[33]

Rethinking Romantic Poetry: Schlegel, the Genre of Dialogue, and the Poetics of the Fragment

For of these forms [of rational inquiry] there are two in particular, the [choicest] vehicles of the great bulk of what generally goes by the name of Philosophy. First, that which is called the systematic form, because it divides the whole field into several particular compartments of sciences.... The second form, neither more rarely used nor less favored, is the fragmentary, which has to deal only with particular investigations, and which, from disconnected pieces, with regard to which it is difficult to be sure whether or no they are real members, or only masses capriciously and unnaturally separated from the whole body, professes, notwithstanding, to make Philosophy comprehensible.

—Friedrich Schleiermacher

Many works of the ancients have become fragments. Many modern works are fragments as soon as they are written.

—Friedrich Schlegel

Philippe Lacoue-Labarthe and Jean-Luc Nancy open *The Literary Absolute* with an important observation concerning a watershed moment in the history of Western culture: "romanticism implies something entirely new, the *production* of something entirely new. The romantics never really succeed in naming this something: they speak of poetry, of the work, of the novel, or . . . of romanticism. In the end, they decide to call it—all things considered—*literature*" (*LA* 11, ellipses in original). This new conception recalls the historical moment when, before an adequate name is available, a variety of local vernacular literary cultures finally begin to crawl out from under the rock of Latin culture which had dominated mediaeval Europe for centuries.[1] Friedrich Schlegel's signature contribution to this cultural transition lies in his efforts to formulate a new conceptual lexicon within which to theorize this historical reconfiguration. After an early attempt at thinking through the issue using ancient Greek poetry as a proof text in *On the Study of Greek Poetry* (1797), Schlegel subsequently seizes on the phenomenon of Socratic dialogue as his interpretive key to understanding modern literature, a literature that would nevertheless remain in dialogue with the past. Throughout the fragments included in the short-lived *Athenäum* (1798–1800), he draws attention to similarities between the historical dissolution of Latin literary culture and the shattering experience one often has reading Socratic dialogue, where one's experiences of intermittent insight are so often followed by the onset of a certain measure of blindness or bewilderment. Schlegel's genius is, among other things, in his simultaneous use of these two parallel, but never quite identical, conceptual and historical registers.

Schlegel sets out to demarcate a new kind of poetry that is, as it were, pure production or, even better, poetry itself [*die Dichtkunst selbst*] (*KA* 2: 183; *LF* 175). For Schlegel, romantic poetry is nothing if not a deeply disturbing skeptical force in thought which is set into motion by, and always at work within, the internal dialogue of the work of art. It is an anarchic force refusing identification with a single genre or particular poetic structure; its work remains within the order of becoming, an always-on-the-way work-in-progress. In the earlier *Critical Fragments*, Schlegel admits that he has already been reconsidering the more or less classical view of poetry he had espoused in *Greek Poetry*. "My essay on the study of Greek poetry," he writes in *Critical Fragment 7*, "is a mannered prose hymn to the objective quality in poetry. The worst thing about it, it seems to me, is the complete lack of necessary irony; and the best, the confident assumption that poetry is infinitely valuable—as if that were a settled thing [*eine ausgemachte Sache*]" (*KA* 2:147-48; *LF* 143-44). In the language of Blanchot, appropriated by Lacoue-Labarthe and Nancy, the romantic work remains workless, unworked [*désoeuvré*] or, as I prefer to put it, unsettled; it exhibits a certain self-withdrawal or self-reserve that Blanchot calls worklessness [*désoeuvrement*], a key turn of phrase (not a concept) in Blanchot's understanding of the fragment. The romantic work simultaneously discloses and yet also withholds itself; its

shortcomings as a work resemble Penelope's weave of creation and anni-
hilation in the *Odyssey* which bends time past the limitations of the clock
and into the realm of the almost or the not yet. Like Penelope's tapestry,
the romantic work of art opens onto an altogether different spatial and
temporal dimension: a dimension that reduces one to waiting for the appearance of another who is at once familiar and strange.

One of the most compelling things about the way Lacoue-Labarthe
and Nancy approach the theory of literature in German romanticism is
how they frame their subject matter in terms of its contemporaneity.
"Our own image," they write, "comes back to us from the literary absolute. And the massive truth flung back at us is that we have not left
the era of the Subject" (*LA* 16). In their reading of German romanticism's rethinking of poetry (in terms of the subject-work of the literary
absolute), Lacoue-Labarthe and Nancy find the current preoccupation
with subjectivity anticipated in the crisis of subjectivity precipitated by
Kant and pursued by the romantics. More specifically, they observe:

> One must set out from this [Kantian] problematic of the subject unpre-
> sentable to itself and from this eradication of all substantialism in order
> to understand what romanticism will receive, not as a bequest but as its
> "own" most difficult and perhaps insoluable question. From the moment
> the subject is emptied of all substance, the pure form it assumes is re-
> duced to nothing more than a function of unity or synthesis. Transcen-
> dental imagination, *Einbildungskraft*, is the function that must form
> (*bilden*) this unity, and that must form it as *Bild*, as a representation or
> picture, in other words as a phenomenon, if by phenomenon one means
> that which is neither of the order of appearance (of the "mere phenome-
> non") nor of the order of manifestation, of *Erscheinung* in the strong
> sense, which can found an ontology of "that which is." (LA 30)

In romanticism's encounter with Kant, Lacoue-Labarthe and Nancy
locate nothing less than the advent of what has come to be known as
the deconstruction or calling-into-question of the subject. What is
interesting is that this so-called deconstruction of the subject turns out
to be an impossible endeavor. That is, it is not altogether clear we are
more human, authentic, or at home in the world without subjectivity,
as with subjectivity, or at least with something of an ego or an identity
to call our own. In which case, we are like Keats's chameleon poet,
shuttling back and forth between having too much personality or
having none at all. To the extent that current thinkers remain committed to reconstituting or reconceptualizing the subject in one form or

another, in rethinking the subject in terms of gender, class, material construction, or continental ethics, they remain within the shadow of romanticism.[2]

For Lacoue-Labarthe and Nancy, the romantic work's worklessness is mirrored by a certain worklessness on the part of the authorial subject as well; or, from another remove, the working and unworking of the work is the very working out of the destiny of the self-seeking subject. With this model, the romantic work of art does not serve as a mirror to nature so much as a mirror to a self-cultivating and self-questioning subject. Thus emerges the particular configuration Lacoue-Labarthe and Nancy call the subject-work of romanticism. The subject imagines itself in terms of the working and unworking of the work of art; and the work becomes a record of the subject's struggle for identity against the relentless external pressure of necessity. The reflexive structure of the romantic work is dizzying—it typically oscillates, for example, between opposites such as system and fragment, subject and work, and, as we have seen, theory and practice. For me, however, the crucial point to remember from all this is the work's demand or exigency, what Blanchot calls *l'exigence fragmentaire* or the fragmentary imperative. For Blanchot, the exigency of the fragmentary work indicates a persistent unsettling of intellectual and artistic territories and ideological positions—even of freedom itself—and constantly holds open the threat of reversal; it is a dull attraction into a space where things are frequently not what we expect them to be. In other words, the exigency of the fragmentary work turns freedom onto an empty ground outside the kingdom of being, where relation tries to take hold but finally cannot. This exigency is a relation without relation; a relation of infinity without a fixed subject or object over which power might gain hold; it robs the very idea of freedom of its liberal comfort, and exposes it to what within it remains to be thought.

The Genre of Dialogue

This interrogation of the subject within German romanticism has its origins in Schlegel's disagreement with Schleiermacher (or Schleiermacher's disagreement with Schlegel) over the question of how to interpret Platonic dialogue, especially the character of Socrates, as well as in (Lacoue-Labarthe and Nancy's view) their varying responses to Kant's reconfiguration of the subject. The early German romantic encounter with the Kantian problematic of the subject, further mediated by Fichte, is underwritten at every step of the way by previous encounters with early Greek writing, especially Plato. In order to approach their questioning of subjectivity, it is necessary to rehearse their critical encounters over the issue of Platonic dialogue and, more specifically, over the issue of Socrates himself.[3]

Traditionally, the first principle of romantic hermeneutics is said to be Schleiermacher's claim that "The task [of hermeneutics] is also to be expressed as follows, to understand the utterance at first just as well and then better than its author. For because we have no immediate knowledge of what is in him, we must seek to bring much to consciousness that can remain unconscious to him, except to the extent to which he himself reflectively becomes his own reader."[4]

Understanding, in this sense, entails projecting oneself into the mind of another. Transforming oneself, so to speak, into the author by means of what Schleiermacher calls the divinatory method. Hans-Georg Gadamer observes that this formulation "has been repeated ever since; and in its changing interpretation the whole history of modern hermeneutics can be read" (*TM* 192). Undoubtedly, the idea is of the utmost importance for the modern history of interpretation.[5] Central as it may be, however, I wish to keep in view another, more elusive (and unsettling) side to romantic hermeneutics that is often overlooked: namely, Schlegel's appropriation (his unworking) of Socratic dialogue in the *Athenäum Fragments* and, more particularly, his acknowledgement of the dark, uncontainable side of words in the essay, "On Incomprehensibility."

Schlegel's fragmentary reflections on the question of understanding or *Verstehen* disclose a more scandalous side to hermeneutics which surrenders the aim of reproducing the inner life or logic of an author's mind and tries to remain with the surface of the text, with the thought provoking back and forth play of language itself. One of the implications of this thought—that romantic hermeneutics straddles the line between sympathetic understanding and a need to acknowledge the claim of language—is that the history of interpretation is not reducible to a single history or tradition but is characterized by dialogue, digression, conversation and conflict. In short, it is characterized by multiple interpretations of what counts as interpretation.[6]

Here within romanticism an important episode within the history of interpretation takes place: a disagreement between Schleiermacher and Schlegel on how Plato's dialogues are to be interpreted and understood. One could say that the difference between their theories amounts to the difference in how the idea of dialogue is to be taken; Schleiermacher works back through dialogue to the unified mind that composed it, while Schlegel finds it more important to remain outside the mind with the surface play of the dialogue itself, with the unsettling, scattering force of its words. Schleiermacher's idea of interpretation places a premium on empathy or self-projection: getting into the mind of another person to see what things look like from the inside. Think of it as a kind of hermeneutical role-playing in which the interpreter duplicates the consciousness of another person in order to experience it as that person experiences it. Richard Palmer describes Schleiermacher's model of the art of understanding as "the reexperiencing of the mental processes of the text's author. It is the reverse of composition, for it starts with the fixed and finished expression and goes back to the mental life from which it arose."[7] So, Schleiermacher's hermeneutics begins with the unwriting or unworking of a text, but an unworking which is a working back to its ethereal origins in the mind of the author at the time of composition. Only, the object is to make the author's mind one's own, to know it as that person knows it. The interpreter must duplicate the author's consciousness at the time of the text's composition as faithfully as possible; it must be reexperienced as the interpreter's own. Reading Schleiermacher through Dilthey's eyes—through the glass of the seminal essay on "The Development of Hermeneutics"[8]—Hans-Georg Gadamer calls this celebrated statement of the aim of understanding as knowing another person's mind as it knows itself "his most characteristic contribution" to hermeneutics (*TM* 186).

To be sure, Dilthey's influential essay underlines the psychological side of Schleiermacher's thought, its internal, mental character, what Schleiermacher calls technical interpretation; it is a hermeneutics which depends on empathy [*Einfühlung*], as Schleiermacher insists, on "the talent for knowledge of individual people" (*H* 78; *HC* 11). Reading Dilthey, it is easy to forget that, in addition to technical or psychological interpretation, Schleiermacher also advocates what he calls grammatical interpretation, the interpretation of statements, even the retrieval of the language as a whole as it existed at the historical moment in which the author lived and wrote. In fact, Schleiermacher, as if able to anticipate Gadamer's objections, regularly links technical and grammatical interpretation. "[These two tasks] are completely equal," he writes, "and it would be wrong to call grammatical interpretation the lower and psychological interpretation the higher [task]" (*H* 77; *HC* 10). Indeed, he thinks of understanding itself as an ongoing reciprocal interplay [*Wechselwirkung*] between these two sides of interpretation:

For the grammatical side to be completed on its own there would have to be a complete knowledge of the language, in the other case [the psychological] a complete knowledge of the person. As there can never be either of these, one must move from one to the other, and no rules can be given for how this is to be done. (*H* 78; *HC* 11)

The idea of reciprocal interplay is crucial, an idea Schlegel, along with Novalis, takes up from Fichte's account of reflection as a back and forth movement between thought and counterthought. But in spite of Schleiermacher's efforts to emphasize such an interplay's mediating role in understanding, the psychological side continually threatens the grammatical side, as in Schleiermacher's description of the appropriate interpretive frame of mind: "Before the application of the art [of interpretation] one must put oneself in the place of the author on the objective and the subjective side" (*H* 84; *HC* 24). As this statement makes clear, no matter how it is qualified, putting oneself in the place of the author is the crucial step in Schleiermacher's romantic hermeneutics.[9]

Assuming the position of the author, once the text has been unwritten or unworked, allows the interpreter to put sense back into an author's words. "The art," Schleiermacher writes, "can only develop its rules from a positive formula and this is the [the] historical and divinatory . . . (prophetic) objective and subjective reconstruction of the given utterance" (*H* 83; *HC* 23). The controversial notion of reconstruction plays an important role in this account of hermeneutics. The notion suggests that the interpreter is a textual carpenter who restores dilapidated, broken down sentences so they can once again house legitimate meanings. Indeed, for Schleiermacher, and especially for Dilthey, hermeneutics is a massive reconstruction project, an attempt to put the mental world of the text—Humpty Dumpty's world, so to speak—back together again (into some kind of intelligible order) after time has laid it to waste. The historical or cultural differences between interpreter and original authorial consciousness are a gulf to be bridged; a difference to be overcome in order for an adequate understanding to emerge.

However, there seems to me to be a more complicated side to romantic hermeneutics that comes out in the story told by Gadamer and Dilthey. Or perhaps it is more correct to say there is another, more playful or ironic side to the usual story of romantic hermeneutics, which complements the story told by Gadamer and Dilthey and that pursues a criticism of Schleiermacher's more or less Kantian hermeneutics one step further or just tries to stay with it. One of Schleiermacher's great achievements, Gadamer says, lies in his distinction "between a looser hermeneutical praxis, in which understanding follows automatically, and a stricter one that begins with the premise that what follows automatically is misunderstanding" (*TM* 185). Or as Schleiermacher has it: "The more strict practice [of the art of interpretation] assumes that misunderstanding results as a matter of course and that understanding must be desired and sought at every point" (*H* 82; *HC* 22). That is, at this juncture in the history of interpretation, a sort of hermeneutical negativity enters into the picture and becomes essential for the practice of the art of interpretation. In a sense, misunderstanding is now where hermeneutics starts. That is, misunderstanding, "what follows automatically," constitutes the normal structure of (our linguistically-mediated) experience, what is given, and the way things initially appear to us in our transactions with the world. "From now on," Gadamer says, "we no longer consider the difficulties and failures of understanding as occasional but as integral elements that have to be prevented in advance" (*TM* 185). This particular line from Gadamer is a little troubling because one wants to know whether for Gadamer, misunderstanding is something to be acknowledged or avoided. Although Gadamer appreciates the role misunderstanding plays—I am thinking of his remarks on the curiously productive meaning of hermeneutical negativity—it still should be avoided, as though interpretation from now on wants (in a Kantian manner) to insure itself against error or confusion as a matter of preliminary procedure (*TM* 353). It may be that all Gadamer wants to say is what Schleiermacher means when he says the goal of the looser practice of hermeneutics is more or less the avoidance of misunderstanding. Anyhow, what one wants to hold onto here is this idea of hermeneutical negativity, the notion that a certain level of inertia or incomprehensibility, misunderstanding or chaos exists, something strangely foreign that goes along with one's linguistically mediated experience of the world.[10]

It is this negative aspect of language, its persistent excessiveness with respect to itself, that Schlegel finds compelling and starts thinking through, first in the *Athenäum Fragments*, and then in the endlessly provocative essay, "On Incomprehensibility." So, well before Gadamer and Dilthey (and certainly before Nietzsche and Derrida), within early German romanticism itself, a reinterpretation of romantic hermeneutics is already taking shape.[11] Dilthey mentions Schlegel's contribution to the development of hermeneutics in his influential essay, but he does so only in an offhand way, referring mainly to the Plato translation undertaken with Schleiermacher (and which Schleiermacher finished alone). Generally the essay furnishes a coherent context for Schleiermacher's achievement: the elevation of hermeneutics from a loose set of rules to something like a science. Schlegel, in the streamlined story Dilthey tells, plays merely a supporting role. As a result, Schlegel's importance to the history of interpretation has been sorely underestimated, if not brushed aside altogether. More recently, however, scholars see Schlegel as more central to romantic hermeneutics, important precisely insofar as he recognizes both the centrality of dialogue and puts into play a persistent negativity of language, which threatens the very possibility of dialogue itself. Words, Schlegel suggests, cannot be shrugged off or turned aside but must be encountered in all their darkness, foreignness, or strangeness.

Schleiermacher and Schlegel, then, assume two related but very different understandings of Socratic dialogue—indeed of Socratic subjectivity itself. Schleiermacher, in Dilthey's view, is concerned with retrieving Plato's state of mind from the reading of texts, locating the unity of the texts in the unified consciousness that produced them. Dilthey writes: "If one follows the relation between the dialogues, their connection, which discloses Plato's central intention, emerges. According to Schleiermacher, only by grasping this methodically developed context does a real understanding of Plato emerge."[12] That is to say, the meaning of a text or a collection of texts is always determinable by intuiting the meaning originally intended by the mind that produced them. In the effort to arrive at a "central [authorial] intention" one has the beginnings of something like E. D. Hirsch's hermeneutics of intentionality, the theory that the meaning of a text can be established by retrieving the author's original state of mind at the time of composition.[13] This form of psychological divination, which secures a model of an author's mind at the expense of the truth of the subject matter, is the side of romantic hermeneutics that Gadamer so relentlessly criticizes.

For Schlegel, however, interpretation as divination of another's mind is overly ambitious, if not foolhardy, because one's consciousness is never that unified to begin with but rather always exists in one of its versions; it is always situated somewhere, as in a relation with another person, or with a text or a subject under discussion. *Athenäum Fragment* 121 acknowledges this being-of-two-minds as basic to the romantic kind of existence:

But to transport oneself arbitrarily now into this, now into that sphere, as if into another world, not merely with one's reason and imagination,

but with one's whole soul; to freely relinquish first one and then another
part of one's being, and confine oneself entirely to an other; to seek and
find now in this, now in that individual the be-all and end-all of existence, and intentionally forget everything else: of this only a mind is
capable that contains within itself simultaneously a plurality of minds and
a whole system of persons, and in whose inner being the universe which,
as they say, should germinate in every monad, has grown to fullness and
maturity. (*KA* 2:185; *LF* 177)

This passage provides an excellent example of what Schlegel describes as the reciprocal interplay of philosophy and poetry, the back and
forth exchange of truth and beauty, which perpetuates itself as a kind of
fruitful tension or strife.[14] Schlegel's own prose moves playfully back and
forth within the very gap he identifies. One can see something like what
Richard Lanham calls "the rhetorical ideal of life," an ancient Greek
ideal of self-formation based on exchange and argument, role-playing
and game playing, verbal gymnastics and wit, rather than on sober
analysis or logical investigation.[15] On this model, one learns arguments
not as positions to be taken up and defended but rather as vocabularies,
taxonomies or anatomies to be mastered, as inventories of proverbial
wisdom to be applied to whatever issue happens to be at stake on a
given occasion. Here the emphasis is on memory as opposed to originality, mental agility as opposed to the systematic development of an argument, and most importantly, on words instead of ideas.

In the *Dialogue on Poetry* (1799), Schlegel writes that, in order to reach
the true (genial and sociable) realm of poetry, "a person keeps going outside of himself, ever certain of finding himself again, in order to seek and
find the completion of his innermost being in the depths of a stranger.
The game of communicating and approaching is the business and the
power of life; absolute completion occurs only in death."[16] Schlegel's reference to "the game of communication and approaching" is interesting
here; later he will say that Kant's philosophy is missing "the category of
the 'almost'," as though philosophy has trouble moving outside the confines of its own concepts. This helps to explain the attraction of Socratic
dialogue for the romantics. In *Athenäum Fragment* 242, Schlegel asks:
"Aren't all systems individuals just as all individuals are systems at least in
embryo and tendency? Isn't every real unity historical? Aren't there individuals who contain within themselves whole systems of individuals?"
(*KA* 2:205; *LF* 196). Schlegel probably has in mind here Socrates,
the Socrates at the close of the *Symposium* whom Alcibiades likens to
a statue of Silenus holding a flute that, once opened, reveals a seemingly
infinite number of smaller images inside (215a-b). This is Socrates the

dissembler, the wily Socrates, the Socrates of many turns, a wandering, polytropic Socrates congenial to Schlegel's notion of the romantic as a figure constituted by a proliferation of identities and always in the process of self-transformation. In this connection, Philippe Lacoue-Labarthe and Jean-Luc Nancy note that for the romantics:

> Socrates (the figure and person) has always represented the anticipatory incarnation or prototype of the Subject itself. The reason for this . . . is that Socrates . . . is what could be called the subject of irony; Socrates, in other words, becomes the locus of the very exchange that, as both a figure and a work, defines irony . . . which is the exchange of form and truth or, and this is strictly identical, of poetry and philosophy. (*LA* 86)

But this endless self-transformation is not all. In contrast to the commonplace that romanticism leads to egotism and self-interest, the fragment suggests that the romantic is characterized by a continual outward motion, a constant beginning or setting out, as though inspired or partly constituted by contact with what is strange or foreign, different or other.

Socrates is also important for Bakhtin's celebrated theory of novelistic discourse, particularly as it informs his intuition of its origins in the broadly satirical impulse of ancient Socratic dialogue. In a well-known essay on "Epic and Novel," Bakhtin speculates on the origins of the novel:

> Moreover, the figure of Socrates himself is characteristic for the genre— he is an outstanding example of heroization in novelistic prose (so very different from epic heroization). It is, finally, profoundly characteristic— and for us this is of utmost significance—that we have laughter, Socratic irony, the entire system of Socratic degradations combined with a serious, lofty and for the first time truly free investigation of the world, of man and of human thought. Socratic laughter (reduced to irony) and Socratic degradations (an entire system of metaphors and comparisons borrowed from the lower spheres of life—from tradespeople, from everyday life, etc.,) bring the world closer and familiarize it in order to investigate it fearlessly and freely.[17]

For Schlegel, the romantic is fully realized when engaged in dialogue with other people, exposed, or subject to their point of view, called onto another's path—not just feeling (empathically), or knowing (cognitively), but by talking out loud, debating, bantering, even arguing. Schlegel gives a decidedly agonistic turn to the Keatsian commonplace of the poet-as-unvirtuous-chameleon; or, better to say Keats downplays the idea of the individual-as-dialogical project in order to arrive at the notion of the poet-as-empath. Here again one can appeal to Philippe Lacoue-Labarthe and Jean-Luc Nancy, who note that for the romantics:

> truth cannot be attained by the solitary path of demonstration (ridiculed in *Athenaeum* fragment 82), but rather by that of exchange, mixing, friend-ship—and love, as we will see. *Symphilosophy* implies the active exchange and confrontation of individuals-philosophers. And thus it implies the dialogue . . . and undoubtedly that perfection of dialogue which becomes the romantic ideal of drama, a hidden but insistent motif that should be traced throughout the *Fragments* in order to extract their particular ideal of natural existence and its correspondingly *natural* staging. (*LA* 45)

By "active exchange and confrontation" Lacoue-Labarthe and Nancy mean the romantics point away from understanding-as-empathy toward something more openly discursive, conversational, or just more outspoken. In any case, Schlegel leads understanding out of the private, mental sphere and back into the public, social, or rhetorical sphere; the sphere of agon and conflict, debate and encounter; the realm of the marketplace or streetcorner, the townsquare or the Temple Mount. One is most oneself, it would seem, when one's word is met, answered or challenged, even refuted, by the stress of another's voice.

Repeatedly in the *Athenäum Fragments*, Schlegel warns against excessive singlemindedness, against identifying oneself too closely with a single mental vantage point: "people . . . who have an understanding of only one thing" are intolerable "not because it's everything to them but because it's the only thing they have, and a thing they're forever repeating" (*KA* 2:220; *LF* 319). Instead, one needs to have (so to speak) a mind of dialogue, as opposed to (say) a mind of winter. Understanding is, or should be, more like a social event, a symposium, a conversation vulnerable to interruptions from the outside. Here one thinks of the ending of Plato's *Symposium*, the point at which Alcibiades visits the dinner party thrown by Agathon for his friends. The goal of romanticism, one might argue, is to develop a genre pliable or flexible enough to accommodate such an unstable event of understanding. *Athenäum Fragment* 77 articulates precisely this need:

> A dialogue is a chain or garland of fragments. An exchange of letters is a dialogue on a larger scale, and memoirs constitute a system of fragments. But as yet no genre exists that is fragmentary in both in matter

and form, simultaneously completely subjective and individual, and completely objective and like a necessary part in a system of all the sciences. (*KA* 2:176; *LF* 170)

This fragment equivocates between a strict and a loose interpretation of dialogue. In fact, one can understand what *Athenäum Fragment* 116 calls romantic poetry as an attempt to answer the question of how strict or loose dialogue should be. The point to mark for now, in any case, is that for the romantics, dialogue remains responsive or answerable to the outside; its fluctuations preserve the integrity (the singularity) of the fragment, and this means preventing it from being subsumed within the larger design of a whole. Dialogue, in this sense, never overcomes the individuality of the fragment: its excessiveness remains. Perhaps this is what Blanchot means by the too much of romanticism. Consider *Athenäum Fragment* 82: "True definitions can't be made at will, but have to come of themselves; a definition which isn't witty is worthless, and there exists an infinite number of real definitions for every individual" (*KA* 2:177; *LF* 171).

In this reading, both subject and the work itself are defined loosely as constituted by the ongoing strife between the one and the indeterminate two, self and other, system and fragment, and finally, philosophy and poetry. Here the text to be consulted (to digress for a moment) is the well-known *Critical Fragment* 42, which begins: "Philosophy is the real homeland of irony, which one would like to define as logical beauty: for wherever philosophy appears in oral or written dialogues—and is not simply systematically philosophized—there irony should be asked for and provided" (*KA* 2:152; *LF* 148). In this fragment, irony is no longer an isolated trope but is located in relation to philosophy, more specifically in relation to philosophical dialogue. Irony belongs (is necessary) to philosophy, has to do with philosophy, but is not simply contained by it. The dialogue does not get all the way around or circumscribe the fragment. On the contrary, what Schlegel means by irony is related to philosophy just in the sense that its habitual attitude toward philosophy is one of outsidedness or estrangement, resistance or refusal, a condition or state of being exiled from that homeland. So, the ironist is understood as one who inhabits the space in between; constantly shuttling back and forth between philosophy and poetry; making a way along a path between reason and madness. The madness in question here would be the madness of words, which insistently interrupt the philosopher's arguments. This is the piece, the fragmentary edge that never quite fits, the word or question one can never quite suppress. For example, *Athenäum Fragment* 204 (written by Schlegel's brother, August Wilhelm): "No matter how good a lecture delivered from the height of the podium might be, the greatest joy is gone because one can't interrupt the speaker. So too with the didactic writer [AW]" (*KA* 2:197; *LF* 189). Note the emphasis on the role of interruption. In the literary-philosophical idiom of the *Fragments*, interruption becomes an unsettling (unsettled) ground that makes dialogue possible; interruption is the (silent) energy of movement that keeps the dialogue from dying out. Again, what kind of work could accommodate (could have already built into it a capacity for) interruption? It should be clear that Schlegel takes un-working in a different sense than Schleiermacher; he takes it not as a working back to the mind of an author, but as the un-working of the work of dialogue itself; a working out or an outward working; the work of remaining open to the outside of (the limits of) the conversation; remaining attentive to what remains to be said, what remains unclear, or what remains for taking up again later.

Schlegel's sense of dialogue can be described as follows: a conversation tending toward the status of a dialogue of fragments rather than a fragmentary dialogue. If Schleiermacher's hermeneutics points behind dialogue to the author's mind, toward a knowledge of people, then Schlegel's self-interpretive poetic work points in front of dialogue to the scattering, unsettling force of words.

All of this explains the direction and force of the turn Schlegel gives to the hermeneutical commonplace that understanding means to understand the text first as well as and then even better than its author. For Schlegel, understanding involves not the retrieval of another's consciousness (implying a possession of it), or an historical account of the language of an era (implying linguistic competence), but rather a step back from these analytical procedures to an acknowledgement of the priority of language. In other words: language keeps the initiative. This is why Schlegel recuperates misunderstanding, incomprehension, chaos, and confusion as modes of resistance to this kind of analysis, as positive values, as in this fragment: "If in communicating a thought, one fluctuates [*abwechselt*] between absolute comprehension and absolute incomprehension, then this process might already be termed a philosophical friendship" (*KA* 2:164; *LF* 160). Complete comprehension (with no remainder) leaves nothing more to be said and so ends a relationship, while endless interpretation, philosophical friendship, has two sides, and so preserves the open-ended (unpredictable) encounter between reader and text.

It may be too much to say that Schlegel wants to establish the historicality of understanding, the way Gadamer does for example, but he does abandon the idea of a single, transcendental point of view for understanding and instead describes interpretation as making one's way through a busy marketplace of voices. It may be that Schlegel's hermeneutics is less ironic in any technical or philosophical sense than just, well, perfectly ordinary.

Schlegel writes: "In order to understand someone who only partially understands himself, you first have to understand him completely and better [*ganz und besser*] than he himself does, but then only partially and precisely [*halb und grade*] as much as he does himself" (*KA* 2:241; *LF* 227-28). This is the first (unprincipled) principle of Schlegel's hermeneutics, that, once one has plumbed the depths of an author's mind, one must back off and let go in order to give back its autonomy or self-determination. This is like saying one must have two interpretations on hand, or think with both hands, beginning with a close study of the logic of the mind and then proceeding, or it may be stepping back, to a more trivial or rhetorical understanding; getting out of the mind's interminable depths and closer to the surface, closer to language and to the sense (understood first as sensation) embodied there.[18] On this reading, Schlegel's hermeneutics has the structure of digression, a readiness or eagerness to stray from the beaten track and follow the hint of words.[19]

Schlegel seems determined to get understanding off track, untracked, or just sidetracked, out from under the direction of a universal set of scientific rules which keep it on the sure-footed Kantian path of understanding-as-knowledge.

One could summarize the tendency of Schlegel's fragments as follows: compelling thoughts lie just off the beaten track.

A Poetics of the Fragment

As is well documented, the *Fragments* provide a new model for the poetic work. In their discussion of "the romantic genre *par excellence*," Lacoue-Labarthe and Nancy note that, although novel, the fragment does not appear from out of nowhere but belongs to a history that includes previous writers like Shaftesbury and La Rochefoucauld. Moreover, "fragments written by members of [the Schlegel circle] are far from constituting a homogeneous and undifferentiated ensemble" (*LA* 40). Only the *Athenaeum Fragments* approach "the fragmentary ideal of romanticism" in that they alone have no object and are "anonymously composed of pieces by several different authors" (*LA* 40). This fact has an important consequence: "Without an objective and without an author, the *Fragments* of the *Athenaeum* strive to be absolutely self-posited" (*LA* 40–41). That is, the *Fragments* look neither to an author nor to a world for their justification; rather, they seek it within themselves. Thus they indirectly raise the question of the role of the aesthetic in founding and articulating the system and the subject. This is their, and our, "*naiveté*" (*LA* 17).

It is important to note at the outset, however, that the fragment or the fragmentary work occupies a curiously duplicitous and unsettled [*désoeuvré*] space within the romantic-era conception of the poetic. That is to say, the fragment, or better, the fragmentary work, is always to be understood in the plural, as constituted by at least two or more fragments. There is no poetics of the fragment as such; it is always a question of the romantic-era poetics of fragments. Lacoue-Labarthe and Nancy put it this way: "Fragmentary individuality is above all that of the multiplicity inherent to the genre. The romantics did not publish a unique *Fragment*; to write the fragment is to write fragments" (*LA* 43–44). In approaching the fragmentary exigency of the romantic work, Lacoue-Labarthe and Nancy settle on the importance of two distinct and continually crossing paths:

> The first, that of Novalis, redefines *Witz*, as simultaneous combination and dissolution. "*Witz*, as a principle of affinity, is at the same time *menstruum universale*" (*Grains of Pollen*) [*Blüthenstaub* fragment 57]. The universal dissolvent undoes the systematic, undoes the identity of the poet and sweeps it toward the "dissolution in song" evoked by a posthumous fragment intended for *Heinrich von Ofterdinger*, a dissolution that includes the sacrifice, in all its ambiguity, of the poet. . . . (*LA* 56).

At the same time, "[t]he second, Schlegelian path," they contend [might be described]

> as the path leading toward "energy" or toward "the energetic man," defined by the "infinitely flexible . . . universal power through which the whole man shapes himself," well beyond the "genius" who "shapes a work." Energy extends to the limit of the work and of the system; its "infinite flexibility," linked to "an incalculable number of projects," effects an infinite fragmentation of work and system. (*LA* 56–57)

"Dissolution and energy, then," Lacoue-Labarthe and Nancy conclude, "the ultimate forms of the fragment, would inevitably lead back to the work-subject" (*LA* 57). This suggests that romanticism, in the wake of the

Kantian crisis of the system and the subject, provides an opportune historical mirror through which to reflect upon a previous crisis in system and subject famously imaged in the form of a single name: Socrates. In the figure of Socrates, arguably the foundational instance of the subject in the Western philosophical tradition, the romantics find a perfect site on which to work through their confrontation with the Kantian legacy of a subject emptied of all substance, a subject reduced to nothing more than a function of unity or synthesis.

Schlegel articulates his fragmentary poetics with special emphasis and eloquence in the well-known *Athenäum Fragment* 116. He writes:

> Romantic poesy is a progressive universal poesy. Its aim isn't merely to reunite all the separate kinds of poetry and put poetry in contact with philosophy and rhetoric. It wants to—and also should—blend and merge poesy with prose, geniality with critique, the poesy of art with the poesy of nature, give life to poesy and render it sociable, make life and society poetic, poeticize wit and fit up and saturate the forms of art with every kind of genuine cultural material, and animate them through the oscillations of humor. It embraces everything that is purely poetic . . . it is also romantic poesy that can hover on the wings of poetic reflection between the presented and the presenting, free from all real and ideal interest, and continually raise this reflection to a higher power, thus multiplying it as in an endless row of mirrors. . . . Romantic poetry is in the arts what wit is in philosophy, and what society and sociability, friendship and love are in life. Other genres [*Dichtarten*] are fixed and capable of being classified in their entirety. The romantic genre [*Dichtart*] is, however, still in the process of becoming; indeed, this is its essence: to be eternally in the process of becoming and never completed. No theory can exhaust romantic poesy, and only a divinatory critique might dare attempt to characterize its ideal. It alone is infinite, just as it alone is free, and it recognizes this as its first law, that the willfulness of the poet [*die Willkür des Dichters*] tolerates no imposition of laws. The romantic genre [*Dichtart*] is the only one that is more than a genre and that itself typifies poetic production; for, in a certain sense, all poesy is or should be romantic. (*KA* 2: 182-83; *LF* 175)

In many ways *Fragment* 116 is the centerpiece of the *Fragments*. It gestures toward an essential incompletion at the heart of the work that is distinct from the roughness that characterizes unfinished texts left behind at a writer's death. This essential incompletion implies that the romantic work is one whose truth resides more in its productivity than in its production of works. The romantic fragment posits, as it were, a version of both the real and the ideal, working with and against one another, gesturing toward infinity while never quite arriving there. Lacoue-Labarthe and Nancy write:

> it is in the very "progressivity" and infinity of its movement that "romantic poetry," since Antiquity and for all the future, forms the truth of all poetry. The actuality of romanticism, as is well known, is never *there* (especially during the period of those who do not call themselves romantics, even while writing fragment 116), and likewise, "there is as yet nothing that is fragmentary" (A 77). But it is indeed in this not being there, this never yet being there, that romanticism and the fragment *are*, absolutely. *Work in progress* henceforth becomes the infinite truth of the work. (*LA* 48)

Lacoue-Labarthe and Nancy thus suggest that romantic poetry unsettles the identity of the work of art. For the romantics, the work is, and is not, a (complete) work. Romantic poetry as "progressive universal" poetry installs an image of the work that is a double image, an overexposure, an image that includes at once itself and its shadow. Simon Critchley usefully describes this is the back and forth movement of wit and irony (112–15). Looked at this way, the truth of the work is no longer a function of the accuracy of its imitation of nature, but rather a form of fulfillment predicated upon its capacity to render the whole mobile while at the same time interrupting it in order to create space for what remains for thinking.

The Otherness of Words

On the lyrical, extravagant side of interpretation there is hardly a more provocative text in romantic hermeneutics than Schlegel's spirited defense of the *Fragments*, the essay "*On Incomprehensibility*."[20] The essay both describes and demonstrates the reciprocal interplay [*Wechselwirkung*] between wit and irony, clarity and obscurity, working and un-working that characterizes the romantic-ironic work, the text in which "everything should be playful and serious, guilelessly open and deeply hidden" (*KA* 2:160; *LF* 156). True to its title, the essay calls into question the assumption that an author should strive for greater clarity and intelligibility; it recuperates instead the value of incomprehensibility, misunderstanding, chaos, and confusion as insurmountable features of reading. Schlegel, wary of construing hermeneutics as trafficking only in enlightenment, gestures toward the dark underside of understanding, the unruly side of things, of words, which understanding-as-knowledge must

overcome in order to be itself. Turning scientific pretensions of interpretation upside down or inside out, Schlegel intimates that the aim of
hermeneutics (understood in a nonenlightenment way) may not be to
raise the subject matter up out of language into conceptual clarity, but
to allow oneself to be drawn into the dark, or perhaps be detained by
the seductive, material dimension of words.

The opening lines of the essay announce one of its chief aims, the dismantling of the idea of a central authorial intention which could govern
interpretation: "Because of something either in them or in us, some subjects of thought stimulate us to ever deeper thought, and the more we are
stimulated and lose ourselves in these subjects, the more do they become
a Single Subject" (*KA* 2:363; *LF* 259). The initial dissimulation between
them and us has its hermeneutic point: the speaker refrains from ground-
ing interpretive authority solely in intention; instead, Schlegel seems to
acknowledge that subjects of human thought have their own disposition.
The question of authority, as a result, is left open. That is to say, the
opening is not just ironic in the sense that you don't get what you would
normally expect, say a point-by-point introduction or exordium, but also
it brackets the essence of what Schleiermacher thought could be re-
trieved from a text: the meaning that the author put there in the first
place. In its place, Schlegel emphasizes the authority of the subject matter and of thinking itself. Schlegel goes on to develop this idea:

> Other subjects perhaps would never be able to attract our attention if we
> were to withdraw into holy seclusion and devote our minds exclusively
> to this subject of subjects, and if we did not have to be in contact with
> people and hence busy our minds with relational concepts which, when
> considered more carefully, always become more numerous and entangled
> and thereby follow the contrary path. (*KA* 2:363; *LF* 259)

Here Schlegel establishes a characteristic opposition between a self-
contained philosophical reading; a private activity of mind complete
unto itself, sealed off from the interventions of other people; and a kind
of reading one could call conversational or social or perhaps, for the
sake of consistency (and not without irony), dialogic, reading which remains exposed to interruption from the outside, vulnerable (or answerable) to the obligations of everyday life, to other people. This would be
reading-as-conversation-with-someone-about-something, as though
reading or interpretation could never be undertaken alone; was never a
solitary mode of coming-to-consciousness about the meaning of a text,

but rather needs the give-and-take of discussion to get a (working) sense of things.

Again, one can see the germ of Bakhtin's theory of novelistic discourse, which is not autonomous and self-contained but in constant contact and struggle with other languages, each of which wants to have its say. Bakhtin's idea is that discourse is constituted by centripetal and centrifugal forces simultaneously at work in any given utterance, unifying and fragmenting forces working and un-working any given speech act. It is precisely in the interaction, strife, or as Bakhtin likes to say, dialogue between these aspects of language that authentic speech is born. Against the traditional view of a word relating logically to its object, Bakhtin emphatically insists that each word, "directed toward its object, enters a dialogically agitated and tension-filled environment of alien words, value judgments and accents, weaves in and out of complex interrelationships, merges with some, recoils from others, intersects with yet a third group: and all this may crucially shape discourse . . ." (*DI* 276). What Bakhtin describes is a kind of discourse thoroughly determined by what *Athenäum Fragment* 116 calls romantic poetry, the dialogically-energized work, which is simultaneously more and less than itself, torn between creation and destruction, wit and irony, working and un-working. Bakhtin appropriates Schlegel's idea and uses it as a way to understand the mainline history of novelistic discourse.

Bakhtin may have had precisely this episode in mind, the disagreement between Schleiermacher and Schlegel, while putting down on paper some rather fragmentary notes on literature and interpretation toward the end of his life. In these notes, Bakhtin excoriates "[t]he false tendency toward reducing everything to a single consciousness, toward dissolving in it the other's consciousness (while being understood)," and at the same time forcefully underlines "[t]he principle advantages of outsidedness (spatially, temporally, and nationally)." He goes on to criticize the romantic notion of empathic understanding: "One cannot understand understanding as emotional empathy [*Einfühlung*] as the placement of the self in the other's position (loss of one's own position). This is required only for peripheral aspects of understanding. One cannot understand understanding as a translation from the other's language into one's own language."[21] Bakhtin seems to follow Schlegel rather than Schleiermacher in placing emphasis upon outsidedness rather than upon empathy, and also in suggesting that it is the novel, or particular forms of what he calls "novelistic discourse," that best captures this consciousness-of-being-outside or, more simply, what one might call "outsidedness."[22]

Schlegel gives notice that, instead of writing in a vacuum, he endeavors to keep himself (and his reader) exposed to the disruptive hiss and clatter of everyday life, the "relational concepts which . . . always become more numerous and entangled and thereby follow (or diverge onto) the contrary path" (*KA* 2:363; *LF* 259). Much like Sterne's narrator in *Tristram Shandy*, his writing (his justification of writing fragments) makes its way, however crookedly and inefficiently, through the confusion of everyday life in order to remain faithful to the excessiveness of experience. This constitutes what he calls his experiments concerning communication: his attempt to recover the otherness of words systematically suppressed by the knowing (comprehending) subject. He explains himself as follows:

> Common sense which is so fond of navigating by the compass of etymologies—so long as they are very close by—probably did not have a difficult time in arriving at the conclusion that the basis of the incomprehensible is to be found in incomprehension. Now, it is a peculiarity of mine that I absolutely detest incomprehension, not only the incomprehension of the uncomprehending but even more the incomprehension of the comprehending. (*KA* 2:363; *LF* 260)

Here Schlegel is in pursuit of what intelligibility must surmount on its way to becoming itself, the conceptually unmanageable dimensions of everyday life. Note the contempt for the incomprehension of the comprehending. To understand too well or too readily (as without a second thought) is not to understand at all. Also recall the remark concerning interpretive single-mindedness, the thorough-going contempt for people "who have an understanding of only one thing . . . they're forever repeating." This is the thinker whose mind has been taken over by a single methodological approach or concern—one for whom a certain thought has become inevitable—for whom thinking (as being open to the discovery of something new) has come to an end.

This is why Schlegel repeatedly insists on the presence of another person, a reader or a clandestine self; someone to think with him as he writes, presumably to keep his writing loose and unstable, open to contingency, alteration, or change. Throughout the essay, Schlegel maintains a sense of audience, someone listening and perhaps talking back; at any rate someone who acts as a co-conspirator in the making and breaking up of meaning. Schlegel writes matter of factly about this:

> For this reason, I made a resolution quite some time ago to have a talk about this matter with my reader, and then create before his eyes—in spite of him as it were—another new reader to my own liking: yes, even

to deduce him if need be. I meant it quite seriously and not without some of my old bent for mysticism. I wanted for once to be really thorough and go through the whole series of my essays, admit their frequent lack of success with complete frankness, and so gradually lead the reader to being similarly frank and straightforward with himself. I wanted to prove that all incomprehension is relative, and show how incomprehensible Garve, for example, is to me. (*KA* 2:363-64; *LF* 260)

Now comes the essay's most provocative line. Over against the notion of a language given over solely to the communication of ideas, to communicative rationality, Schlegel places the sheer material fact (the unavoidability) of words, the physical existence of language which understanding must get under control in order to be logical, self-consistent, clear. The idea of writing fragments, he says, is to recover, against philosophical (procedure-governed) interpretation, the material side of words. Schlegel writes:

I wanted to demonstrate that words often understand themselves better than do those who use them, wanted to point out that there must be a connection of some secret brotherhood among philosophical words that, like a host of spirits too soon aroused, bring everything into confusion in their writings and exert the invisible power of the World Spirit on even those who try to deny it. (*KA* 2:364; *LF* 260)

The worst or most unthinking comprehension, Schlegel says, is one that ignores the material fact of language or remains at a safe distance, disdaining to engage the text at the level of the unregenrate (unreconstructed) word. This attitude toward language ultimately has to do with one's attitude toward reading. For Schlegel, reading is more than comprehension, more than getting clear about one's concepts or ideas, or extracting them from a text; it means, first of all, acknowledging the words of the text, listening to and for them, before anything else; listening to the phonic and material dimensions of words precedes the understanding of ideas.

There are two points to be made here. First, what Schlegel describes as the self-understanding of words precedes whatever understanding can be extracted from them. This rational comprehension, the kind of understanding which can be put into assertions or statements, is always secondary or derivative of a prior understanding, the self-understanding of words. This prior self-understanding (of words) is what Schlegel is after.[23] Schlegel underscores this point by opposing a more material, Joycean view of language with what he somewhat scornfully calls a real language [*eine reelle Sprache*] (*KA* 2:364; *LF* 260). This is the old idea of a philosophical language or character; a language that serves as a transparent vehicle for concepts. The kind of language that will allow us to "stop rummaging about for words and pay attention to the power and source of all activity" (*KA* 2:364; *LF* 260). As though words just get in the way of rational understanding. Schlegel lampoons this notion of a real (philosophical) language with the whimsical transition to the story of Girtanner, a German chemist and physician, who believed that in the nineteenth century, science would find a way to manufacture gold. Just as crazy as the prospect of making gold is the prospect of a real language, perfect and unequivocal, and conceptually consistent. Second, the basic tendency of words, left to themselves, is always toward chaos rather than order, or toward an order that is not quite recognizable as such. The instinctive power of language to rise up and create chaos or confusion out of an orderly set of terms or concepts prevents the kind of reconstructed account of another's mind or world-view Schleiermacher is looking for. The self-understanding of words (not to be trusted) always, it would now appear, intervenes.[24]

Language in its everyday sense never stands still, keeps its place, or says what you want it to all the time. *Athenäum Fragment* 19: "The best way to be understood or, rather, to be misunderstood, is to use words in their original meanings, especially words from the ancient languages" (*KA* 2:168; *LF* 163). As though what the later Heidegger calls thinking is buried in the sounds of words, and what we need to do is listen for it (entertain it) by listening to words. Schlegel says that this wayward nature of language, its tendency to refuse conceptual control and to throw everything into utter confusion, is precisely what makes understanding as thinking possible. He writes:

> Why should I provide misunderstandings when no one wants to take them up? And so now I let irony go to the winds and declare point-blank that in the dialect of the Fragments the word means that everything now is only a tendency, that the age is the Age of Tendencies. (*KA* 2:367; *LF* 264)

Far from preventing understanding, incomprehension makes understanding (now understood as thinking) possible. But more than this: comprehension is grounded on incomprehension. Some misunderstanding or incomprehension is necessary to initiate nonstrategic thinking, to set one upon the way of thinking. The way to enlightenment passes through darkness. The upshot is that understanding now acknowledges a dependence on the reciprocal interplay between comprehension and incomprehension. Only now understanding is not exactly understanding as Schleiermacher thought of it (not exactly *Verstehen*) but is partly something else, partly other or, better, excessive with respect to itself so that it can't be reduced to a concept, for example, the concept of understanding, but will always be tied to the situations in which it is called for or in which it occurs. Note how Schlegel describes his attitude toward words as one of freeing or releasing, as a letting-be or letting-go: "And so now," he says, "I let [*lasse*] irony go to the winds" (*KA* 2:367; *LF* 264). Rather than tightening the conceptual screws, Schlegel loosens his grip on irony, allowing it to go its own way. In this view, words (in order to be themselves) need to be turned loose from conceptual constraint, need to be left to go [*lassen*] into their own tendencies, their own wayward (unspeakably dark) ways. For Schlegel, irony is connected to (bound to) such releasement, such freeing up or letting-go.

Schlegel's parody of scientific classification offers an instructive example of how irony works to loosen our grip on things by loosening our grip on our conceptual (linguistic) categories. Somewhat like the opening sentences, in which Schlegel begins with the idea of a single thought but then quickly acknowledges the outside pressures (their exertion of a claim) on that thought, Schlegel's classification of all the ironies both describes and demonstrates irony's basic tendency toward proliferation:

> In order to facilitate a survey of the whole system of irony, we would like to mention here a few of the choicest kinds. . . . Finally, there is the irony of irony. Generally speaking, the most fundamental irony of irony probably is that even it becomes tiresome if we are always confronted with it. But what we want this irony to mean in the first place is something that happens in more ways than one. (*KA* 2:369; *LF* 266)

This is a hermeneutics which traffics in the singular, which tries to think several paths at once, resists forcing the otherness of words (of existence itself) into preexisting categories of thinking or understanding. It is a hermeneutics only too answerable to the claim of the contrary path. Toward the end of the essay, Schlegel reaches the point where even he longs for the end, longs for a Hegelian synthesis of all the big and little ironies of the world into a single, logically coherent scheme. In the end, however, the inertia or otherness of words defers just that possibility:

What gods will rescue us from all these ironies? The only solution is to find an irony that might be able to swallow up all these big and little ironies and leave no trace of them at all. I must confess that at precisely this moment that mine has a real urge to do just that. But even this would only be a short-term solution. I fear that if I understand correctly what destiny seems to be hinting at, then soon there will arise a new generation of little ironies: for truly the stars augur the fantastic. (*KA* 2:369-70; *LF* 267)

This ironic setting free of words to the winds, implying a release of words from conceptual constraint into their own natural tendencies as characteristic of the ironist or the poet, sets the stage for what is arguably the highpoint of the essay, the climactic passage in which Schlegel comes closest to describing what he means by incomprehensibility. Here again, Schlegel describes the ironist's attitude toward words as one of releasement:

But is incomprehensibility really something so unmitigatedly contemptible and evil? Methinks the salvation of families and nations rests upon it. . . . Yes, even man's most precious possession, his own inner happiness, depends in the last analysis, as anybody can easily verify, on some such point of strength that must be left in the dark, but that nonetheless shores up and supports the whole burden and would lose this power the moment one wished to resolve it into rational understanding. Verily, it would be frightening for you if, as you demand, the whole world were just once, in all seriousness, to become wholly comprehensible. And isn't this entire, unending world constructed by the understanding out of incomprehensibility or chaos? (*KA* 2:370; *LF* 268)

Schlegel implies that back-and-forth reciprocal work between comprehension and incomprehension is basic to the experience of the work of art, now understood, romantically, as being inscribed by the quarrel between philosophy and poetry, what *Athenäum Fragment* 116 calls the romantic kind of poetry. The essay works toward acknowledgement of a certain chaotic foundation or underground that underwrites the world, an underwriting (a writing beneath or beyond comprehension) which escapes our human categories and our rational terms for understanding it. The romantic kind of poetry is writing which, tending outside the confines of the classical genres, seeks not to control but to put into play, turn loose, the chaotic energies of words themselves and set them ringing. The thought here is that the otherness or incomprehensibility of words must be recuperated, maintained, and cultivated, not overcome; our happiness depends on "some such point of strength that must be left in the dark." This ongoing tension between possession and dispossession as modes of understanding, light and dark regions of thinking, is basic to the essay. Schlegel holds the two together in fruitful tension, arguing that the world (as we know it) depends on a region that must be both allowed or left to go [*muß gelassen werden*]. Things cannot be known by analytically forcing them into the glare of conceptual clarity but by setting them free into tendencies they already possess—or are already possessed by. This succeptibility to digression, wandering, lingering, or straying, Schlegel would say, is what the science of hermeneutics (as Schleiermacher thinks of it) can learn from the language of the work of art.

One Word More

One might conclude here by recalling Schlegel's observation that "what we want this irony [of the fragmentary work] to mean in the first place is something that happens in more ways than one" (*KA* 2:369; *LF* 267). There are two points to consider here. First, the reserve or refusal of the fragmentary work in the face of the knowing subject is more like the experience of an occurrence or an event than like the grasping of an object of knowledge. It is resistant to, and inaccessible with respect to, critical-historical method. That is to say, there can be no literary theory, strictly speaking, which might be able to "divine" its essence because, to begin with, it is not a rule-governed activity; it disregards (as if in response to Kant) the usual conditions under which it is supposed to make its appearance and tends to erupt instead at the most inconvenient times and places, and in the most embarrassing ways. Better to think of it as a way language, apart from any human willing or desiring, comports itself. Second, it is irreducibly plural, heterogeneous, more than or other than itself, singular, and excessive with respect to sense. So it is never a question of a fragmentary genre per se; rather, one is doomed to tracing it out in its various forms and living with it in its different versions, with the plurality and multiplicity of its historical manifestations.

This uncontrollable movement of words is what disturbed Søren Kierkegaard most about irony as practiced (or undergone) by the early German romantics. Presumably, this is why he tried, for the remainder of his life, to get a manageable handle on it; to slow it down, to still its incessant motion. Kierkegaard remained unsettled by romanticism's embrace of irony; drawn to it and yet wary of it. Here is Kierkegaard in *The Concept of Irony*, characteristically caught between impulses toward freedom and self-mastery: "irony simultaneously makes the poem and the poet free. But for this to happen, the poet himself must be master over the irony."[25] Given Kierkegaard's anxiety, it should not be surprising that literary criticism perpetually tries to put back the lid to Pandora's box. Kierkegaard calls for containment in the conclusion to his doctoral thesis, an abandonment of romantic discourse's wanton recklessness and a return to a kinder, a more controlled (a more responsible) use of irony:

> To be controlled in this way, to be halted in the wild infinity into which it rushes ravenously, by no means indicates that irony should now lose its meaning or be totally discarded. On the contrary, when the individual is properly situated—and this he is through the curtailment of irony— only then does irony have its proper meaning, its true validity. In our age there has been much talk about the importance of doubt for science and scholarship, but what doubt is to science, irony is to personal life. Just as scientists maintain that there is no true science without doubt, so it may be maintained with the same right that no genuinely human life is possible without irony. As soon as irony is controlled, it makes a movement opposite to that in which uncontrolled irony declares its life. Irony limits, finitizes, and circumscribes and thereby yields truth, actuality, content; it disciplines and punishes and thereby yields balance and consistency. Irony is a disciplinarian feared only by those who do not know it but loved by those who do. Anyone who does not understand at all, who has no ear for its whispering, lacks eo ipso (precisely thereby) what could be called the absolute beginning of personal life; he lacks what is momentarily indispensable for personal life; he lacks the bath of regeneration and rejuvenation, irony's baptism of purification that rescues the soul from having its life in finitude even though it is living energetically and robustly in it. (326)

One of the striking things about Kierkegaard's account is the way it combines ironic destruction and humorous regeneration, or tragic ending and comic beginning, as though the romantic work is constituted by a serio-comical duplicity, a back and forth play between the serious and the trivial. Furthermore, this in-betweenness suggests a family resemblance between the linguistic experience of the romantic work's worklessness and hermeneutic experience, that is, the experience of understanding, which is often said to have its primal scene in the ancient quarrel between philosophy and poetry. What romanticism is most concerned with is making a beginning, moving toward or gesturing toward a beginning, as though writing never really begins as such, but is always beginning again.

Again one thinks of Kierkegaard's description: "If I have conceived . . . of the romantic position as a teeter-totter, the ends of which are characterized by irony and humor, then it follows naturally that the path of its oscillation is extremely varied, all the way from the most heaven-storming humor to the most desperate bowing down in irony"(*CI* 430). Kierkegaard's account of irony's duplicity is quite similar to Schlegel's point about the heterogeneity of irony or, to put it differently, the idea that irony is excessive with respect to the conceptual. What is excessive is precisely what Kierkegaard mentions, namely, the unstable humor of irony, and the tendency of humor to turn to irony and vice versa. One could call this the weakness of language; its tendency to fall to the earth or to go around in a circle, the failure of words to stay put; to mean always what they say, as if their material mode of being exerts a claim on one prior to their meaning. One could think of this reluctance as part of the intrinsic humor of words. What is important in terms of interpretation is the strange humor of language philosophy cannot acknowledge and still remain philosophical. To retain its seriousness and respectability, philosophy has to maintain control over words, has to get words straight, get their sense out in the open, so it can begin to think clearly. To put it another way, the humor of words is what philosophy remains constitutionally unable to cope with. The fragment, in this case, is the comically weak (uncontrollable) participant in a romantic-ironic dialogue, the fragmentary word that in its ludicrous wandering undoes philosophy's pious seriousness. One can read the *Fragments* as a collection of forms of ironic life—each bearing a family resemblance to every other—that spring up in the rift between philosophy and poetry: Socratic irony, the novel, the dialogue, the compendia or the encyclopedia, symphilosophy, the fragmentary work, romantic poetry, the idea, comic wit, the fragment itself, transcendental poetry, and so on.

So, romantic poetry, as it begins within German romanticism, constitutes an attempt to think by means other than the closed system, the foundation, or the logical framework. More than anything else, it represents an attempt to think from the margins or from the outside of reason, in the plural, to think by means of the plurality of language. Discussing the romantics, Blanchot writes:

if all these traits are recognized as being equally necessary, inasmuch as they are opposed to one another, what then becomes the dominant tone is not the ideological meaning of any one of them in particular, but rather their opposition: the necessity of contradiction, the scission and the fact of being divided—what Brentano calls *die Geteilheit*. Thereby characterized as the requirement or the experience of contradiction, romanticism does no more than confirm its vocation of disorder—menace for some, promise for others, futile threat or sterile promise. (*EI* 516; *IC* 352)

Blanchot concedes the apparent open-endedness of the romantic mindset which is not primarily a paradigm of consciousness but more like a mode of writing, or more precisely, a mode of thinking-as-writing. He attempts to redirect such thinking toward the outside, the singular, the uncontainable or exceptional. Here Blanchot points to the signature genre of romanticism, the fragment:

Just as genius is nothing other than a multiple person (Novalis) or a system of talents (Schlegel), what is important is to introduce into writing, through the fragment, the plurality that in each of us is virtual, in all of us real, and that corresponds to "the unceasing, autocreative alternance of different or opposed thoughts." Discontinuous form: the sole form befitting romantic irony, since it alone can make coincide discourse and silence, the playful and the serious, the declarative, even oracular exigency and the indecision of a thought that is unstable and divided, finally, the mind's obligation to be systematic and its abhorrence for system: "Having a system is as moral for the mind as not having one: it must, then, decide to lose both these tendencies" (Schlegel). (*EI* 526; *IC* 358)

This observation is a powerful insight into German romanticism, which begins to take one out of romanticism construed as a literary category or an historical marker and into a region that is closer to being a form of life. One might call it (with Blanchot) the realm of the essential solitude of the work of art, of literature; the tentative region opened up by the work itself, the space for thinking or being fostered by the working of the work which, however, in the light of day is just plain nonsense, unintelligibility, and anarchy.

3

Nothing so Difficult as a Beginning: Byron's Pilgrimage to the Origin of the Work of Art and the Inspiration of Exile

Nothing so difficult as a beginning
In poesy, unless perhaps the end . . .

—Byron

Exile is one of the saddest of fates. In premodern times banishment was a particularly dreadful punishment since it did not only mean years of aimless wandering away from family and familiar places, but also meant being a sort of permanent outcast, someone who never felt at home, and was always at odds with the environment. There has always been an association between the idea of exile and the terrors of being a leper, a social and moral untouchable.

—Edward Said

In 1834, a decade after Byron's death at Missolonghi in Greece, writer and civil servant Henry Taylor offered his assessment of the poet: "Had [Byron] united a philosophical intellect to his peculiarly poetical temperament, he would probably have been the greatest poet of his age."[1] For much of the twentieth-century, critics have agreed, dismissing Byron's obsession with the ironic negativity of poetic experience as the result of an adolescent temperament rather than as a constitutive aspect of his poetics. T. S. Eliot, who was partly responsible for establishing this view, regarded Byron as a poet for schoolboys rather than a mature artist and damned the poet with faint praise in a notorious dismissal.[2] Not until the 1960s did less partisan critics begin to take the full measure of

Byron as a deeply thoughtful and widely influential, if profoundly skeptical, poet.[3] Even so, most of these critics limit themselves to thematic
issues such as the myth of the Fall, or, more recently, the historical con-
vulsions that inform the poetry, rather than the fragmentary force of
his poetics.[4] Byron's writing, however, explores fragmentation and ruin
not merely in thematic terms but also in terms of the centrifugal force
of poetry itself; its need to pass beyond itself in order to confront what
remains unthought in thinking. Moreover, when one begins to think of
Byron's work in terms of what Schlegel calls *romantische Poesie*, a dialogic
work whose essence is "to be eternally in the process of becoming and
never completed," a far more philosophically prescient, and profoundly
unsettling, dimension of his poetics emerges: the fragmentary weakness
of the romantic work of art. Thought of in this way, some of Byron's
greatest poems, including *Childe Harold's Pilgrimage* and *Don Juan*,
can be read not so much as an ironic counter-voice to the mainline
British tradition but rather as some of the most compelling instances
of romantic poetry in world literature.[5]

In a seminal discussion of *Don Juan*, Elizabeth French Boyd calls the
poem a novel in verse, a work

> written in defiance of the world, in an atmosphere of increasing intellec-
> tual freedom. Freedom is not only one of *Don Juan's* powerful themes
> but breathes in its scope and variety, and in the originality of its mixture
> of forms and styles.[6]

One can further explore this novelistic dimension of Byron's poetics by
appealing to the work of the critic Mikhail Bakhtin. In two suggestive
essays, Bakhtin describes the novel in terms that echo Schlegel's theory
in some striking ways. "[T]he novel," Bakhtin writes in "Epic and
Novel," "is the sole genre that continues to develop, that is as yet un-
completed. The forces that define it as a genre are at work before our
very eyes: the birth and development of the novel as a genre takes place
in the full light of historical day" (*DI* 3). Bakhtin cites Byron's works as
key examples of the "novelization" of epic. He writes:

> Of particular interest are those eras when the novel becomes the domi-
> nant genre. All literature is then caught up in the process of "becoming,"
> and in a special kind of "generic criticism." This occurred several times in
> the Hellenic period, again during the late Middle Ages and the Renais-
> sance, but with special force and clarity beginning in the second half of the

eighteenth century. In an era when the novel reigns supreme, almost all the remaining genres are to a greater or lesser extent "novelized": drama (for example Ibsen, Hauptmann, the whole of Naturalist drama), epic poetry (for example, *Childe Harold* and especially Byron's *Don Juan*), even lyric poetry (as an extreme example, Heine's lyrical verse). (*DI* 5–6)

For Bakhtin, the rise of the novel and the novelization of other genres by means of irony, dialogue, and fragmentation contribute to the breakup of epic consciousness and announce the emergence of a more historically circumspect plurality.[7] Novelistic modes of discourse engage in a parodic-travestying dialogue with the serious genres, breaking down their prim and proper palace walls, releasing them from the prison-house of their own high seriousness and opening their borders to the exotic and the foreign, the alien and the strange, the comical and the satirical registers of human experience.[8]

Ultimately, Bakhtin traces novelization to the unsettling force of Socratic dialogue. "This [deconstruction of epic consciousness]," he writes, "applies in particular to the Socratic dialogues, which may be called—to rephrase Friedrich Schlegel—"the novels of their time," and also to Menippean satire (including the *Satyricon* of Petronius), whose role in the history of the novel is immense and as yet inadequately appreciated by scholarship. These serio-comical genres were the first authentic and essential step in the evolution of the novel as the genre of becoming" (*DI* 22). Eschewing the epic's univocal mythic narrative consciousness and drawn instead to the intellectual drama that characterizes dialogue, Bakhtin presents a Socrates who is more at home on the street corner than in the ivory tower. Inspired by the romantics and their rethinking of Platonic dialogue, Bakhtin places the elusive Socrates at the very center of novelistic discourse:

Moreover the figure of Socrates himself is characteristic for the genre—he is an outstanding example of heroization in novelistic prose (so very different from epic heroization). It is, finally, profoundly characteristic—and for us of the utmost importance—that we have laughter, Socratic irony, the entire system of Socratic degradations combined with a serious, lofty and for the first time truly free investigation of the world, of man and of human thought. Socratic laughter (reduced to irony) and Socratic degradations (an entire system of metaphors and comparisons borrowed from the lower spheres of life—from tradespeople, from everyday life, etc.) bring the world closer and familiarize it in order to investigate it fearlessly and freely. (*DI* 25)

Bakhtin thus re-casts Plato as an intellectual provocateur who special-izes in the theater of ideas but who never intended his dialogues to be taken as doctrine by overzealous students. Rather, the dialogic word (embodied in Socratic irony) must remain fully open, two-sided, tenta-tive and on the edge, and, most important, unfulfilled in order to pro-voke a thoughtful response.

For Bakhtin some doubt about the meaning of words is appropriate and plays an important role in ensuring the truth of literature. Skepti-cism, for him, is not so much a problem as the region in which poetry takes up its abode; there is an internal connection, that is, between poetry and skepticism. In an essay entitled "From the Prehistory of Novelistic Discourse," Bakhtin explores this idea:

> These parodic-travestying forms prepared the ground for the novel in one very important way. They liberated the object from the power of language in which it had become entangled as if in a net; they destroyed the ho-mogenizing power of myth over language; they freed consciousness from the power of the direct word, destroyed the thick walls that had impris-oned consciousness within its own discourse, within its own language. A distance arose between language and reality that was to prove an indispen-sable condition for authentically realistic forms of discourse. (*DI* 60)

Bakhtin makes three crucial observations here. First, because of its di-alogic nature, novelistic discourse frees the world of objects from the stranglehold of a single point of view. This gives things or entities, to say nothing of characters or incidents, space to be what they are, apart from human desires. Second, such deliberately self-conscious discourse de-stroys the ideal of transparency according to which language is merely an instrument used for the transmission of doctrines or ideas. Finally, such a view unsettles the myth of a homogenous tradition that underwrites consciousness with a single worldview. The novel exposes consciousness to the truth that there are two sides to every story, two ways of seeing every problem, or, in this case, two senses to every word.

According to Bakhtin, novelistic discourse exposes homogeneous ways of looking at the world to the answering voices of the heterogeneous mar-gins, allowing such voices to counter the absolutism of the epic. In order to account for the impact romantic poetry has had on epic consciousness Bakhtin uses an analogy drawn from the early modern history of science:

> The novel is the expression of a Galilean perception of language, one that denies the absolutism of a single and unitary language—that is, that *refuses to acknowledge its own language as the sole verbal and semantic center*

of the ideological world. . . . The novel begins by presuming a verbal and semantic decentering of the ideological world, a certain *linguistic home-lessness* of literary consciousness, which no longer possesses a sacrosanct and unitary linguistic medium for containing ideological thought. (*DI* 366-67, emphases mine)

One consequence of the novel's critique of the pre-modern or Ptole-maic worldview is that literary consciousness no longer depends on a single world picture. In the spirit of Fontenelle's *Conversations on the Plurality of Worlds* (1686), in which a Marquise and her mentor reflect on the possibility of other worlds, the novel as a dialogic genre acknowl-edges the existence of multiple narratives interacting with one another on a variety of planes.[9] In *Don Juan*, a work that champions the Galilean or Copernican alternative, Byron puts the matter this way: "There's more than one edition, and the readings / Are various, but they none of them are dull."[10]

Edward Said provides a useful way to complicate such an analysis. In a lecture entitled "Intellectual Exile," Said reflects upon the question of exile in terms of its currency as an existential mood or a mode of being, rather than simply a territorial condition or temporary state. Reflecting on "[those] who because of exile *cannot*, or, more to the point, will not [work out an accommodation with a new or emerging dominant power]," preferring instead to remain outside the mainstream, unaccommodated, uncoopted, resistant," Said focuses on Theodor Adorno, a Jewish intel-lectual who fled first the horrors of Europe during the 1930s and subse-quently the crassness of American consumerism.[11] For Said, this sort of exile—exile as an impossible choice—involves an individual who, having been forced into exile by an authoritarian regime, subsequently (and un-thinkably) chooses exile as the mode of being that allows for the greatest degree of authenticity.

Said pursues this line of thinking by adding two important qualifica-tions. First, he complicates the notion, expanding it so that it appears as both a physical or material condition and at the same time a meta-phorical or metaphysical frame of mind or way of being: "while it is an *actual* condition, exile is also for my purposes a *metaphorical* condition." Said explains:

> The pattern that sets the course for the intellectual as outsider is best exemplified by the condition of exile, the state of never being fully ad-justed, always feeling outside the chatty, familiar world inhabited by natives, so to speak, tending to avoid and even dislike the trappings of accommodation and national well-being. Exile for the intellectual in

this metaphysical sense is restlessness, movement, constantly being un-settled, and unsettling others. You cannot go back to some earlier and perhaps more stable condition of being at home; and, alas, you can never fully arrive, be at one with your new home or situation. (373)

Second, Said extends the application of the concept of exile so that "while it is an *actual* condition," a state of being in exile or banishment, "[it] is also . . . a *metaphorical* condition," a way of belonging-by-being-outside, or of belonging-by-not-belonging. In this sense, exile desig-nates more than geopolitical dislocation; it implies, in the metaphorical and metaphysical senses Said invokes, a way of being-in-the-world, a "restlessness, movement, [a state of] constantly being unsettled, and [of] unsettling others." Such a conception recalls Heidegger's analysis of ex-istence in *Being and Time* in which he underscores the unfinished na-ture of human life: the "structural factor of care tells us unambiguously that something is always still *outstanding* [*aussteht*] in Da-sein [Heideg-ger's word for human beings] which has not yet become "real" as a potentiality-of-its-being. A *constant unfinished quality* thus lies in the essence of the constitution of Da-sein."[12]

Said develops this analysis further by suggesting that the condition of exile can revisit an individual as a metaphorical or metaphysical op-portunity. "Secondly," Said says, "—and I find myself somewhat sur-prised by this observation even as I make it—,"

the intellectual as exile tends to be happy with the idea of unhappiness, so that dissatisfaction bordering on dyspepsia, a kind of curmudgeonly disagreeableness, can become not only a style of thought, but also a new, if temporary, habitation. The intellectual as ranting Thersites perhaps. A great historical prototype for what I have in mind is a powerful eighteenth century figure, Jonathan Swift, who never got over his fall from influ-ence and prestige in England after the Tories left office in 1714, and spent the rest of his life in exile in Ireland. (373)

For Said, the intellectual can break through to the other side until it becomes an enabling condition to view the world through the eyes of exile. For Said, this quasi-occult state of belonging-by-not-belonging, neither here nor there, is the condition of the exile par excellence. According to Said, the trauma of exile can paradoxically become a habitation—a way of being-in-the-world that brings life's ambiguities, contradictions, disappointments, and reversals to the surface. Swift, "[a]n almost legendary figure of bitterness and anger—*saeve indignatio* he said of himself in his own epitaph," was in the end a deeply divided writer, "furious at Ireland, and yet its defender against British tyranny, a man whose towering Irish works *Gulliver's Travels* and *The Drapier's Letters* show a mind flourishing, not to say benefiting, from such productive anguish" (373).

In Byron's works, the ambiguity that surfaces for those who dwell at the margins comes dramatically into view, illustrating Bakhtin's claim that the novelist looks both through, and at, language, seeing it as an object of aesthetic and ethical interest as well as a medium of expression. As a result, such a writer experiences not only the dialogism of individual words but also the competing claims of the multiple worldviews inscribed within any given discourse. Julia Kristeva builds upon Bakhtin's revolutionary insight into the dialogic structure of literary language by extending the ironic richness of novelistic discourse to poetry: "The poetic word," she writes, "polyvalent and multi-determined, adheres to a logic exceeding that of codified discourse and fully comes into being only in the margins of recognized culture."[13] The poetic word, in other words, drifts outside the logic of sense and nonsense or, better, truth and falsity, and discloses a fundamental ambiguity in its material thickness. The poet-narrator in *Don Juan* affirms this thought: "But words are things, and a small drop of ink, / Falling like dew, upon a thought, produces / That which makes thousands, perhaps millions, think" (III, 88). In these few lines, Byron asserts a profound connection involving poetry, language, and thought.

Such a view of poetic language returns us to Boyd's claim that *Don Juan* centers on the issue of freedom, although the freedom in question is not so much free will, or the freedom of the autonomous self, as the freedom of the world to be what it is in the first place. Understood this way, the essence of romantic poetry as *romantische Poesie* is to release the world as a gift, the gift of being or existence, the freedom, that is, of world to be itself. The preservation of this freedom, Bakhtin implies, is contingent on the ironic negativity of poetic discourse. Kristeva examines the negativity of poetic language in detail, calling it "the fourth 'term' of the [Hegelian] dialectic":

> The notion of *negativity* [*Negativität*], which may be thought of as both the cause and the organizing principle of the *process*, comes from Hegel. The concept of negativity, distinct from that of nothingness [*Nichts*] and negation [*Negation*], figures as the indissoluble relation between an "ineffable" mobility and its "particular determination." Negativity is the

mediation . . . of the "pure abstractions" of being and nothingness in the concrete where they are both only moments. Although negativity is a concept and therefore belongs to a contemplative (theoretical) system, it reformulates the static *terms* of pure abstraction as a process, dissolving and binding them within a mobile law. . . . Negativity constitutes the logical impetus beneath the thesis of negation and that of the negation of negation, but is identical to neither since it is, instead, the logical functioning of the movement that produces the theses.[14]

Such an account of poetry's fondness for inhabiting the hinterland between being [*Sein*] and nothingness [*Nichts*] provides a touchstone for romantic period writing. Wordsworth frequently, even morbidly, meditates on the mystery of human finitude, while P. B. Shelley's "Mont Blanc" and Keats's "Ode to a Nightingale" address the question of what separates being from nonbeing and what it might be like to experience the transition from one to the other. In recent work exploring connections between Byron's poetics and his audience, Jane Stabler reminds us that, for contemporary poets like Felicia Hemans and Elizabeth Barrett Browning, "Byron [was] associated with a violent collision of presence and absence."[15] For her part, Kristeva explores the complexity of a negativity that, in terms of the poetics articulated by German romanticism and recounted by Lacoue-Labarthe and Nancy (following Heidegger), "has no essence, not even in its inessentiality" (*LA* 83). It is rather an indissoluble relation between the originating play of the world and its concrete and historical determinations. Negativity as *Negativität* is a persistent remainder in experience that the gears of dialectic can never recuperate. One can think of it as that part of the process that allows the process to go on.

In an essay on "Byron's Phenomenology of Negation," John Watkins makes a case for the view that the poet's ongoing fascination with negation, nothingness, and negativity is foundational for his mature poetic practice.[16] Although Watkins relies on Heidegger rather than Bakhtin or Kristeva, his analysis of Byron's fragmentary poetics reinforces my own. "Byron not only speculates about the abyss," Watkins writes, "but incorporates it as a principle of formal fragmentation in his mature work. His confrontation with it in [his] poems . . . frees him from an inherited teleology of narrative that threatens to deny him direct engagement with experience" (396). Watkins gives the issue of freedom dramatic new application and force; it is no longer simply a thematic issue but is now integral to the structure of Byron's mature work.

Watkins goes on to argue (with some success) for a kinship between Byron and Heidegger: "Like Heidegger in his attack on the static metaphysics of previous philosophy, Byron confronts the nothing that is the matrix of individual beings to discover their vulnerability to the eventual and certain negation that is part of the truth of being. For Byron, too, *Angst* in the face of nihilation engenders freedom" (404). Watkins emphasizes that freedom in this sense operates simultaneously on thematic and formal levels, complicating the boundaries between the two in order to serve as a ground or first principle for thinking with poetry. In this view, some of Byron's most beloved poetic works, including *Childe Harold's Pilgrimage* and *Don Juan*, embody a dialogue between narrative clarity and lyrical obscurity in which the origin of the work of art is not so much a starting point as a projected (and always provisional) goal.

The Wandering Outlaw of His Own Dark Mind

Written during his travels in the Levant in 1809–11 and by all accounts the poem that made him famous, Byron's *Childe Harold's Pilgrimage* I–II (1812) announces a preoccupation with the condition of exile. Creating a new kind of hero, one introduced, as Byron says in the "Preface," "for the sake of giving some connexion [sic] to the piece" (*CPW* II, 4), the poem begins by posing the question of what to do when one finds oneself at the end of the story with the balance of one's life still left to live. Here the outstanding [*aussteht*] quality of human existence comes dramatically into view. The impetus for the events of the narrative comes not as the result of a specific crisis exerting pressure on Harold as from the existential restlessness or ennui that settles into Harold's mind and body as a matter of course. Canto I begins with Harold already at loose ends: "ere scarce a third of his pass'd by, / Worse than adversity the Childe befell; / He felt the fulness of satiety" (I, 4). Harold has met a fate worse than slow agonizing death: the satisfaction of his earthly needs. "Then loath'd he in his native land to dwell, / Which seem'd to him more lone than Eremite's sad cell" (I, 4). Byron parodies the logic of romance and builds the poem out of the conflict between Harold's desire to leave his father's "vast and venerable pile" (I, 7) and the inertia of epic consciousness. The poem's self-consciously archaic title and opening lines—"Whilome in Albion's isle there dwelt a youth / Who ne in virtue's ways did take delight" (I, 2)—establish a signature opposition between the weight of an antiquarian, oppressive, even funereal tradition and the need to exercise individual talent on behalf of the present and future.[17]

However, lest one assume that Byron sides entirely with iconoclastic Harold against epic consciousness, the Preface acknowledges a semblance of propriety. Byron writes that

> it had been easy to varnish over [Harold's] faults, to make him do more and express less, but he never was intended as an example, further than to show that early perversion of mind and morals leads to satiety of past pleasures and disappointment in new ones, and that even the beauties of nature, and the stimulus of travel . . . are lost on a soul so constituted, or rather misdirected. (*CPW* II, 6)

Byron thus calls attention to his hero's shortcomings, promising the reader that over the course of the pilgrimage he will be enlightened as to the true nature of virtue—much like Dante the pilgrim, made to understand the meaning of justice. Although Byron constructs a different sort of pilgrimage, the poet's voice is nonetheless surprisingly sincere and one would do well not to ignore the normative moral framework against which Harold's adventures play themselves out.[18] Canto I proceeds with Harold's story:

5

For he through Sin's long labyrinth had run,
Nor made atonement when he did amiss,
Had sigh'd to many though he lov'd but one,
And that lov'd one, alas! could ne'er be his.
Ah, happy she! to 'scape from him whose kiss
Had been pollution unto aught so chaste;
Who soon had left her charms for vulgar bliss,
And spoil'd her goodly lands to gild his waste,
Nor calm domestic peace had ever deign'd to taste.

6

And now Childe Harold was sore sick at heart,
And from his fellow bacchanals would flee;
'Tis said, at times the sullen tear would start,
But Pride congeal'd the drop within his ee:
Apart he stalk'd in joyless reverie,
And from his native land resolv'd to go,
And visit scorching climes beyond the sea;
With pleasure drugg'd he almost long'd for woe,
And e'en for change of scene would seek the shades below.

In a useful discussion of the poem, Frederick Shilstone observes, "[t]he conflict between self and tradition informs Byron's early lyrics and emerges fully defined in . . . *Childe Harold's Pilgrimage*" (1). Shilstone identifies this as "a confident attempt by the conservative Byron to guide his wrongheaded other self, Harold the iconoclast, to an awareness of the value of inherited myths," a sort of pilgrim's progress through modernity intended to teach Harold the virtues of myth and tradition. However, Shilstone admits, "the work ultimately succumbs to the personal tragedies and historical ironies its stanzas encounter" (1). Similar to Schlegel's defense of classical poetry against the encroachment of modernity in *On the Study of Greek Poetry*, Byron is at first inclined to defend tradition against the rising tide of vernacular culture.

When Harold sets out from his ancestral home, it is not a pilgrimage in the usual sense but a more reluctant passage out into the world of the ordinary, where age, sickness, war, disillusionment, and death hold sway. "Onward he flies," the narrator says, "nor fix'd as yet the goal / Where he shall rest him on his pilgrimage; / And o'er him many changing seasons must roll / Ere his thirst for travel can assuage" (I, 28). Rather than progress toward a goal that one can physically perceive somewhere in the distance, Harold's (and the poet-narrator's) way embodies what Gadamer calls hermeneutic experience. Experience in this sense, argues Gadamer, is a process often leading to unpredictable results:

> In fact, this process is essentially negative. It cannot be described simply as the unbroken generation of typical universals. Rather, this generation takes place as false generalizations are continually refuted by experience . . . Language shows this when we use the word "experience" in two different senses: the experiences that conform to our expectation and confirm it and the new experiences that occur to us. This latter— "experience" in the genuine sense—is always negative. If a new experience of an object occurs to us, this means hitherto we have not seen the thing correctly and now know it better. Thus the negativity of experience has a curiously productive meaning. (*TM* 353)

As Harold leaves home, the poet-narrator reminds us that, like Harold, our aims and goals are rarely determined entirely in advance, but rather undergo frequent modification as a result of the journey. McGann argues that this happens to the poet-narrator as well as to Harold: over the course of the poem he, too, undergoes a pilgrimage in order to find his voice as a writer.[19] A close reading of the poem bears this out: one can see the journey as a heuristic through which the poet identifies the aim of the search along the way. Even so, with a portion of the pilgrimage completed, Byron admitted in a letter to John Murray in November of 1813 "C[hil]d[e] Ha[rol]d is & I rather think always will be unconcluded" (*BLJ* III, 182). Although one detects discouragement in Byron's words, M. K. Joseph notes that over the course of the first two Cantos, "Byron discovers what is to become the master-device of the poem, the use of ruined monuments as the link between present and past, and opens what is to be its central theme, the triumph of time and the transience of human glory."[20]

Written in the years following the publication of *Childe Harold* I-II, the Eastern Tales reinforced Byron's growing reputation. These verse narratives turned out to be so popular that Bryon wrote Thomas Moore to offer what sounds like inside information: "Stick to the East;—the oracle, Staël, told me it was the only poetical policy" (*BLJ* III, 101). In *The Giaour, A Fragment of a Turkish Tale* (1813), the first and most instructive of the Eastern Tales, Byron further examines the limits of narrative and the productive experience of exile. Composition of the poem, as McGann writes in his notes to the text (*CPW* III, 406–24), proceeded in a piecemeal fashion, and the first version of the poem was only 344 lines long (*CPW* III, 413). As Byron later told Francis Hodgson, a subsequent sketch consisted of a 407-line fragment, to which he then made "additions to the amount of ten pages, *text* and *margin* (*chiefly* the last)" that increased the length to 685 lines; further revised and expanded, the final version runs to 1334 lines (*BLJ* III, 96, emphasis in original). Ironically, the more lines Byron added to the poem, the more he underlined its essential incompleteness.

Amidst all the excitement surrounding his newfound celebrity, Byron admitted to Murray some reservations regarding his new poem. He wrote:

> The general horror of *fragments* makes me tremulous for the "Giaour" but you would publish it—I presume by this time to your repentance— but as I consented—whatever be it's fate I won't now quarrel with you—even though I detect it in my pastry—but I shall not open a pye without apprehension for some weeks. (*BLJ* III, 62, emphasis in the original)

Some of the apprehension resulted from negative criticism received by Samuel Rogers's poem, *The Voyage of Columbus* (1812), an experimental work that, like *The Giaour*, makes unusual demands on its reader. In a gesture of fraternal support, Byron dedicates his poem to Rogers, while in the Advertisement, he attempts to disarm critics by foregrounding the historical forces at play in its textual transmission. He writes:

> The tale which these disjointed fragments present is founded upon circumstances now less common in the East than formerly. . . . The story, when entire, contained the adventures of a female slave, who was thrown, in the Musselman manner, into the sea for infidelity, and avenged by a young Venetian, her lover, at the time the Seven Islands were possessed by the Republic of Venice. (*CPW* III, 39)

Adopting the role of editor and redactor, Byron links the instability of the poem to the ravages of time. Once a completed work, *The Giaour* now gives only tantalizing hints of its former brilliance. Together, McGann argues, the Eastern Tales reflect the collapse of the Roman world and the emergence of a more heterogeneous political and social order. These Tales "are not merely a set of exotic adventure stories. They constitute a series of symbolic historical and political meditations on current European ideology and politics in the context of the relations between East and West after the break-up of the Roman Empire and the emergence of Islam."[21] Employing historical and socio-political categories rather than generic or linguistic ones, McGann nevertheless confirms many of Bakhtin's insights regarding the emergence of the novel and the irony of novelistic discourse.

Many of these questions surface with redoubled force in relation to the poem's title. According to the *OED*, the word *giaour* is originally a term of reproach applied by Turks to non-Muslims, especially Christians; it denotes an unbeliever or an infidel, and, even more disparagingly, a dog. Byron may have come across it in William Beckford's oriental tale, *Vathek*, originally written in French in 1782 and translated into English by Samuel Henley in 1786 under Beckford's supervision. Most important, it is difficult for a native English speaker to know how to pronounce this unfamiliar word. In Jane Austen's novel *Persuasion*, the heroine Ann Elliott is engaged in conversation with Captain Benwick on the relative merits of Byron and Scott, the two great poets of the age. Benwick reflects on "whether *Marmion* or *The Lady of the Lake* were to be preferred, and how ranked the *Giaour* and *The Bride of Abydos*;

and, moreover, how the *Giaour* was to be pronounced."[22] Often re-marked upon, this is a telling passage. Shilstone writes, "[t]he voice that Byron uses in this and other early narratives is derived from the works of writers like Sir Walter Scott, especially from the oral bard who most obviously found his way onto the printed page in Scott's *The Lay of the Last Minstrel* (1805)" (47). However, unlike Scott, Byron is determined to complicate this oral voice, to juxtapose its superficial unity with more complex and elusive depths. What eventually results in a one thousand three hundred and thirty-four-line narrative, Shilstone says, "seems more an attempt to conceal its plot than straightforwardly to reveal it and comment upon its significance" (48–49).

This word, the first (or, more precisely, second) pronounced by an English speaking reader, places one in an unusual, even uncomfortable position: inside the worldview of one who sees a Christian as an infidel— i.e. a Muslim. The poem forces the reader to experience the events of the poem through the eyes of a poet-narrator who sees in Christianity, not Islam, a heterodox persuasion and an outlaw worldview. Byron's use of the word *giaour* as the title resituates the gentle reader at the oppo-site end of the high table of the hermeneutic conversation: outside the circle of orthodoxy and in the position of the one who must justify her very being.

In part, Byron wishes to draw the reader's attention to the opposi-tion between religious orthodoxy and freedom of conscience, ideologi-cal conformity and intellectual independence. "The desertion of the Mainotes," writes Byron in the Advertisement, "on being refused the plunder of Misitra, led to the abandonment of that enterprise, and to the desolation of the Morea, during which the cruelty exercised on all side was unparalleled even in the annals of the faithful" (*CPW* III, 40). This intersection of narratives, the exposure of one to another, culminates in the giaour's reflections on his beloved Leila during his confession: "Howe'er deserv'd her doom might be, / Her treachery was truth to me" (*CPW* III, 73). In these powerful lines, Byron not only speculates on the textual transmission of tradition over time but also on how dif-ferent worldviews collide in the present.

These anxieties regarding multiple worldviews surface again in the poem's opening lines. As it begins, the reader finds herself at the water's edge, floating near the surface below an anonymous "Athenian's grave" (*CPW* III, 40). It is a wonderful, almost cinematic moment. Our atten-tion is quickly drawn from the water's surface to a breathtaking height: "High o'er the land he saved in vain" the dead man rests, and the speaker asks, "When shall such hero live again?" (*CPW* III, 40). As we know, Byron will return to this question later in his career: "I want a hero: an uncommon want," begins *Don Juan*; "When every year and month sends forth a new one" (I, 1). This power vacuum is a signature moment in Byron's poetry, like the moment of going into exile, signifying not just thematically but also structurally and ontologically the absent presence of the romantic subject.

The second verse paragraph of the second narrative fragment of the poem begins with a haunting tableau in which the poet-narrator imagines himself standing over a decaying human corpse. It is as though, inspired by the heart-rending epigraph from Thomas Moore, the entire poem stems from a devastating personal loss. Byron writes:

> He who hath bent him o'er the dead,
> Ere the first day of death is fled;
> The first dark day of nothingness,
> The last of danger and distress,
> (Before Decay's effacing fingers
> Have swept the lines where beauty lingers,)
> And mark'd the mild angelic air—
> The rapture of repose that's there— . . . (*CPW* III, 42)

Byron situates us in the in-between region bounded by the no longer and the not yet of the conquering hero. Like the young drug-dealer in the Sam Mendes film *American Beauty* who experiences a momentary ecstasy standing next to the lifeless body of his neighbor, the anonymous speaker of this poem witnesses something profound and illuminating in the face of death. Byron's note to the lines is worth quoting in full:

> I trust that few readers have ever had an opportunity of witnessing what is here attempted in description, but those who have will probably retain a painful remembrance of that singular beauty which pervades, with few exceptions, the features of the dead, a few hours, and but for a few hours, after 'the spirit is not there'. It is to be remarked in cases of violent death by gun-shot wounds, the expression is always that of languor, whatever the natural energy of the sufferer's character; but in death from a stab the countenance preserves its traits of feeling or ferocity, and the mind its bias, to the last. (*CPW* III, 416)

The narrator surrenders himself to a moment of intense attention that threatens to stop the poem in its tracks: "The rapture of repose that's there." It is an ecstatic but deeply unsettling moment. The observer (in the case of both the poem and the film) witnesses the luminous trace of a once-living human being die out slowly as the body becomes permanently still; he embarks on a journey provoked by the experience of another's death.

As the speaker describes the experience, his speech registers the shattering force of the encounter: "And—but for that sad shrouded eye, / That fires not—wins not—weeps not—now— . . . " (*CPW* III, 42). Multiple negations rise to the surface—rippling through and ripping apart the syntax—before finally breaking off into silence. In a chilling extension of the initial comparison, the narrator juxtaposes the living encounter with the dead body and a contemporary English traveler's experience of the lifeless but still luminous ruins of Greece:

> So fair—so calm—so softly seal'd
> The first—last look—by death reveal'd!
> Such is the aspect of this shore—
> 'Tis Greece—but living Greece no more!
> So coldly sweet, so deadly fair,
> We start—for soul is wanting there.
> Hers is the loveliness in death,
> That parts not quite with parting breath;
> But beauty with that fearful bloom,
> That hue which haunts it to the tomb—
> Expression's last receding ray,
> A gilded halo hovering round decay,
> The farewell beam of Feeling past away! (*CPW* III, 42–43)

The mighty ruins of the once-proud archipelago lies sprawled across the water like a constellation of lifeless body parts, its once incandescent brilliance calling attention to itself even in death. This opening sequence throws an Orphic shadow behind the poem, suggesting that the music of the poem predicates itself upon the dismemberment of the ancient Athenian body. With a mixture of aesthetic perfection and political tragedy that will surface again, the lines introduce the reader to ruins of Europe, Greece, and the Middle East which cut both diachronically and synchronically across tradition.

Childe Harold's Pilgrimage III (1816) presses these issues even further; for Shilstone the Canto represents "the literary embodiment of Byron's exiled consciousness" (118). Written comparatively quickly during the spring and summer of 1816 and published later that same year, the Canto begins with one of the most affecting scenes in all of Byron's poetry, recounting the poet's farewell to his nine-month-old daughter, Ada. At the time of his departure, Byron had not seen his daughter for almost eight months; and as we know, he was never to see her again. Byron writes:

I

Is thy face like thy mother's, my fair child!
Ada! sole daughter of my house and heart?
When last I saw thy young blue eyes they smiled,
And then we parted,—not as now we part,
But with a hope.—
Awaking with a start,
The waters heave around me; and on high
The winds lift up their voices: I depart,
Whither I know not; but the hour's gone by,
When Albion's lessening shores could grieve or glad mine eye.

2

Once more upon waters! yet once more!
And the waves bound beneath me as a steed
That knows his rider. Welcome, to their roar!
Swift be their guidance, wheresoe'er it lead!
Though the strain'd mast should quiver as a reed,
And the rent canvas fluttering strew the gale,
Still must I on; for I am as a weed,
Flung from the rock, on Ocean's foam, to sail
Where'er the surge may sweep, or tempest's breath prevail.

Opening with a departure similar to the one portrayed in Canto I, Byron shifts his focus from the journey of the fictitious pilgrim to the exile of the poet-narrator himself, repeating and in the process deepening its significance. The pain of leave-taking is underscored in the formal structure of the first stanza, which breaks off in the middle: "And then we parted,—not as now we part,/But with a hope." It is a powerful moment, with real-life trauma interrupting fictional melodrama.

    Over the course of the poem, Byron finds his voice and, finding it, dedicates his powers to the original subject matter of his song: Harold. Byron inserts himself into the fabric of the poem, not simply as its author

but as its ground and source, its abiding genius and spirit, and ultimately as the prize for which the journey into exile began in the first
place. Byron writes to discover who he will be when he has finished the
poem. He writes:

6

'Tis to create, and in creating live
A being more intense, that we endow
With form our fancy, gaining as we give
The life we imagine, even as I do now.
What am I? Nothing; but not so art thou,
Soul of my thought! with whom I traverse earth,
Invisible but gazing, as I glow
Mix'd with thy spirit, blended with thy birth,
And feeling still with thee in my crush'd feelings' dearth.

7

Yet must I think less wildly:—I *have* thought
Too long and darkly, till my brain became,
In its own eddy boiling and o'erwrought,
A whirling gulf of phantasy and flame:
And thus, untaught in youth my heart to tame,
My springs of life were poison'd. 'Tis too late!
Yet am I chang'd; though still enough the same
In strength to bear what time can not abate,
And feed on bitter fruits without accusing Fate.

In these lines one finds the best articulation in romantic period literature of what Lacoue-Labarthe and Nancy call the subject-work of
the romantic work of art: a working outward of the subject from itself
into the field of the work of art that confers existence or being onto
the subject. As Philip Barnard and Cheryl Lester, translators of
The Literary Absolute, put it, the subject-work is "the paradigmatic
model of the romantic subject's auto-production in the (literary)
work of art" (*LA* xi). Byron becomes the poet he is by virtue of the
poems he has created and set free as autonomous ontological and ethical entities.

Begun in the Swiss Alps in the autumn of 1816 and completed in
Venice early the next year, *Manfred, A Dramatic Poem* (1817) demonstrates Byron's deepening investment in a philosophically prescient
poetics. The poem, which echoes both Goethe's *Faust* and Shakespeare's

Hamlet, ultimately reaches all the way back to the origins of philosophy itself in Plato's *Apology*. Philosophy, as every student knows, teaches one how to die, and Socrates' trial, conviction, sentencing, and death represent the primal scene for understanding philosophy in this sense. Byron seems in fact to have conceived of the poem as an experiment in Socratic dialogue, a testing of the limits of dialogue for later use. He gave the poem a revealing subtitle, "A Dramatic Poem," and referred to it in a letter as a "poem in dialogue" (*BLJ* V, 209). In recent years, scholars and critics have sought to understand more precisely the role drama plays in the development of Byron's poetic personae.[23] While *Manfred* embodies Byron's dramatic re-interpretation of Socrates' trial and death, his attempt to re-inscribe the injunction to "Know Thyself " into the margins of his own historical moment, it is also a cautionary tale concerning the limits of human, and even superhuman, knowledge.

The drama takes place, as the stage directions tell us, "amongst the Higher Alps—partly in the Castle of Manfred, and partly in the Mountains" (*CPW* IV, 52). Manfred's romantic agony remains at the center of the reader's attention throughout. The poem begins, Byron tells us, in "a Gothic gallery" at "Midnight" (*CPW* IV, 53), as the title character seeks the solace of what Geoffrey Hartman calls "anti-self-consciousness":

> My slumbers—if I slumber—are not sleep,
> But a continuance of enduring thought,
> Which then I can resist not: in my heart
> There is a vigil, and these eyes but close
> To look within; and yet I live, and bear
> The aspect and the form of breathing men.
> But grief should be the instructor of the wise;
> Sorrow is knowledge: they who know the most
> Must mourn the deepest o'er the fatal truth,
> The Tree of Knowledge is not that of Life. (I, i, 3–12)

Exhausted and at an impasse, Byron negotiates a way between the Scylla and Charybdis of tradition and individual talent, communal life and autonomy, responsibility and authenticity. Neither tradition nor imaginative vision, however, is enough to allow Manfred to cope successfully with the tremendous weight of human consciousness.[24]

These lines articulate a problem many view as emblematic of modern philosophy, especially in the analytic tradition: the inability to see that, as Stanley Cavell says, we need not only better ways of knowing but also the ability to learn when to surrender the need to know. Byron, on this issue at least, agrees with Wordsworth, who famously laments: "Our meddling intellect / Mis-shapes the beauteous forms of things; / We murder to dissect."[25]

In Cavell's view, Shakespeare's tragedies, especially *Othello* and *King Lear*, map out the borderland between certainty and doubt in an effort to measure their respective roles in creating conditions conducive to maintaining human sanity, if not survival. In a reading of *King Lear* entitled "The Avoidance of Love," Cavell wonders:

> But how do we stop? How do we learn that what we need is not more knowledge but the willingness to forego knowing? For this sounds to us as though we are being asked to abandon reason for irrationality (for we know what these are and we know these are alternatives), or to trade knowledge for superstition (for we know when conviction is the one and when it is the other—the thing the superstitious always take for granted). This is why we think skepticism must mean that we cannot know the world exists, and hence that perhaps there isn't one (a conclusion some profess to admire and others to fear). Whereas what skepticism suggests is that since we cannot know the world exists, its presentness to us cannot be a function of knowing. The world is to be accepted; as the presentness of other minds is not to be known, but acknowledged.[26]

Byron's works often involve a similar questioning. In fact, one can read *Manfred* as an attempt to show how such a murderous desire for God-like knowledge can be ended, how anti-self-consciousness might be achieved, how the world might be regained for its own sake; unfortunately, it is an ending that comes at an extreme, one might say excessive, cost. In fact, one way to read *Manfred* and its quest for anti-self-consciousness is to see it as the desperate conclusion Byron's later poetry painstakingly attempts to unsettle.

Some critics have understood Byron's career in terms of an extended exercise in self-examination, self-criticism, and self-correction. One can read *Childe Harold* IV (1818) as Byron's most visible attempt to meet this challenge. No longer inclined simply to abandon "[t]he burning wreck of a demolish'd world" that Manfred leaves behind (I, i, 5), Byron applies himself in *Child Harold* IV to exploring analogues for the cultural and moral decay he sees all around. In some of his most moving poetry, Byron meditates on the ruins of medieval Venice and ancient Rome in an effort to come to terms with the stark reality of fragmentation. This rich history gives Byron footing for his restless thoughts as he acknowledges in Canto IV:

25
But my soul wanders: I demand it back
To meditate amongst decay, and stand
A ruin amidst ruins; there to track
Fall'n states and buried greatness, o'er a land
Which was the mightiest in its old command,
And is the loveliest, and must ever be
The master mould of Nature's heavenly hand . . .

In his powerful conclusion Byron seems to be speaking as an author directly to the character he created in *Manfred*:

127
Yet let us ponder boldly—'tis a base
Abandonment of reason to resign
Our right of thought—our last and only place
Of refuge; this, at least, shall still be mine:
Though from our birth the faculty divine
Is chain'd and tortured—cabin'd, cribb'd, confined,
And bred in darkness, lest the truth should shine
Too brightly on the unprepareè mind,
The beam pours in, for time and skill will couch the blind.

128
Arches on arches! as it were that Rome,
Collecting the chief trophies of her line,
Would build up all her triumphs in one dome,
Her coliseum stands; the moonbeams shine
As 'twere its natural torches, for divine
Should be the light which streams here to illume
This long-explored but still exhaustless mine
Of contemplation; and the azure gloom
Of an Italian night, where the deep skies assume

129
Hues which have words, and speak to ye of heaven,
Floats o'er this vast and wondrous monument,
And shadows forth its glory. There is given
Unto the things of earth, which Time hath bent
A spirit's feeling, and where he hath leant
His hand, but broke his scythe, there is a power
And magic in the ruin'd battlement,
For which the palace of the present hour
Must yield its pomp, and wait till ages are its dower.

130

Oh Time! the beautifier of the dead,
Adorner of the ruin, comforter
And only healer when the heart hath bled;
Time! the corrector where our judgments err,
The test of truth, love,—sole philosopher,
For all beside are sophists—from thy thrift,
Which never loses though it doth defer—
Time, the avenger! unto thee I lift
My hands, and eyes, and heart, and crave of thee a gift:

131

Amidst this wreck, where thou hast made a shrine
And temple more divinely desolate,
Among thy mightier offerings here are mine,
Ruins of years, though few, yet full of fate:
If thou hast ever seen me too elate,
Hear me not; but if calmly I have borne
Good, and reserved my pride against the hate
Which shall not whelm me, let me not have worn
This iron in my soul in vain—shall they not mourn?

Byron is in effect defying his earlier defiance in defense of time and
history as the inevitable conditions at human existence.

143

A ruin—yet what a ruin! from its mass
Walls, palaces, half-cities, have been rear'd;
Yet oft the enormous skeleton ye pass,
And marvel where the spoil could have appear'd.
Hath it indeed been plunder'd, or but clear'd?
Alas! developed, opens the decay,
When the colossal fabric's form is near'd:
It will not bear the brightness of the day,
Which streams too much on all—years—man—have reft away.

With the completion of *Childe Harold* IV, Byron has tentatively stepped
back from the abyss of *Manfred* and reclaimed his place as a mortal
being among the ruins of time and history. It is "a base/Abandonment
of reason," he confesses in stanza 127, "to resign/Our right of thought—
our last and only place/Of refuge." Standing firm with the Enlightenment's contempt for vulgar superstition but now more accepting of the

limits of reason, Byron begins to come to term with his role as a poet. Rather than rejecting the ruined and imperfect world, as he had in *Manfred*, Byron now delves deeper into its essential ambiguity to create some of his greatest art.

Wandering with Pedestrian Muses

Byron's masterpiece, *Don Juan* is perhaps the finest example of *romantische Poesie* in world literature. Begun during the last few years of the poet's life and left unfinished at his death, "Donny Johnny"—as Byron called it (*BLJ* VI, 207)—continues to explore the border between wit and irony, knowledge and doubt, narrative and lyric, being and non-being. What is remarkable when readers come to the poem for the first time is how they must learn, in the absence of an editorial note, how to pronounce the name of the title character. At first, the name appears to rhyme with (and first-time readers almost invariably do rhyme it with) a word like "swan." However, as one reads on, it becomes obvious that the name rhymes instead with a word like "ruin." Indeed, the name of the hero, pronounced "Don JOO-an" in order to rhyme with "new one" and "true one" (I, 1), is a deliberately clumsy, vulgar, even ethnocentric mispronunciation that evokes English bigotry toward its colonial possessions and European neighbors.

The name of the main character and the title of the poem, Don Juan derives from the Spanish legend of a libertine who is tireless in his amorous pursuits and, besides that, devilishly clever. In a recent study, Moyra Haslett points out how important the legend actually is for an informed reading of the poem.[27] Byron takes pains to inform us that, in addition to relying on the legend, he also models his efforts upon the wooden puppet of the popular street show. As the narrator says, "We all have seen him in the pantomime/Sent to the devil, somewhat ere his time" (I, 1). This less idealized and more commonplace source has the generic advantage of foregrounding the puppet's dependence on the puppeteer, the one who pulls the strings, much as the narrator in the poem, and behind the narrator the poet himself, does for Juan.

The epigraph Byron selected for the poem comes from Horace: "*Difficile est proprie communia dicere*" (*CPW* V, 1). In a juvenile version, Byron himself had translated the line: " 'tis no small task to write on common things" (*CPW* I, 296). The epigraph carries the sense, roughly, of the difficulty of writing on the usual themes, the typical subjects, that poets are wont to write about; but it also connotes the difficulty of writing about what is closest to one's self, what is most private or personal, and, further-more, by extension, what is most ordinary and everyday; what is com-monplace. As an interpretive point of reference, the epigraph exhibits provocative ambiguities deriving almost exclusively from the single phrase translated as "common things" or what is common. How is this word or phrase to be understood—as something private or ordinary or shared, as in a shared sense of a community or world? Or as something more like the mundane or the trivial, the ordinary and the common-place? Perhaps we are to take it as an ironic boast about the extraordinary powers of the poet—that he can create a poem out of anything? It is pos-sible to take the epigraph as proof of the value of ordinary life as opposed to visionary, mythical, or ideal realms, that is, as a statement of belief in the mystery of the everyday world, the way that the ordinary is the cru-cial site for the appearance of the strange or other. The commonplace world contains more than enough romantic agony to go around, and it is not so much foundational as an ongoing task and responsibility.

One can see how Byron appreciates the futility of trying too hard to exercise control over words—as though the question of originality is a non-issue for him, as though one always appropriates words—or as though words always appropriate the poet, as in Novalis's celebrated "Monologue." Indeed, Byron's language refuses conceptual control, as though the truth itself is double. Byron's language, actually, is not "Byron's language." It belongs rather to Spanish legend and to the Roman poet Horace, respectively. One of Byron's favorite gestures is to produce the words of another author, either in the form of a quotation or a paraphrase, then draw attention to his indiscretion. At the conclu-sion of Canto I, for example, the narrator proclaims: "[t]he four first rhymes are Southey's every line:/For God's sake, reader! take them not for mine" (I, 222). Or more simply: "I like so much to quote" (II, 17). As Byron admits (in the Preface to Cantos VI. – VII. – and VIII.), much of the middle Cantos originate form a French history of Russia, " '*His-toire de la Nouvelle Russie*' " (*CPW* V, 295). The elusiveness of these tainted words and phrases, mini-dialogues involving strange and famil-iar languages—English, Spanish, Latin, Greek, Hebrew, and others—is a substantial part of their (and the poem's) meaning. Incidentally, it is also a fine piece of transcendental buffoonery that such an emphasis on the commonplace usages of words is inscribed within an obscure (and for many readers probably unintelligible) Latin text.

The Preface, probably started after the completion of Cantos I and II but soon abandoned (Byron inserted the "Dedication" in its place), underscores the idea that the language of the poem will be a form of borderline discourse or in-between speech, rather than the utterance of a single self-contained consciousness. In its creation of a composite, or at least bilingual narrator, the Preface foregrounds the dialogic interaction between languages-as-worldviews that is crucial for novelistic discourse, discourse in which two languages intersect and are double-crossed with one another. Beginning with a parody of Wordsworth's note to "The Thorn," Byron informs us that we are "requested to suppose by a like exertion of imagination that the following epic narrative [the story of Don Juan] is told by a Spanish gentleman in a village in the Sierra Morena on the road between Monasterio & Seville— . . ." (*CPW* V, 82). Furthermore, "The reader is further requested to suppose him (to account for his knowledge of English) either an Englishman settled in Spain—or a Spaniard who had travelled in England" (*CPW* V, 83).

In this text, later abandoned, Byron creates a narrator who inhabits the English language only partially, understands its limitations as they unfold by means of interaction with another language—Spanish or any other with which it might come into contact. The conversation between different worldviews that appears in the title and in the epigraph, adumbrated in the Preface, militates against the idea of a single authoritative consciousness behind the poem. As critics often remark, one of the main issues of the poem is the striking passivity of the main character, how little initiative Don Juan actually takes in his affairs and engagements, a passivity shared by the narrator, specifically, in his use of language.[28] It is important to see that the narrator of *Don Juan* claims to have no real authority over his words, and he even admits that, "note or text,/I never know the word which will come next" (IX, 41). This confession raises the question of how language speaks, as Heidegger likes to say, how language comes to speech in the hands of a poet. Or, more radically, it anticipates the "radical passivity" many see in Blanchot's poetics; a persistent passivity and a passion that, finally surrendering the will to refuse, slips outside.[29] For now, it is enough to notice how Byron displaces narrative consciousness and, simultaneously, shows how words are not fixed in their meanings like terms but are more open-ended and ambiguous, dependent for their meanings on their use rather than on their power to designate or signify objects.

The Dedication, which replaced the rejected Preface, further elaborates the idea of a heterogeneous work whose words have been liberated from the narrowness of a single language-view; it is composed out of words which appear to resist the authority of a pious omniscient narrator and strike off on their own, their fortune for to seek. Think of this as the word's protest against the usurpation of poetic authority by epic consciousness. The idea of protest against a centralized authority links together the two main objects of the poet's wrath in the piece, poets (represented by the Lake School poets) and politicians (represented by Robert Stewart, Viscount Castlereagh), both of whom situate themselves at the center of their small worlds. In the first lines of the Dedication, Byron the poet lord addresses Southey the poet laureate as informally and as dismissively as possible, by his shortened first name, "Bob":

> I
> Bob Southey! You're a poet—poet Laureate,
> And representative of all the race;
> Although 'tis true you turn'd out a Tory at
> Last,—yours has lately been a common case:—
> And now, my epic renegade! where are ye at,
> With all the lakers in and out of place?
> A nest of tuneful persons, to my eye
> Like four and twenty blackbirds in a pie . . .

Byron opens with a metrical bang: the spondaic or, better, trochaic "Bob Southey! You're a poet!" This emphasizes the difficulty of finding one's place in the world, raising the perhaps scurrilous question of what it might mean to be in and out of place. This version of Southey's name also happens to be part of a Regency joke on sexual incompetence (a "dry bob" being Regency slang for sexual intercourse without ejaculation or, as McGann says [in fine Byronic form], "coition without emission" [CPW V, 671, n.24]). Byron (not one to miss such an opportunity) fully exploits the pathetic plight of this modern day Icarus in the third stanza: "you soar too high, Bob,/And fall, for lack of moisture, quite adry, Bob!" (*CPW* V, 4). It is as though Southey's name is, when turned loose, an accomplice in a comical critique of the poet's attempt to scale visionary heights; a bawdy linguistic self-reproach, which, appropriately enough, leads back to the grotesque human body, made conspicuous by its failure to function. One cannot help noticing the rude, rough, coarse language, indicative of the novelist's rejection of the sublime registers of epic speech. The narrator represents himself as an exile from the majestic language proper to the poetical establishment, the high style and moral tone of "the lakers." As opposed to these "epic renegades," he is a connoisseur of linguistic scandal and of verbal impropriety. The narrator reaffirms this commitment to chaos following the sequence describing the siege of Ismail when he says, "carelessly I sing" (VIII, 138).

For now, it is enough to notice Byron's use of vulgar language, which represents more than just the appropriation of a common style. It marks a refusal of style altogether, a refusal to exert authority over words and so to silence the talk, laughter, and waywardness of words. The poem is, at least in part, an allegory of scandalous intercourse; the salacious unauthorized commingling of different senses of everyday words. Byron here anticipates "the Nichtian glossery" of Joyce's great work-in-progress, *Finnegans Wake*. An appropriate index of Donna Inez 's parochial view is her reluctance in Canto I to acknowledge this commingling of tongues:

> 14
> She liked the English and the Hebrew tongue,
>   And said there was analogy between 'em;
> She proved it somehow out of sacred song,
>   But I must leave the proofs to those who've seen 'em,
> But this I heard her say, and can't be wrong,
>   And all may think which way their judgments lean 'em,
> 'Tis strange—the Hebrew noun which means "I am,"
> The English always use to govern d—n.'

Along with Donna Inez's inability to acknowledge the linguistic comedy of such a juxtaposition of sacredness and profanity, the narrator's familiar language puts him at odds with her high seriousness. It is this overly serious language-as-worldview Juan will spend the rest of the poem trying to cope with. The narrator's abuse of Southey's name brings him comically, ridiculously, close to both poet and reader. He is no longer depicted using the reverent language of the epic but in the stylistically mixed language of the novel, a language which preserves a counter-meaning concerning Southey's name which might otherwise remain hidden.

Byron's familiarization of the world through informal language liberates it from the narrow frame of epic representation and rehabilitates it. It releases it or frees it in order that it may go into its own way of being. This vernacular style brings people and things comically close (as though familiarity itself, what Bakhtin calls proximity, were a form of meaning or truth) and undermines the high-minded, authoritative and normative significance of epic representation. In the Dedication, Byron has words of ridicule not only for Southey but also for Wordsworth (in *Don Juan* he calls him the "poet Wordy" [IV, 109] and in his letters far worse) and Coleridge (slightly less self-important) for their presumption in writing poetry which assumes authority and which centers on the individual mind. Byron savages these writers for their persistence in pursuing such solpsistic points of view:

> 5
> You, Gentlemen! by dint of long seclusion
>   From better company have kept your own
> At Keswick, and through still continued fusion
>   Of one another's minds at last have grown
> To deem as a most logical conclusion
>   That poesy has wreaths for you alone;
> There is a narrowness in such a notion
> Which makes me wish you'd change your lakes for ocean.

It is, of course, the exclusivity of the worldview—and by extension all such views—that Byron categorically rejects. In this case, Byron objects to poetry masquerading as metaphysics; poetry as a form of authoritative knowledge. The poet's relation to the world (from Byron's point of view) is not one of cognition, knowing, or logical conclusions. It is not one of conceptual grasp; it not epistemological or a function of the way the mind links up (or fails to link up) with the world. Byron is adamant about this, and he criticizes practically by name such a view:

> 15
> If we may judge of matter by the mind,
>   Emasculated to the marrow, *It*
> Hath but two objects—how to serve, and bind,
>   Deeming the chain it wears even men may fit;
> Eutropius of its many masters—blind
>   To worth as freedom, wisdom as to wit—
> Fearless, because *no* feeling dwells in ice,
> Its very courage stagnates to a vice.

Byron equates excessive seriousness with slavery; a form of coercion or subjugation, a struggle for power between those at the center and those on the periphery. Knowledge of this kind is simply a way of getting the upper hand over someone else. As opposed to the Lakers' epistemological orientation to the world, their relating to it as a master, Byron suggests the poet's relation to the world is closer to travel, swimming or sailing on the surface of existence, a vigorous and enabling activity which nonetheless preserves a good deal of danger and uncertainty. One can contrast the poets' dominance of their narrow lakes with the narrator's submission to the ocean; it is a matter of recognizing the limits of one's own world-view and being able to view it with some self-conscious distance. As the narrator of *Don Juan* knowingly says in Canto II of Juan's departure from Seville (which the narrator rhymes with revel [I, 148, 4] and devil [I, 203, 8]),

12

I can't but say it is an awkward sight
   To see one's native land receding through
The growing waters; it unmans one quite,
   Especially when life is rather new:
I recollect Great Britain's coast looks white,
   But almost every other country's blue,
When gazing on them, mystified by distance,
We enter on our nautical existence.

This entrance or passage into exile, into a nautical existence, as the narrator puts it, is one of the most frequently played out dramas in all of Byron's poetical works. The representation of the poet's life as a nautical existence serves as an emblem to remind us of an identity that is composite and always in progress, in pursuit of a further role or character to play, always on the way somewhere else, in process. This is in stark contrast to the stasis of the Lakers, a group of tuneful persons confined to their insular nest, or to the tyranny of Castlereagh, who from his centralized position dominates all that is around him, "pant[ing]" for "wider carnage" (*CPW* V, 6). What links the poets and the politician of the Dedication are their one-sided (humorless) languages or points of view and how such perspectives do violence to those who live (like the Irish [or the Turks]) on the outskirts.

To protest against such acts, language in the Dedication takes on a visceral, material quality charged with an energy that is almost out of control. The words tend toward the status of words in ancient satire, toward the status of objects, rocks, sticks, or stones the narrator hurls at those he singles out for abuse. Words fly back and forth less as expressive or even speculative instruments than as projectiles, bombs, or missiles. It may be that here Byron's language is close to the language of satire, criticism or protest from the vantage point of the underdog, David's word against that of Goliath. ("I was born for opposition," the narrator says [XV, 22].) This aspect of satirical language, its tendency toward the status of the physical object, is a quality it shares with the laughing word of the novel. The Dedication begins with an exclamation rather than a descriptive statement: the words "Bob Southey!" (the first draft reads "Southey! you're a poet!" [*CPW* V, 3]) ring out of the opening stanza like a curse, death threat, or piece of blasphemy. Byron instinctively knows how far one's words can go once they are let go into the air or onto the page, in spite of the rhymes one uses as a kind of counter charm or antidote, to hurt us. There is a sense in which it is good, perhaps, not to take words seriously.

To acknowledge the material dimension of words is to become an outsider or an exile from the master narrative, transformed into one who takes a skeptical or nominal view of language, especially one's own. This figure of the poet as outsider is a self-representation Byron cultivated all his life and, as critics like McGann remind us, has roots in biographical, historical, social, and political events. The Dedication vividly underscores this point:

8
<blockquote>
For me who, wandering with pedestrian Muses,
    Contend not with you on the winged steed,
I wish your fate may yield ye, when she chooses,
    The fame you envy, and the skill you need;
And recollect a poet nothing loses
    In giving to his brethren their full meed
Of merit, and complaint of present days
Is not the *certain* path to future praise.
</blockquote>

One must not underestimate the importance of this self-description, for it goes a long way toward providing a useful emblem for the poet throughout the poem. Byron's description of himself deconstructs the romantic myth of the poet as mighty seer, or prophet blest. It also qualifies the superiority of the sustained high style of the epic over the truth of doggerel verse, anecdotes, parodies or puns. The phrase points to Byron's effort to turn language away from winged flight and keep it on a more common or pedestrian level, as though words are best used when made to walk and not canter or march, much less fly. From the vantage point of this phrase, one views *Don Juan*'s pursuit of "questions answerless, and yet incessant" (VI, 63) as the pursuit of identity from the ground up and not from a transcendental perspective. The romantic, engaged with existence at the messy level of everyday life, does not have access to an over-arching scheme according to which differences dissipate. Order, in such a world, is not a deep structure waiting for analysis or logic or allegory to lay bare; order is, rather, a task or a project to pursue in the face of disorder and confusion. The footloose figure inscribed in the word *pedestrian* illustrates the comic weakness of ordinary words, the way language questions or repudiate itself.

The Fragment, which editors have (since 1832) used as a headpiece for *Don Juan*, furnishes an appropriately upside down context for such a reading of the poem. One finds the poet (finding himself) "seem[ing] to stand upon the ceiling," in a disrupted physical, mental, and emotional state, suffering through the discomfort of a hangover (*CPW* V, 88). Presumably such discomfort is the point of wishing one were made of "so much Clay" (oblivious to memories of, as well as suffering caused by, the past) rather than all the things he is made of—"blood, bone, marrow, passion, feeling"—stubborn flesh which refuses to go away. (From the drunk's vantage point, the Cartesian fiction of the disembodied subject sometimes sounds like a good idea.) The Fragment furnishes an opening distinctly different from that of the epic. The epic poet speaks from a reverent and culturally central perspective, a standpoint outside the past action but at the center of present cultural authority, and with an eye toward underlining the normative significance of past actions. This cast-off rhyme (Byron left it out of Canto I) calls into question the authority of the representative leader, the one who occupies a centralized perspective. From this point of view, one encounters a work with a considerably altered perspective, not the usual reverent perspective but a trivializing perspective, the vantage point of a poet with a hangover—a rake, a fop, a clown, a buffoon, a rascal, or a fool. Along with this upside down view, the poem also calls for its own jocular grammar in which sober precepts are suspended or rescinded and words pledge their allegiance to the grammar of the pun.

Byron presents the conflict between idealism and skepticism not as conflict taking place within the imagination but as a struggle between narrative wit and lyric fragmentation—a struggle, that is, within the space opened by the work of art itself. One must also focus on Byron's propensity for generating contexts and then, after exploring the possibilities and limits of these contexts, abandoning them for new possibilities tempered by the realization that no context, however powerful as a hermeneutic tool, is ever absolute. That is, one must repeatedly negotiate the nothing at the heart of being. Here Byron anticipates the insight found in the later Wittgenstein: that is, the tendency to come up

against the limitations of any single language-game or set of criteria
and so to be forced to look for possibilities offered by other language-
games or sets of criteria. No single language-game, or path of thinking, ever suffices; we are always traveling on more than one path at a
time.[30]

Now and Then Narrating, Now Pondering

Don Juan takes on a fascinating new shape when seen this way, as epic
consciousness interrupted and cross-fertilized by novelistic discourse.
The poem reorients literature toward the historical present as opposed
to the mythical past; a history, moreover, whose meaning is as of
yet undetermined and so remains open to interpretation. Against the
example of mythic work, Byron's real epic is modeled after *Tristram
Shandy*, and endeavors to maintain a difficult relation with ordinary life,
the unappealing, distasteful or even ugly aspects of everyday experience.
Significantly, this experience is what Donna Inez tries to exclude from
Juan's moral education, what's "loose,/Or hints continuation of the
species . . ." (I, 40), that is, the body of knowledge that is repressed by civ-
ilized societies in their efforts to raise human beings to a higher moral
level. In contrast to the Miltonic aim to justify God's ways to man, Byron
sets to work within the precincts of ordinary human existence. Instead of
taking the first person perspective of Wordsworth's man speaking to
men, the perspective of the representative individual who looks down
from above and defines the sprit of the age, Byron takes a different cultural perspective. Installing the topic of the world upside, Byron com-
poses his poem from the ground up, from the point of view of the messy,
unruly, conceptually unmanageable side of life typically excluded by epic.
Moreover, through his buffoonish narrator he establishes the upside
down perspective of language itself, of the material reality of language
that will not remain subject to the constraints of the speaking subject
but will rise in rebellion. In Canto I he says:

6

Most epic poets plunge in 'medias res',
    (Horace makes this the heroic turnpike road)
And then your hero tells, whene'er you please,
    What went before—by way of episode,
While seated after dinner at his ease,
    Beside his mistress in some soft abode,
Palace, or garden, paradise, or cavern,
Which serves the happy couple for a tavern.

7

That is the usual method, but not mine—
    My way is to begin with the beginning;
The regularity of my design
    Forbids all wandering as the worst of sinning,
And therefore I shall open with a line
    (Although it cost me half an hour in spinning)
Narrating somewhat of Don Juan's father,
And also of his mother, if you'd rather.

The distinction between method and way provides a hint of what is to come. Working against traditional models for writing epics, in which the story tells of a completed past heroic action from the relatively secure position of present, Byron's narrator remains interested and engaged in, even partially exposed to, the difficulty of the events he describes. Action taking place in the historical present interrupts narrative progress because it is not clear what the outcome of the action will be. Byron gives this exposure to the prospect of interruption a hilarious twist when little Juan accidentally (?) pours out "[a] pail of housemaid's water" onto the narrator's unsuspecting head (I, 24). Here the story, prompted by the "little curly-headed, good-for-nothing/ And mischief-making monkey," actually bites back (I, 25). The narrator, swept up in the action of the poem, is not exactly sure where he or it is going. The poem's perspective does not even pretend to be sweeping or objective, a point reinforced by the furtive deference to the wishes of his audience.[31] In fact, the narrator refuses authority for his interpretation of the story of Juan and Julia. His insistence on his ignorance, easily interpretable as a Socratic ploy, or an appropriately ironic pretense of ignorance, is a refusal of a typically reverent perspective of the past from the more or less objective standpoint of the present.

Don Juan proper begins with several easily underestimated acknowledgments of a doubled, crazed, or ambiguous language. The mispronunciation of the title embodies precisely the generically unstable sort of discourse I have been describing. As pronounced in Canto I, to rhyme not with "Don" or with "wan" but with "new one" and "true one," the name represents a linguistic or phonetic mistake; as such, it becomes an emblem for the language of the poem as a whole. Consider the opening of Canto I:

1

I want a hero: an uncommon want,
    When every year and month sends forth a new one,

> Till, after cloying the gazettes with cant,
>   The age discovers he is not the true one;
> Of such as these I should not care to vaunt,
>   I'll therefore take our ancient friend Don Juan,
> We all have seen him in the pantomime
> Sent to the devil, somewhat ere his time.

Now one might recall Geoffrey Hartman's observation that the slip of the tongue or the joke serves as the basic unit of poetic discourse: "What we get to see [in poetic language] is always a palimpsest or a contaminated form of some kind: a stratum of legitimate, sacred, or exalted words purifying a stratum of guilty, forbidden, or debased words."[32] Although Hartman makes this point with reference to Christopher Smart's exorbitant rhetoric in *Jubilate Agno*, Byron's work certainly makes sense in light of such an account. In *Don Juan* the contamination often takes the form of an English defilement of another language, as in the narrator's (mis) pronunciation of the name of Juan's mother, Donna Inez, which he rhymes with "so fine as" (I, 11). If not exactly exorbitant as poetic rhetoric, this is surely pushing the envelope. Over the course of the poem, the narrator takes increasing pleasure in noting how one language thrives at the expense of another, as in his amusing contrast of the Russian and the English versions of general Suvaroff's last name: "Suvaroff, or anglicè Suwarrow, / Who loved blood as an Alderman loves marrow" (VII, 8). The English misappropriates the Russian (mediated by the French), and the effect is a demystification of the ideal of heroism. Byron's verses repeatedly suggest how such play can represent a form of resistance. The English tendency to mispronounce the name of a Russian military leader involuntarily (and yet deliberately) represents an elemental rebellion against the government of the tongue. By themselves, these mistakes seem to harm no one and are part of what Byron calls his lack of a plan, his intention merely "to be a moment merry" (IV, 5). However, the mispronunciation of these names bears significantly on the poem's vision, for they show how the language of romantic poetry refuses the univocal perspective of the epic and remains doubled or indeterminate—like the pun, or the double exposure, an open question. This rejection of epic omniscience in favor of the perspective of language is one of the most telling features of Byron's poem, from the title to the last words of Canto XVI, a crude, lewd, and quite possibly obscene pun on the earthly preoccupation of a ghost who, one night at Norman abbey, enters Juan's room, "[t]he phantom of her frolic grace—Fitz-Fulke!" (XVI, 123)

In other words, Byron's way with words has a serious point. The instability of these names embodies a protest against dignity and decorum, as well as the austerity of epic vision. Embodied in the poet-narrator's mispronunciation of Don Juan's name is not just a recognition of two different languages, one English and one Spanish, one regrettably insular and one pleasantly cosmopolitan, but the recognition of a dialogized conflict of linguistic world views; how one does unutterable violence to the other. The reality of the Spanish name is one the narrator's language has trouble containing. The historical tendency of English, Byron suggests, has been to appropriate other forms of life by anglicizing them, by bastardizing and domesticating them until they are English. Byron's poem militates against this ethic of assimilation; it suggests that there is value in what refuses appropriation by a single language, vision, program or ethos. This ragged and unpredictable dimension Byron welcomes back into the realm of poetry. Put differently: Byron creates low or everyday art, avant-garde art made out of leftover scraps; the errors of other people's words. The poem's first words refuse the rules of serious, epic discourse and constitute a movement away from a consciousness fully in control of its speech and toward restoration of the ancient multiplicity of words. This wordplay allows a contradictory reality otherwise occluded by serious, one-sided representation to come back into view, to seep back into the epic-length work.

The poem opens with the call for a hero, an uncommon want for an epic. Cataloguing a series of potential heroes, he rejects them all—mostly embodiments of the traditional hero, the military man—because the world is already saturated, "every year and month send[ing] forth a new one." The poet-narrator informs us that his poem calls for a different kind of hero, someone unfamiliar with or resistant to the martial system of the conventional epic. Such heroes and veterans of various wars come and go, but a real hero is hard to find. The narrator settles on Don Juan, whose absolutely trivial accomplishments (on the epic view) are underscored by the narrator's mention of the way his (Juan's) story has been culturally transmitted, namely "in the pantomime" or dumb show, a form more suited to a folk or emergent popular culture than to the epic elite, fit audience though few. Byron's hero is a lover and not a fighter, one whose first battle takes place in the metaphorical war-room of Donna Julia's bedchamber. What is more, Juan's chief qualification for the role (aside from his notorious reputation as a love maker) is nothing more than the sound of his name, a mellifluous appellation that the narrator says is well "adapted to [his] rhymes" (I, 3) and for that reason "fit for [his] poem" (I, 5). From the start it is clear that *Don*

Juan is an extraordinary version of the epic, an uncommon poem in which the usual high moral tone has been suspended in favor of a more mundane and therefore scandalous mood.

Canto I illustrates Byron's characteristic juxtaposition of the serious and the playful, the high and the low, with the movement through their back and forth play leading not to a contradiction but rather to an acknowledgment of the bodily, earthly, ordinary, and human, along with the infinite complexity that surrounds it. First, the narrow view of his mother's attitude toward education represents a one-sided view of life against which the remainder of the poem will situate itself. Following Don Jóse's death, Donna Inez, "[s]agest of women, even of widows, she / Resolved that Juan should be quite a paragon, / and worthy of the noblest pedigree" (I, 38). Her sober ideal of education calls to mind much of what is considered the province of the noble world of the romance epic: "In case our lord the king should go to war again, / He learn'd the arts of riding, fencing, gunnery, / And how to scale a fortress—or a nunnery" (I, 38). The dominant principle governing Juan's social formation is Inez's belief "that his breeding should be strictly moral" (I, 39), that strict morality should govern all that his teachers transmit to him. What Juan does learn is telling:

40

The languages, especially the dead,
   The sciences, and most of all the abstruse,
The arts, at least all such as could be said
   To be the most remote from common use,
In all these he was much and deeply read;
   But not a page of anything that's loose,
Or hints at continuation of the species,
Was ever suffer'd, lest he should grow vicious.

What Inez thinks of as the strictly moral character of Juan's learning closely resembles the epic's preoccupation with the heroic (or just the dead) past and its contempt for the (living) present, a preoccupation which justifies itself by suppressing the human body, what's loose or not reducible to the categories of a virtuous program. The body is that part of us which refuses to remain under control, and rebels at every chance, speaking out or drawing attention to itself when we least expect it. It is the material fact of the body that Donna Inez seeks to remove from her son's education:

44

Juan was taught from out the best edition,
   Expurgated by learned men, who place,
Judiciously, from out the schoolboy's vision,
   The grosser parts; but fearful to deface
Too much their modest bard by this omission,
   And pitying sore his mutilated case,
They only add them all in an appendix,
Which saves, in fact, the trouble of an index;

45

For there we have them all at one fell swoop,
   Instead of being scatter'd through the pages;
They stand forth marshall'd in a handsome troop,
   To meet the ingenuous youth of future ages,
Till some less rigid editor shall stoop
   To call them back into their separate cages,
Instead of standing staring altogether,
Like garden gods—and not so decent either.

Juan is tutored from the "best edition,/expurgated by learned men," taught from a single proper and unselfconscious point of view, an epic point of view which looks unquestioningly through its own language at the object of study. Such language has no self-critical mechanism, no way to stand outside itself and question itself. Along with the narrator's qualification of these noble pursuits, the stanzas present the ideal education in a telling light: an education governed by strict morality is presented as a consciously constructed product, a cultural ideal, like any other culturally-specific ideal, assembled by Donna Inez and a team of experts and inscribed on Juan's blank tablet. Byron portrays it as though it were one of many artificially constructed languages, a language with certain limitations that nonetheless (from Inez's point of view) provides a semblance of order for Juan (especially in the wake of the untimely death of his father, Don Jóse). In other words, Canto I foregrounds the social construction of the epic subject, a consciously monitored construction which is by no means ideology free but which carries with it the baggage of a hierarchy of values, none of which is more important than the suppression of the body.

It is interesting to see just how Juan's early education proceeds at the expense of all that is normally associated with the human body and the ordinary world, whatever's "loose/Or hints at continuation of the species." Nothing that suggests the existence of the unsavory or unpleasant underworld of human sexuality or bodily pleasure can enter into Juan's moral and intellectual formation. To his credit, the buffoonish narrator remarks on this insular mode of education, the value of which he persistently questions. Like a modern day Socrates, he admits, "I had my doubts, perhaps I have them still,/But what I say is neither here nor there" (I, 51). In a wonderfully pregnant locution, Byron links the skepticism of this Socrates manqué to a deliberate refusal to take sides. "What I say is neither here nor there" may be a throwaway line, but it is certainly also a dig at the political ideologues of Byron's day who were so entrenched in their positions that they could not even consider alternative possibilities. The narrator takes the reader aside in a conspiratorial way:

52

For my part I say nothing—nothing—but
   This I will say—my reasons are my own—
That if I had an only son to put
   To school (as God be praised that I have none)
'Tis not with Donna Inez I would shut
   Him up to learn his catechism alone,
No—No—I'd send him out betimes to college,
For there it was I pick'd up my own knowledge.

53

For there one learns—'tis not for me to boast,
   Though I acquired—but I pass over *that,*
As well as all the Greek I since have lost:
   I say that there's the place—but '*Verbum sat*',
I think I pick'd up too, as well as most,
   Knowledge of matters—but no matter *what*—
I never married—but, I think, I know
That sons should not be educated so.

The narrator's preference for social intercourse over splendid isolation, whatever its sexual suggestion (and the suggestion is considerable), underlines a point to which the poem returns again and again: that such a narrow-minded and serious view as Donna Inez's overlooks the most basic fact about human beings, that they have physical bodies (or matter) which (no matter what) do matter. Given the narrator's knowledge of matters, and his eagerness to pursue this frivolous (but rewarding) education, it is tempting to dismiss his criticism of Juan's education as a weakness of the flesh, a kind of pathology or deviance.

The poem's fascination with obtrusive bodies, however, makes it clear that such fleshly matter, far from being the personal idiosyncrasy of the narrator or the poet, is meant to remind us of how much our bodies influence everyday life.

This relentless self-questioning creates a skeptical opening in the midst of the story that in turn introduces a kind of linguistic cushion between subject and object. No pure access to another person's thoughts exists; the story relegates us to the outside. Thus:

<blockquote>

68

I can't tell whether Julia saw the affair
   With other people's eyes, or if her own
Discoveries made, but none could be aware
   Of this, at least no symptom e'er was shown;
Perhaps she did not know, or did not care,
   Indifferent from the first, or callous grown:
I'm really puzzled what to think or say,
She kept her counsel in so close a way.

</blockquote>

So there remains knowledge that is off limits to the narrator; he remains outside the inner life of the other person, whether he is narrating the story of Inez and Jóse or Juan and Julia or, indeed, his own story. The skepticism of the poem reaches even into the narrator's mind, into his failure to know his own mind. This, Byron wants us somehow to see, is not necessarily a bad thing.

The second half of Canto I represents a progressive degradation of the seriousness instilled in Juan by Donna Inez, and leads back to an acknowledgment of the body and to the brink of the promise of regeneration, embodied in the passionate sexual love between Juan and Julia. The narrator, consistently unable to establish the facts of the story with certainty—"and who can tell?" (I, 78); "to such doings I'm a stranger" (I, 80); "I really don't know what" (I, 81); "I only say suppose it—*inter nos*—" (I, 84); "I only say suppose this supposition" (I, 85); "The poet meant, no doubt" (I, 89)–turns his own uncertainty into a theme. In this uneasy frame of mind, he describes the effect that such a single-minded education has had on Juan:

<blockquote>

91

He, Juan (and not Wordsworth), so pursued
   His self-communion with his own high soul,

</blockquote>

Until his mighty heart, in its great mood,
   Had mitigated part, though not the whole
Of its disease; he did the best he could
   With things not very subject to his control,
And turn'd, without perceiving his condition,
Like Coleridge, into a metaphysician.

92

He thought about himself, and the whole earth,
   Of man the wonderful, and of the stars,
And how the deuce they ever could have birth;
   And then he thought of earthquakes, and of wars,
How many miles the moon might have in girth,
   Of air-balloons, and of the many bars
To perfect knowledge of the boundless skies;
And then he thought of Donn Julia's eyes.

93

In thoughts like these true wisdom may discern
   Longings sublime, and aspirations high,
Which some are born with, but the most part learn
   To plague themselves withal, they know not why:
'Twas strange that one so young should thus concern
   His brain about the action of the sky;
If *you* think 'twas philosophy that this did,
I can't help thinking puberty assisted.

Byron clearly sees exclusive self-communion as disastrous for healthy social interaction. Such obsessive introspection turns inward and perpetuates the illusion that one controls one's entire being: "he did the best he could/With things not very subject to his control." Here we see played out a tension between self-control and self-abandonment, between the desire to keep to oneself and the desire to give oneself away to another. As the tension builds, the narrator exhibits an exaggerated squeamishness concerning the climax of the clandestine interview between Juan and Julia:

III

The hand which still held Juan's, by degrees
   Gently, but palpably confirm'd its grasp,
And if it said 'detain me, if you please;'
   Yet there's no doubt she only meant to clasp

His fingers with a pure Platonic squeeze;
  She would have shrunk as from a toad, or asp,
Had she imagined such a thing could rouse
A feeling dangerous to a prudent spouse.

Reverting to characteristic skepticism concerning his own narrative, he admits: "I cannot know what Juan thought of this,/But what he did, is much what you would do;/His young lip thank'd it with a grateful kiss . . ." (I, 112). Then comes one of the great moments of the poem, the passage in Canto I describing the precise moment when, as Julia and Juan sway back and forth, lost in one another, giddily tossed between the opposing claims of religious propriety and the heat of their desires, unrestrained love (or is it lust?) becomes conscious of itself:

115

And Julia sate with Juan, half embraced
  And half retiring from the glowing arm,
Which trembled like the bosom where 'twas placed;
  Yet still she must have thought there was no harm,
Or else 'twere easy to withdraw her waist;
  But then the situation had its charm,
And then—God knows what next—I can't go on;
I'm almost sorry that I e'er began.

Indeed, beginnings can be dangerous. In a celebrated essay entitled "What Is Freedom?", Hannah Arendt reflects on the origin of humankind as a sort of quintessential embodiment and confirmation of freedom: "Because he *is* a beginning, man can begin; to be human and to be free are one and the same. God created man in order to introduce into the world the faculty of beginning: freedom." At the same time, Arendt acknowledges that every authentic act of origination, no matter how small or insignificant at the time of its occurrence, must in retrospect be viewed as a sort of miracle, as a miraculous interruption of the prevailing automatism—something which could not be anticipated.[33]

Much Too Poetical

In Canto IX, the narrator admits that his manner of writing at times remains "[m]uch too poetical. Men should know why/They write, and for what end; but, note or text,/I never know the word which will come next" (IX, 41). Here Byron draws on the notion of poetry as exorbitant with respect to means and ends, causes and effects, problems and solutions. Perhaps most forcefully presented in the work of Georges Bataille, this is the idea that poetry stands over against the world of utility as its persistent other. "Human activity," Bataille says, "is not entirely reducible to processes of production and conservation, and consumption must be divided into two distinct parts." If the first part involves those activities needed for survival, Bataille insists, "[t]he second part is represented by so-called unproductive expenditures: luxury, war, cults, the construction of sumptuary monuments, games, spectacles, arts, perverse sexual activity (i.e. deflected from genital finality)—all these represent activities which, at least in primitive circumstances, have no end beyond themselves."[34]

In this way, too, Byron distances himself from epic poetics, emphasizing not the end or goal for which he writes but rather the material fact of words and the opportunities for thinking this dimension casts his way. Canto IX, for example, begins by focusing on the pronunciation of a great English war hero's name:

I

Oh, Wellington! (Or 'Vilainton'—for Fame
  Sounds the heroic syllables both ways;
France could not even conquer your great name,
  But punned it down to this facetious phrase—
Beating or beaten she will laugh the same)—
  You have obtained great pensions and much praise;
Glory like yours should any dare gainsay,
Humanity would rise, and thunder 'Nay!'

Here Byron juxtaposes two narratives, one victorious English and the other vanquished French, one denoting a stable narrative frame of reference and the other set inside (and awkwardly interrupting) the first, demonstrating what Bakhtin means by ironized or novelized discourse. The first, English, voice adoringly addresses the great leader: "Oh, Wellington! . . . —/You have obtained great pensions and much praise." While the second, countering voice surmises with far less confidence on the value of heroism. Note how even the second, parenthetical voice carries with it strains of English contempt. An English sensibility invades the French worldview even in ignominious defeat.

This ambiguity within the material dimension of words points to another, more dramatic and more profound, ambiguity. The connection between the linguistic ambiguity of Wellington's name and the moral and historical ambiguity of the art of war resonates deeply within Byron. The narrator again addresses Wellington concerning his profession:

4

You are 'the best of cut-throats:'—do not start;
    The phrase is Shakespeare's, and not misapplied:—
War's a brain-spattering, windpipe-slitting art,
    Unless her cause by Right be sanctified.
If you have acted *once* a generous part,
    The World, not the World's masters, will decide,
And I shall be delighted to learn who,
Save you and yours, have gained by Waterloo?

Here Byron suggests that taking positions assumes too much; that it is extremely hard to tell whether one's cause is in fact by Right sanctified. That is, our vision is too dim; we have too little perspective on events taking place in the world for us to settle for simplistic definitions of right and wrong. We decide things too quickly.

14

'To be or not to be! that is the question,'
    Says Shakespeare, who just now is much in fashion.
I am neither Alexander nor Hephaestion,
    Nor ever had for *abstract* fame much passion;
But would much rather have a sound digestion,
    Than Buonaparte's cancer:—could I dash on
Through fifty victories to shame or fame,
Without a stomach—what were a good name? . . .

16

'To be or not to be?'–Ere I decide,
    I should be glad to know that which *is being*?
'Tis true we speculate both far and wide,
    And deem, because we *see*, we are *all-seeing*:
For my part, I'll enlist on neither side,
    Until I se both sides for once agreeing.
For me, I sometimes think that Life is Death,
Rather than Life a mere affair of breath.

17

'Que sçais-je?' was the motto of Montaigne,
    As also of the first Academicians:

That all is dubious which Man may attain,
   Was one of their most favorite positions.
There's no such thing as certainty, that's plain
   As any of Mortality's Conditions:
So little do we know what we're about in
This world, I doubt if doubt itself be doubting.

18

It is a pleasant voyage perhaps to float,
   Like Pyrrho, on a sea of speculation;
But what if carrying sail capsize the boat?
   Your wise men don't know much of navigation;
And swimming long in the abyss of thought
   Is apt to tire: a calm and shallow station
Well nigh the shore, where one stoops down and gathers
Some pretty shell, is best for moderate bathers.

Here Byron rehearses the step back from the logical impasse of the analytic attitude in order to take a broader hermeneutic view, and to reflect upon the assumptions that put one in the position of having to decide one way or another in the first place.

Byron approaches the edge of philosophical anarchy, which sees all ideological, political, military positions, right and left, up and down, here and there, all forms of strategic thinking and assessment of optimal conditions, as contributing to unending conflict. He writes, then, of another form of resistance to war:

24

And I will war, at least in words (and—should
   My chance so happen—deeds) with all who war
     With Thought;—and of Thought's foes by far most rude,
   Tyrants and Sycophants have been and are.
I know not who may conquer: if I could
   Have such a prescience, it should be no bar
To this my plain, sworn, downright detestation
Of every despotism in every nation.

25

It is not that I adulate the people:
   Without *me*, there are Demagogues enough,
And Infidels, to pull down every steeple
   And set up in their stead some proper stuff.

Whether they may sow Skepticism to reap Hell,
   As is the Christian dogma rather rough,
I do not know;—I wish men to be free
As much from mobs as kings—from you as me.

26

The consequence is, being of no party,
   I shall offend all parties:—never mind!
My words, at least, are more sincere and hearty
   Than if I sought to sail before the wind.
He who has nought to gain can have small art: he
   Who neither wishes to be bound nor bind,
May still expatiate freely, as will I,
Nor give my voice to Slavery's jackal cry.

In reply to those who call for censorship, Byron proclaims himself a
new kind of freedom fighter, an anarchist unwilling to side with either
Whigs or Tories, in order that freedom, not slavery, or the selfish aims
of individual men and women, may flourish. In a belated recognition of
where his commitment to romantic poetry has led him, Byron resigns
himself to the limitations of his own calling as an artist. He returns
(never really having left) to the regulating themes and forms of Shakespeare's great play, while also indicating the distance he has traveled
from Plato and, especially, Aristotle:

41

But I am apt to grow too metaphysical:
   'The time is out of joint,'—and so am I;
I quite forget this poem's merely quizzical,
   And deviate into matters rather dry.
I ne'er decide what I shall say, and this I call
   Much too poetical. Men should know why
They write, and for what end; but, note or text,
I never know the word which will come next.

42

So on I ramble, now and then narrating,
   Now pondering:—it is time we should narrate:
I left Don Juan with his horses baiting—
   Now we'll get o'er the ground at a great rate.
I shall not be particular in stating
   His journey, we've so many tours of late:

> Suppose him then at Petersburgh; suppose
> That pleasant capital of painted Snows . . .

Note the revolutionary transposition of the mental action of Shake-speare's play to the serio-comical, satirical, and almost burlesque regis-ters of *Don Juan*. Such reflection on the competing claims of plot and character, action and psychological drama, suggests a sustained intellec-tual engagement with the issues at the core of the play: how to respond to the fact of death, how to measure the weight of painstaking thought against the call to some form of action?

Wittgenstein's Problem

Byron's mature poetic works, especially *Childe Harold's Pilgrimage* and *Don Juan*, portray in exemplary fashion the poetic pilgrimage to dis-cover the constitutive tension between narrative and lyrical impulses characteristic of romantic poetry. As I have suggested, this shares a family resemblance to what one might call (after Blanchot) Wittgen-stein's problem, the problem of being able to find meaning only through an essential detour across a vast terrain of different languages, none of which alone can ever yield a definitive standpoint. To remain exposed to the outside, a community must remain a weak community; a community where the promotion of forgiveness and the curtailment of revenge makes possible the freedom to make and break promises that allow human beings to be as they are and (among other things) to change their minds. Part of the price paid for interruption is a manner of being-outside where, instead of escaping from an authoritative worldview into the open (into the ritualized exuberance of the carni-val), one must undergo the negativity of poetic experience; one must move from language to language, from place to place, as a matter of course. The romantic work consolidates the inside and exposes one to the outside; the work names what it can within the terms of its own worldview but acknowledges what it cannot. This is the double imper-ative of the fragmentary work. The linguistic consciousness and perva-sive becoming of romantic poetry, in other words, are not merely restorative or conciliatory. They do not restore a Golden Age or an Eden but unleash the unsettling ambiguity of words, so that words no longer belong to one as a possession but appear otherwise.

The romantic work causes one to be skeptical of those who would establish permanent dwelling-places with their words. Better to ac-knowledge, with Byron's narrator in *Don Juan*, that "[t]here's more than one edition, and the readings/Are various, but they are none of them dull." Just so: meanings are protean and often ambiguous, but they are rarely dull or boring. A touchstone for the romantics on this point is *Tristram Shandy*, a book that rehearses the old idea from the *Symposium* that poetry constitutes an attempt to create something out of nothing (205 b-c). Sterne's reflections on this issue are certainly not lost on Byron. In a letter to Douglas Kinnaird dated April 24, 1823, less than a year before his death, Byron defended *Don Juan* as best he could: "You must not mind occasional rambling [.] I mean it for a poetical T[ristram] Shandy—or Montaigne's Essays with a story for a hinge" (*BLJ* IX, 150). Looking back over Byron's meteoric career at the time of his death, William Hazlitt also found a useful analogue in Sterne's novel. Hazlitt's assessment is surely an apt description of Byron's poem and, moreover, one that points to a deeper truth about Byron's poetic achievement, namely, it can be understood to persist in an effort to confront the existential challenge of the nothing.

In *The Space of Literature*, Blanchot links the original nothing out of which springs the work of art to the freedom that grounds it. Blanchot's reflections on poetry furnish a vital connection between the lessons of Platonic dialogue, especially the *Symposium*, and Byron's search for a beginning (out of the nothing) for his greatest poetic work. In a discussion of this kind of experience in Mallarmé, Blanchot writes,

> Yes, we can understand that the work is thus pure beginning, the first and last moment when being presents itself by way of the jeopardized freedom which makes us exclude it imperiously, without, however, again including it in the appearance of beings. But this exigency [*exigence*] which makes the work declare being in the unique moment of rupture— "those very words: it is," the point which the work brilliantly illuminates even while receiving its consuming burst of light—we must also comprehend and feel that this point renders the work impossible, because it never permits arrival at the work. It is a region anterior to the beginning where nothing is made of being, and in which nothing is accomplished. It is the depth of being's inertia [*désoeuvrement*]. (*EL* 49; *SL* 46)

Ostensibly about Mallarmé's experience of the nothing, this passage also informs much of what I have to say about Byron's poetics. For Blanchot, the jeopardized freedom that facilitates a beginning is always a hazardous, risky, unpredictable venturing forth from out of the reserve of the nothing. Significantly, freedom risks itself here. Nothing can guarantee the outcome of such a venture; no one can foresee its eventual design. Such pursuit of the origin of the work of art in this strange region has the effect of turning one into an itinerant or a traveler, a wanderer over the face of the earth.

In the end, the work of romantic poetry simultaneously reveals and conceals the truth as an event that one can never simply grasp as a correspondence between word and thing. Rather, the romantic work persists, as Lacoue-Labarthe and Nancy observe, as a questioning that "bear[s] only upon an indistinct, indeterminate thing, indefinitely retreating as it is approached, open to (almost) any name and suffering none: a thing that is unnameable, shapeless, faceless [*sans figure*]–in the last instance, 'nothing' " (*LA* 83). In effect, Lacoue-Labarthe and Nancy follow Heidegger in rethinking the essence [*wesen*] of poetry as less the making of images or worlds than discourse having to do with the revelatory interaction of being [*Sein*] and nothing [*Nichts*]. Now this is a conception of poetry that Byron would surely have understood.

4

Narrative and Its Discontents; or, The Novel as Fragmentary Work: Joyce at the Limits of Romantic Poetry

—Are you going to write it? Mr Best asked. You ought to make it a dialogue, don't you know, like the Platonic dialogues Wilde wrote.

—James Joyce

Twenty years ago, in the *Introduction to the 'Origin of Geometry'* . . . at the very centre of the book, I compared the strategies of Husserl and Joyce: two great models, two paradigms with respect to thought, but also with respect to a certain 'operation' of the relationship between language and history. Both try to grasp a pure historicity. To do this, Husserl proposes to render language as transparent as possible. . . . The other great paradigm would be the Joyce of *Finnegans Wake*. He repeats and mobilizes and babelizes the (asymptotic) totality of the equivocal, he makes this his theme and his operation. . . .

—Jacques Derrida

Of all the works in the modernist literary canon, Joyce's *Ulysses* best embodies the fragmentary work Schlegel calls *romantische Poesie*. However, such an observation immediately leads one away from one of the most long-standing and deeply entrenched assumptions about Joyce's mature works: that the narrative structure of *Ulysses*—and to a lesser extent, *Finnegans Wake*—is based upon the foundation of epic poetry, especially Homer's *Odyssey*.[1] This assumption originates with the essay, "*Ulysses*, Order and Myth" (1923), in which T. S. Eliot famously argues that Joyce's use of Homer opens up artistic space that comes to be known as modernism.[2] In fact, Joyce himself invited this assumption when he furnished his friend Stuart Gilbert with a map of Homeric parallels to use in the authorized study of his book.[3] No doubt the *Odyssey* plays a large role in setting the agenda for both the structure and themes of the novel. Nonetheless, compelling reasons remain for reading Joyce's mature works in terms of a genealogy of writing based upon the example of Socratic dialogue, especially the forms of parody and satire Bakhtin associates with "the prehistory of novelistic discourse" (*DI* 41–83). These reasons certainly begin, but are by no means exhausted by, Joyce's placement of a farcical, satirical, and self-parodying dialogue concerning *Hamlet* at precisely the structural center of the novel, the discussion at the National Library in the "Scylla and Charybdis" episode. This episode is the pivot on which the entire dialogic structure, and the two-headed theme, of the novel turns.

However, much evidence suggests Joyce questions even the Greek origins of romantic poetry and novelistic discourse by making the novel's hero a middle-aged Jewish no-one-in-particular who makes himself at home, when he can, in the gaping maw of the Irish metropolis.[4] Here, Joyce extends a thought that informs much of the work of Schlegel and Byron: that fragmentary forms often entail not only a formal experimentation leading to what one might call indeterminacy or openness, but that such forms also embody a quasi-ethical imperative: that to think and to write in such a way is to remain responsive to what remains unthought in thinking, is to be responsive to what remains hidden or tacit in the mainline narratives in which we live, to what these narratives, by themselves, cannot contain.[5] This is a concern that has frequently animated the work of the philosopher Jacques Derrida. Derrida speaks warmly of his first encounter with Joyce's writings in 1956–1957 at Harvard University, especially *Ulysses*, an encounter that left an indelible imprint on his thinking.[6] More specifically, at the end of "Violence and Metaphysics," a long and difficult early essay devoted to the thought of the Jewish philosopher Emmanuel Levinas, Derrida raises the question of the possibility of an encounter between Greek and Hebrew forms of life:

> Are we Greeks? Are we Jews? But who, we? Are we (not a chronological, but a pre-logical question) *first* Jews or *first* Greeks? And does the strange dialogue between the Jew and the Greek, peace itself, have the form of the absolute, speculative logic of Hegel, the living logic which *rec-*

onciles formal tautology and empirical heterology after having thought prophetic discourse in the preface to the *Phenomenology of the Mind?* Or, on the contrary, does this peace have the form of infinite separation and of the unthinkable, unsayable transcendence of the other? To what horizon of peace does the language [that] asks this question belong? From whence does it draw the energy of its question? Can it account for the historical *coupling* of Judaism and Hellenism? And what is the legitimacy, what is the meaning of the *copula* in this proposition from perhaps the most Hegelian of modern novelists: "Jewgreek is greekjew. Extremes meet"?[7]

In this provocative conclusion, Derrida, quoting Joyce (*U* 15.2098–99) sets a course for much of what follows in this chapter, for the guiding thought that Joyce's development of a dialogic and fragmentary poetics in *Ulysses* and *Finnegans Wake* is not so much an avant-garde aberration but rather occupies a central place in romantic and postromantic poetics. Furthermore, it suggests that such a poetic opens onto, or leads finally to, a profound awareness of a fragmentary exigency that is also an ethical responsibility. That is, that the fragmentary exigency is an ethical imperative to set out in order to maintain the possibility of justice, of a just relation, as Blanchot puts it. As it happens, this idea is also perfectly consistent with Lacoue-Labarthe and Nancy's insistent claim that German romanticism inaugurates the genre of literature *par excellence*; such a conception of literature also informs, in my view, the work of Byron, Joyce, and, in a more extreme form, Blanchot. The upshot of this deployment of a fragmentary poetic is that both of Joyce's late works can be seen as governed by an essential ambiguity internal to both the romantic work of art and the unsettling worklessness of poetic language itself. The main difference between the two books, to oversimplify things greatly, is that while *Ulysses* embodies this ambiguity on the macrocosmic level of narrative structure (though with Joyce this requires a lot of qualification), *Finnegans Wake* embodies it on the microcosmic level of the lowly unregenerate word. That is, Joyce rethinks the romantic era appropriation of Socratic dialogue and locates its capacity for truth not so much within the domain of narrative or storytelling as within the sentence, phrase, word, or even (at times) the individual syllable itself.[8]

What links these works at the deepest level, as Hugh Kenner has observed, is the emergence of language as a major character in Joyce's episodic Greco-Hebrew-Irish drama: "language is what we now confront [in *Ulysses*]," Kenner writes, "as in *Dubliners* we had confronted the characters. . . . Language is doing very much what the characters had previously done: playing roles, striking postures, contorting itself into expressive patterns which offer to clarify what is going on and instead, like Gabriel Conroy's speech [in "The Dead"], mislead: introducing dissonance into the ancient doctrine of stylistic decorum."[9] Kenner of course builds upon the earlier observation of a "Neopolitan critic" cited by Stuart Gilbert who remarked that the "protagonist [of *Ulysses*] is neither Mr Bloom nor Stephen but the *language* [of the work]."[10] In fact, this is precisely the same kind of point urged upon the reader by Schlegel in his defense of the *Fragments*: there exists a reserve within language that understanding can never completely absorb or assimilate but that nevertheless shores up and supports everything else involved in the art of interpretation. In *Finnegans Wake*, this point is memorably made:

> Hang coersion everyhow! And smotthermock Gramm's laws! But we're a drippindhrue gayleague all at ones. In the buginning is the woid, in the muddle is the sounddance and thereinofter you're in the unbewised zagain, vund vulsyvolsy. (*FW* 378.27–31)

The narrator's pun here on the word *"woid"* (signifying both word or Word and void or abyss) nicely echoes what Heidegger, in his lecture "What Is Metaphysics?" (1929), calls the being disclosed by language and the revelation of the nothing internal to Being that attends such disclosures.[11] Furthermore, this pun suggests the fragmentary work of art consists of a complex play of opposites, in whose intercourse the truth of whatever is at stake is set into motion. Levinas puts this thought as a series of questions: "Does not the function of art lie in not understanding? Does not obscurity provide it with its very element and a completion *sui generis*, foreign to dialectics and the life of ideas? Will we then say that the artist knows and expresses the very obscurity of the real?"[12] This is the question at stake in this chapter on Joyce.

Husserl versus Joyce; or, Apollo versus Dionysus

The signature movement of Joyce's late texts is a stepping down from the omniscient univocal perspective of the Martello Tower into the ambiguity of the warp and woof of everyday life. In this sense, Joyce's text repeats the opening gesture of *Don Juan*, stepping down as it does into the mire of the commonplace from the tremendous heights of the epic. *Ulysses* opens with a well-known scene in which Stephen, after confronting Mulligan about their English roommate, Haines, and about Mulligan's borderline behavior toward him, resolves to leave the Tower. Stephen formulates his decision, "I will not sleep here tonight. Home also I cannot go" (*U* 1.739–40). Thus Stephen, his dignity and exaggerated sense of self-importance slighted, leaves the tower and becomes an exile in his native city of Dublin. The events leading up to Stephen's open disagreement with Buck Mulligan, and his ensuing decision to leave, are worth considering because they establish a pattern of conflict between levity and seriousness that continues throughout most of the novel. This conflict gradually leaks out of the level of character into the level of narrative and threatens to bring the book to a premature end. That is, irony is displaced from character and plot to language and inspires a rebellion on the part of words, a resistance to narrative progression, lucidity, and point. This begins to happen in earnest when Mulligan returns to goad Stephen on to nonsensical (intoxicated) brilliance in the National Library.

As the novel opens, Mulligan, a medical student, appears atop the Martello Tower, where he, Stephen Daedalus, and a young Englishman named Haines, are living together. Mulligan, preparing for a shave, blithely and unexpectedly breaks into a parody of the opening words of the Roman Catholic sacrifice of the mass: "—*Introibo ad altare Dei*" (*U* 3.5). Mulligan's performance is directed at overturning the solemnity of the mass and the centralized authority it represents, turning its seriousness upside down and establishing a more subversive levity in its place. In fact, he is initially described as a jovial and perhaps distracted priest: "The plump shadowed face and sullen oval jowl recalled a prelate, patron of arts in the middle ages. A pleasant smile broke quietly over his lips" (*U* 3.31–33). Now one can immediately contrast this description of Mulligan as a jolly monk with Stephen's image of himself in *A Portrait of the Artist as a Young Man* as "a priest of eternal imagination, transmuting the daily bread of experience into the radiant body of everliving life" (*P* 240). Buck Mulligan and Stephen Dedalus represent two competing conceptions of the aesthetic priest, the artist or thinker, one more or less serious and the other subversively ironic and satirical. One can contrast the two conceptions of the artist as, on the one hand, an original genius, and on the other, an inventor, arranger, and plagiarist. Mulligan, the second kind of artist, always inhabiting another's words, offers up a solemn parody of Stephen's seriousness in an effort to shake Stephen loose from a foul temper that has overshadowed him since his mother's death. So while Stephen's brooding holds him captive, Mulligan plays tirelessly at his games of mockery.

Yet if Mulligan's shenanigans are at times excessive, his joyful enthusiasm for serendipitous wordplay certainly bears the imprint of his maker; a wordplay that the rest of the novel redeems from its crude beginnings in the mouth of the Buck. Mulligan's sheer unselfconscious delight in the material presence and etymological possibilities of words is far closer to the talents of the gnomic Shem the Penman (and later Joyce) than Stephen's excessively earnest and pious forgeries. The signal tension between Stephen and Mulligan is replayed in the *Wake* in the persons of Shaun the Postman and Shem the Penman. Recall Kenner's observation that "We should note, too, that in the terminology of *Finnegans Wake* [Stephen] spends many hours playing Shaun the Post, delivering letters, while Mulligan is permitted to play Shem the Penman, literary and insufferable."[13] What is potentially more interesting, however, is how this opening quarrel between Stephen and Mulligan, in which Stephen is usually figured as the Christ-figure and Mulligan the wily fiend, presents a balanced view of the strife between Mulligan and Stephen, ever a view that tips the scales in Mulligan's favor. Here, one can appeal to Nietzsche's Zarathustra for an analogue to Mulligan's attitude toward everything that is serious:

> You look up when you feel the need for elevation. And I look down because I am elevated. Who among you can laugh and be elevated at the same time? Whoever climbs the highest mountains laughs at all tragic plays and tragic seriousness.[14]

Zarathustra challenges his followers to search for a more difficult way of thinking, which leads beyond the security of one-sided seriousness. It is a thinking that is simultaneously serious and playful; a laughing wisdom never content to rest on what it already knows but always setting out anew. As he sets out into the water for a morning swim, with Haines watching from a rock on the shore, Buck Mulligan cannot resist one last performance before he and Stephen go their seperate ways:

> —My twelfth rib is gone, he cried. I'm the *Übermensch*. Toothless Kinch and I, the supermen. (*U* 1.708–09)

Mulligan thus issues a challenge to Stephen, a challenge to think less seriously about art, to abandon his reliance on external authorities, to let go of his efforts to control words, and become more attentive to their own soundings.

A text within the history of philosophy furnishing a compelling ana-logue to the conflict between Buck and Stephen is Nietzsche's *The Birth of Tragedy out of the Spirit of Music* (1872). This book-length essay, a copy of which Joyce owned, contains a powerful allegory of the history of art, and even culture itself, and it reads in part as an interpretation of romantic poetry.[15] Lacoue-Labarthe and Nancy observe:

> The Schlegels invent what becomes known (under various names) as the opposition of the Apollonian and Dionysian. And what they also estab-lish, because they have arrived (however unwittingly) at the "matrix" that produces it, is indeed—as Heidegger emphasizes—the philosophy of history. (*LA* 10)

The opposition Nietzsche articulates between Apollo and Dionysus calls to mind Schlegel's claim that the romantic work should combine seriousness and playfulness, wit and irony. The romantic work should emerge within "the continually self-creating interchange of two con-flicting thoughts" (*KA* 2: 184; *LF* 176); it also articulates precisely what seems to be at issue for Joyce in the opening pages of *Ulysses*. Consider Nietzsche's famous description of the opposition between the gods Apollo and Dionysus:

> The continuous evolution of art is bound up with the duality of the *Apolline* and the *Dionysiac* in much the same way as reproduction de-pends on there being two sexes which co-exist in a state of perpetual conflict interrupted only occasionally by periods of reconciliation. We have borrowed these names from the Greeks who reveal the profound mysteries of their view of art to those with insight, not in concepts [*Be-griffen*], admittedly, but through the penetratingly vivid figures [*Gestalten*] of their gods. Their two deities of art, Apollo and Dionysos, provide the starting-point for our recognition that there exists in the world of the Greeks an enormous opposition, both in origin and goals, between the Apolline art of the image-maker or sculptor and the image-less art of music, which is that of Dionysos.[16]

Apollo and Dionysus thus represent two antithetical impulses of art, "the separate art-worlds of dream and intoxication" (*GT* 26; *BT* 14–15). The one impulse is geared toward upholding intellectual distinctions, while the other is geared specifically toward dissolving them. The op-position offers an intriguing account of the history of art as the history

of perpetual conflict interrupted only occasionally by periods of reconciliation between the plastic, visual arts and the musical, nonvisual arts,
an animating tension or strife that resides to a greater or a lesser degree
within all art. So the history of art for Nietzsche embodies conflict,
back and forth movement, attraction and repulsion that maintains the
equilibrium of the aesthetic realm.

The Apollonian impulse, the impulse of the plastic or visual arts,
represents the idealizing, clarifying, rationalizing, ordering side of the
Greek mind, the side responsible for painting, sculpture, architecture,
and epic narrative. The Apollonian impulse governs the art of maintaining dreams or illusions and is closely attuned, for Nietzsche, to the
eyes:

> The Greeks also expressed the joyous necessity of dream-experience in
> their Apollo: as the god of all image-making energies, Apollo is also the
> god of prophecy. According to the etymological root of his name, he is
> 'the luminous one,' the god of light; as such, he also governs the lovely
> semblance produced by the inner world of fantasy. . . . But the image of
> Apollo must also contain that delicate line which the dream-image may
> not overstep if its effect is not to become pathological, so that, in the
> worst case, the semblance would deceive us as if it were crude reality; his
> image must include that measured limitation, that freedom from wilder
> impulses, that wise calm of the image-making god. (*GT* 27; *BT* 16)

Apollo is described as the luminous one, the god of light. The suggestion here is that Apollo governs the dream of human rationality or enlightenment; the history of philosophy thought as the progress of the
intellect. By contrast, the more skeptical (Dionysian) thinker is the one
who dwells or gropes a way through the dark; abandons the hope of
unequivocal enlightenment; and remains content following a crooked
or winding path. One of the most important aspects of the image of
Apollo provided here is the idea that he is the god of limits, boundaries, and separations; the codes and regulations that create the very
possibility of transgression. Transgression without an Apollonian world
of moral and rational order would make little or no sense, have no
meaning, no force or point. Art as Apollonian dream needs to establish
firm and clearly discernible limits in order to maintain its power, identity, and self-sameness. Apollonian art depends on keeping straight
what is one thing and what is another, where one entity ends and where
another begins. The Apollonian realm of art is the realm sanctioned by
law, custom, authority, reason.

By contrast, the Dionysian impulse represents the more subversive, dark, obscure, irrational, and chaotic frame of mind; the aesthetic impulse that governs music, dancing, and also the impulse most closely attuned to the ear. The Dionysian impulse begins with a primitive and uncontrollable urge toward unconscious creation, a mode of existence in which one's being is taken over by another; usurped, transformed, changed into something else:

> In the same passage Schopenhauer has described for us the enormous horror which seizes people when they suddenly become confused and lose faith in the cognitive forms of the phenomenal world because the principle of sufficient reason, in one or other of its modes, appears to sustain an exception. If we add to this horror the blissful ecstasy [that] arises from the innermost ground of man, indeed of nature itself, whenever this breakdown of the *principium individuationis* occurs, we catch a glimpse of the essence of the Dionysiac, which is best conveyed by the analogy of intoxication. These Dionysiac stirrings, which, as they grow in intensity, cause subjectivity to vanish to the point of complete self-forgetting, awaken either under the influence of narcotic drink, of which all human beings and peoples who are close to the origin of things speak in their hymns, or at the approach of spring when the whole of nature is pervaded by lust for life. In the German Middle Ages, too, ever-growing throngs roamed from place to place, impelled by the same Dionysiac power, singing and dancing as they went . . . (*GT* 28; *BT* 17)

The force of Dionysian rapture is so great that, as Nietzsche says, "the principle of sufficient reason . . . appears to sustain an exception." Another, illogical logic comes into play, another set of unruly rules come into force according to which the rules of daytime thought no longer apply. The person under the influence of the Dionysian impulse begins to doubt cognitive modes of experience, becomes more skeptical about the use of reason, and is less inclined to see thinking confined within the limits of logic. Causal relations are suspended, and, in the breakdown of the principle of individuation, one experiences a loss of the self as a discrete entity clearly separated from other people—one becomes part of a totality, a throbbing mass; a joyous, pulsating throng. The image of the wayward crowd wandering across the German countryside is especially worth noting here, for at various points Nietzsche derives his most specific sense of the Dionysian from the festival, fair, or carnival. If the Apollonian upholds the discreetness of the individual, the Dionysian dissolves the boundaries between one person and another and one becomes taken up in rapture as part of a multitude, which moves in unison; a homeless, drifting, wayfaring mass. If the Apollonian impulse in art produces art as dream and art as the creation and maintenance of illusion by means of a set of laws, regulations, and rules, then the Dionysian impulse produces a state of intoxication and transport; a deliverance or liberation, which militates toward the overcoming of the dream, limits, boundaries, or barriers.

In the passage pertaining most directly to the tension between Stephen and Mulligan, Nietzsche explicitly addresses the question of the character types represented by Apollo and Dionysus. Apollo represents self-control, self-possession, and transfiguration into a higher state of being, while Dionysus represents self-abandonment and self-abnegation, transformation into another. Apollo requires self-knowledge, careful introspection, while Dionysus calls for spirit and passion, intensity, and commitment:

> If one thinks of it as in any sense imperative and prescriptive, this deification of individuation knows just one law: the individual, which is to say, respect for the limits of the individual, measure [*sophrosyne*] in the Hellenic sense. As an ethical divinity Apollo demands measure from all who belong to him and, so that they may respect that measure, knowledge of themselves. Thus the aesthetic necessity of beauty is accompanied by the demands: 'Know thyself' and 'Not too much!', whereas getting above oneself [*hubris*] and excess were regarded as the true hostile demons of the non-Apolline sphere, and thus as qualities of the pre-Apolline period, the age of the Titans, and of the extra-Apolline world, that of the barbarians. . . .
>
> The Apolline Greek, too, felt the effect aroused by the Dionysiac to be 'Titanic' and 'barbaric'; at the same time he could not conceal from himself the fact that he too was related inwardly to those overthrown Titans and heroes. Indeed he was bound to feel more than this: his entire existence, with all its beauty and moderation, rested on a hidden ground of suffering and knowledge which was exposed to his gaze once more by the Dionysiac. And behold! Apollo could not live without Dionysos. (*GT* 40; *BT* 27)

The tension between *sophrosyne* and *hubris* in Nietzsche's account of how art has developed can be taken as the informing opposition behind the tension between Stephen and Buck at the outset of (and indeed throughout) the novel. In the character of Stephen one can see the overwhelming desire for *sophrosyne*, for the gift of Apollo, god of self-mastery, knowledge, soothsaying, epic narrative and vision; the art born of the eye; symmetry, precision, clarity, intensity and proportion. Stephen guards his identity jealously and he is afraid of giving himself over to Mulligan's high jinks; he remains fearful of being taken over by another intelligence, fearful of losing himself. Stephen tries desperately to remain in control, resists Mulligan's counsel of humor, and finds in it a constant threat to his identity. Stephen must preserve his visionary powers in order to compose the great Irish epic the people of Ireland long for.

By contrast, Mulligan represents the attribute of *hubris*, gaiety, and mockery; a mood in which song, dance, satire, and role-playing dominate; a life of self-divestment and metamorphosis; a constant breakdown of the barriers between self and other. Stephen is constantly erecting distance between himself and Mulligan; Mulligan is constantly dissolving that distance and inhabiting what Stephen thinks or wants to think is his own private world. He anticipates (thinking like Mulligan) how Mulligan will react to his aiding Mr. Deasy in the battle against the foot and mouth disease: "Mulligan will dub me a new name: the bullockbefriending bard" (*U* 2.430–31). (One can think of this taking sides as crucial: the foot and [or in] mouth disease describes [after a fashion] just what plagues [possesses] the second narrator, that is, language, the desire to get things absolutely [equivocally] wrong. Bloom muses over this fact in the cabman's shelter in the wee hours of the morning: "Text: open thy mouth and put thy foot in" [*U* 16.1269].) In terms of the general structure of the novel, the first half of the book belongs to Stephen, *sophrosyne*, narrative, lucidity, vision, rational progression; keeping things discrete and separated. The second half belongs to Buck Mulligan, the Dionysian impulse, the attitude of hubris, a letting go of words, a ludicrous abandonment of boundaries, borders, limits, decorums, orders and structures. The opposition between Stephen and Buck, Apollo and Dionysus, *sophrosyne* and *hubris*, self-control and self-abandonment, can be said to come down to the opposition between narrative and lyric.

One can pursue this Nietzschean dissatisfaction with an excessive seriousness of thought by focusing more specifically on the quarrel between Stephen and Mulligan. As the book begins and he first appears, Stephen's every movement is weighted down by a worldly burden: "Stephen Dedalus, displeased and sleepy, leaned his arms on the top of the staircase and looked coldly at the shaking gurgling face that blessed him, equine in its length, and at the light untonsured hair, grained and hued like pale oak" (*U* 1.13–16). Even as Stephen follows Mulligan to

the parapet, he is immune to Mulligan's friendly jest. Instead of attempting (or feigning) to play along with Mulligan, Stephen will be
only himself: "Stephen Dedalus stepped up, followed him wearily
halfway and sat down on the edge of the gunrest, watching him still as
he propped his mirror on the parapet, dipped the brush in the bowl and
lathered cheeks and neck" (*U* 1.36–39). Stephen, more sinned against
than sinning, cannot forget himself for a moment. Mulligan, on the
contrary, is full of lighthearted mockery, a figure of energy, spirit, wit, a
lively absurdity that inheres even in his name: "—My name is absurd
too: Malachi Mulligan, two dactyls. But it has a Hellenic ring, hasn't it?
Tripping and sunny like the buck himself" (*U* 1.41–42).

After listening to Stephen's pouting, his complaint about Haines's
nightmares involving black panthers, Mulligan draws from Stephen a
hint as to what's been troubling him. Stephen, one learns, has been
holding a yearlong grudge against Mulligan for something Stephen
overheard Mulligan say to his mother at the time of Stephen's mother's
death: "—You said, Stephen answered, *O, it's only Dedalus whose mother
is beastly dead*" (*U* 1.198–99). For Stephen to remember this slight after
the passage of a full year is remarkable; for him to hold a grudge against
Mulligan for so long says something about Stephen's character that
calls into question the central role many critics claim for him and puts
him fundamentally at odds with the profoundly ambiguous but life-
(and death-) affirming spirit of laughter, which erupts over the course
of the book and comes to a poignant crescendo in Molly Bloom's
last words. Stephen assigns weighty blame to Mulligan for his transgression against the law of gravity and so maintains a more or less
principled grudge. The attitude Mulligan takes toward life is at this
point absolutely unthinkable for Stephen, who remains imprisoned in
melancholy.

Mulligan's response to Stephen's complaint by no means reveals the
straightforward or binary oppositions between death and seriousness
and life and laughter, which animates the entire novel:

—And what is death, he asked, your mother's or yours or my own? You
saw only your mother die. I see them pop off every day in the Mater and
Richmond and cut up into tripes in the dissecting room. It's a beastly
thing and nothing else. It simply doesn't matter. You wouldn't kneel
down to pray for your mother on her deathbed when she asked you.
Why? Because you have the cursed jesuit strain in you, only it's injected
the wrong way. To me it's all a mockery and beastly. Her cerebral lobes

are not functioning. She calls the doctor Sir Peter Teazle and picks but-tercups off the quilt. Humour her till it's over. (*U* 1.204–12)

Here one sees elements of a discernibly Nietzschean struggle against the weight of a mummified, fetishized past and in favor of life; a strug-gle to overcome the heaviness of a past that crushes life with its weight. What is usually downplayed or ignored altogether in this celebration of the living present is Nietzsche's insistent emphasis on humor, parody, comedy, and wit as modes of coping with the dead weight of an excess of history. In a famous essay Nietzsche berates overly serious philoso-phizing and turns to celebrate the contemporary German Eduard von Hartmann as a philosophical parodist who, for Nietzsche, has put his finger on the pulse of the modern age by viewing it as the age of irony. Nietzsche finds himself carried away by Hartmann's witty parody of philosophy and its pretensions. Of his reading von Hartmann he writes:

> I have seldom seen a more humorous invention or read anything so full of philosophical roguishness as this work of Hartmann's; anyone whom it fails to enlighten on the subject of *becoming*—indeed, anyone whom it does not set a right—is truly fit to be called a has-been. The beginning and goal of the world process, from the first startled jolt of consciousness to the point at which it is flung back into nothingness . . . all of this so deceptively imitated and immersed in such an upstanding seriousness, as though it were in fact a serious philosophy [*Ernst-Philosophie*] and not merely a philosophical joke [*Spass-Philosophie*] . . . what cure could pos-sibly be more effective against the excess of historical cultivation than Hartmann's parody of all world history?[17]

Nietzsche finds in Hartmann's parody of world philosophy a wonder-fully ludic doubleness, which parallels his own freely ranging wordplay and reveals his contempt for one-sided, straight-faced thinking. Nietzsche also finds in Hartmann's writings a key to the idea of life as a never-ending process of becoming, an idea which becomes impor-tant in Nietzsche's later outlook. What is notable about Mulligan's de-scription of his side of the story is how his coldness in the face of death, somewhat understandable in light of his status as a medical stu-dent, is counterbalanced by a piece of genuine advice he gives to Stephen. He tells Stephen that he should try a less serious approach in dealing with such matters, tells him that he could be more flexible or more accommodating. He tells Stephen that, rather than sticking stubbornly to the idea of a self-identical or self-consistent subject, a quasi-philosophical subject that sticks to its rules of behavior no matter what the situation, it would have been more appropriate for Stephen to have humour[ed] his mother. A conflict is established here between two fundamentally different attitudes toward death (and toward life): on the one hand, an attitude that is serious, iron-willed, unforgetting (and unforgiving) and, on the other, one that is more comically adaptable, flexible, and all too forgetful. Without trying to place too much weight on this single word, humour, one can nonetheless say that the pun or play on the word is highly effective, joining together the senses of to content or to soothe, and also to induce into a humor or to cause to laugh. For Mulligan, there is an internal connection between the face one shows to someone in an effort to play along with them in their condition or state and the reality in which it, the face or mask, partakes. As a verb, it also means to adapt oneself to something, as though to humor is to change oneself. That is to say, had Stephen deigned to humour his mother on her deathbed, Mulligan says, it would have been a performance with authenticity in it, a certain agreement with the mode of behavior called for by the situation. The idea is that rather than masking an alternative or different interior identity already in place, roles carry their authenticity with them and confer identity from the outside, from the discursive situation in which they come into play.

After Mulligan's explanation, Stephen keeps on, in a stubbornly petulant effort to keep Mulligan under the spell of his own lingering wound. Mulligan, for his part, continues to try to shake Stephen out of his gloom, an effort Stephen consistently and deeply resents: "—Look at the sea. What does it care about offences? Chuck Loyola, Kinch, and come on down. The Sassenach wants his morning rashers" (*U* 1.231–32). Then, after pausing, the pressure intensifies: "Don't mope over it all day, he said. I'm inconsequent. Give up the moody brooding" (*U* 1.235–36). Stephen, however, continues to slip into ghostly reveries in which he sees his mother's "wasted body within its loose graveclothes giving off an odour of wax and rosewood, bent over him with mute secret words, a faint odour of wetted ashes" (*U* 1.270–72). In the profoundest sense, his struggle is a life-or-death struggle against the hardening, rarefying power of memory to solidify the past into a burdensome monument: "No mother. Let me be and let me live" (*U* 1.279), Stephen finally cries out to himself. Mulligan, to his credit, senses Stephen's predicament (or just exhibits good timing and appears at a propitious moment) and calls out to him, in a singing voice, "—Kinch ahoy!"

(*U* 1.280). In view of the circumstances, that is Stephen's moody brooding, most of Mulligan's jesting is appropriate, indeed, precisely what is
called for.

The most crucial early instance of the animating tension between
these two personalities, or principles, of seriousness and laughter occurs
toward the end of "Telemachus." One will remember that prior to
Stephen's decision to leave the Tower, just before the chapter's end,
Buck Mulligan, having failed to get much of a reaction out of Stephen
Dedalus earlier on top of the tower or inside of it, and now walking out
with Stephen and Haines toward town, pulls out all the stops and gives
one last rousing performance of an irreverent ballad in an attempt to
free Stephen from his ghosts:

> He moved a doll's head to and fro, the brims of his Panama hat quiver-
> ing, and began to chant in a quiet happy foolish voice:
> —*I'm the queerest young fellow that ever you heard.*
> *My mother's a jew, my father's a bird.* (*U* 1.581–85)

In this festive but unsettling scene, Mulligan is taken hold of by the
verses he chants. His personality is usurped by the song itself. While
Stephen continues walking, hardly interested, and for the most part
unimpressed with a routine that he has heard and seen before, Haines
has been taken up in the gay theatricals. Here is how Joyce's narrator
describes this particular moment: Haines, who had been laughing guard-
edly, walked on beside Stephen and said:

> —We oughtn't to laugh, I suppose. He's rather blasphemous. I'm not a
> believer myself, that is to say. Still his gaiety takes the harm out of it
> some-how, doesn't it? What did he call it? Joseph the Joiner?
> —The ballad of Joking Jesus, Stephen answered.
> —O, Haines said, you have heard it before? (*U* 1.605–09)

Haines is a little mixed up here, unable to sort out how he feels and
how he should react. Haines is caught between Stephen and Mulligan,
but also caught within a primal, visceral reaction to Mulligan's artistry,
which he tries to justify as best he can. A question worth asking oneself
here: what role does Haines play? After this scene, he more or less dis-
appears from the book. One possible answer is that Haines's apparently
trivial internal dilemma is at the heart of the book. Whether Stephen
has heard it all before or not, the issue that Mulligan's song and
Haines's deeply divided reaction puts forcefully before the reader (the

question the character of Haines exists to formulate) is the question of the value of laughter; laughter provoked by a prankish, exuberant, mocking song, which takes one outside of oneself and exposes one to the being of another person.

Stephen, who has just left the Tower, is determined to prevent the spirit of laughter from taking hold in him, and is committed to preserving his self-control, while Mulligan is just as intent on foisting the spirit of gay mockery, in whatever fashion, upon him, this wild, uncontrollable, and dissolving spirit of decadent, irreverent, humorous song. The argument between gravity and lightheartedness elaborated here by Joyce, far from being merely a dramatic device to create character conflict, or even just a thematic concern, the difference between art and mere mockery, is a major structural principle of the book. The tension between seriousness and laughter is not just something that happens in this book, but it is also just what the book is and is about; that is, *Ulysses* is, among other things, precisely a profoundly self-divided work in the sense that its narrative is progressively pulled apart by the laughing chaos of its rebellious words, which refuse to remain yoked, for any length of time, to an epic narrative or storyline. Hugh Kenner makes this point concisely and eloquently in *Joyce's Voices* when he describes the narrative as "a sort of duet for two narrators, or perhaps a conspiracy between them" (67). The first narrator dominates the first third of the book and is a more straightforward storyteller, "mov[ing] characters about, and report[ing] their doings, in fluent unemphatic novelese, barely to be distinguished from a neutral idiom . . ." (70). The second narrator, who comes into his (or her) own (roughly) in the Sirens episode, is a more rebellious, anarchic, lyrical presence, a prankish, unpredictable trickster or punster who mocks the blandness of the first narrator's story and insists on asserting another, more ironic, comical, satirical, and farcical point of view. Kenner observes:

> This second narrator is letting us know that he is there, and that he will not necessarily remain content to serve the needs of the narrative, even supposing the improbable, that its needs can be simply defined. No, he is *reading* the narrative, and reserves the privilege of letting us know what he thinks of it (75).

The farcical narrative point of view reaches its zenith (or its nadir) in "Circe" in which daylight logic has been suspended and things move in a completely different nocturnal atmosphere. "Circe" is the book turned completely inside out by the second narrator's prankish skill, undone, reversed, and replayed at a different speed for comic effect. What Kenner's reading starts to underline is how Stephen and Mulligan represent more than just character types; they embody the age-old struggle between storytelling and song, narrative and lyric.

Navigating the streets of Dublin on his unlikely odyssey, Bloom's situation illustrates two features of the romantic-poetic work. First, Joyce's hero finds himself in the role of the outsider, the exile, the pariah, the Wandering Jew, or the person who doesn't know enough physics to take certain things for granted, one who dwells on the margins of a particular language and so begins to notice things anyone else would consider (perfectly or painfully) obvious. Try as he may, Bloom's efforts to belong to a circle of Dubliners earn him mostly ridicule and abuse. More routinely, he finds himself in the opposite position, on the outside looking in; remaining on the outside and availing himself to other (perhaps less fortunate) outsiders, by establishing for a time, "in orthodox Samaritan fashion" (*U* 16.3), comically weak, unstable, and provisional communities, communities another person is always free to refuse.

Second, this exile causes him to take specific language views of the world less seriously and to adopt a more parodic, playful, or frivolous attitude toward words; to begin to allow room for them to play on their own and to notice their clumsiness or material heaviness. The language of an ironic outlook comports itself differently than philosophical or schoolroom speech. It withholds sense as often as it delivers it, turns back into itself, and falls to the earth in mute laughter or jocoserious silence. The strange humor of Joyce's later works is a function of the fact that gravity persistently pulls words out of the realm of the worldly or intelligible and back down into the duplicitous realm of the earthly or material. This refusal of sense can be thought of in the terms of Schlegel's idea of romantic poetry, in which the communicative side of language is called into question by another, darkly comical side, which refuses the communication of ideas and reverts to a different mode of being; a more anarchic mode in which words withdraw from the realm of communication to inhabit a space other than the space of intelligibility or meaning.

In "Hades" Joyce provides a perfect example of this gravity. Deprived of its seriousness, a serio-comical and duplicitous gravity brings things crashing back to earth by means of a strange humor and sends words, by the same illogic, rising into the air or, away from the world of lucidity or sense. Driving to the cemetery together, Martin Cunningham, Simon

Dedalus, and Mr. Power remember the time "when the hearse capsized round Dunphy's and upset the coffin on to the road" (*U* 6.415–16). Bloom reimagines this scene to himself: "Bom! Upset. A coffin bumped out on to the road. Burst open. Paddy Dignam shot out and rolling over stiff in the dust in a brown habit too large for him" (*U* 6.421–23). Here gravity produces a bizarre comedy of the body, Dignam's body which impolitely falls out into street, sprawling down the hill. It is as though gravity has been serio-comically divided against itself, deprived of its one-sided seriousness. Moments later, as Dignam's body is taken to its graveplot, Bloom's thoughts turn impulsively to song: "The ree the ra the ree the ra the roo. Lord, I mustn't lilt here" (*U* 6.640). Again, here is the constant tension between narrative control and lyrical abandon. Bloom finds himself at a critical moment, between grave and lilting impulses, between the seriousness and self-possession appropriate at the funeral of a friend, and the natural tendency of words to disrupt that seriousness.[18]

Work-in-Progress: The Apotheosis of Romantic Poetry

Ulysses is filled with of clowns, wits, artists, fools, buffoons, and unstable figures of mockery, laughter, wit, and folly; those who mimic or echo others and those who change into other forms of life and metamorphose with disturbing ease. "If we were all suddenly somebody else," Bloom muses (*U* 6.836).

Almost everyone in the book plays more than one role, and that is how Joyce seems to have thought of character; in a dramatic sense, as role-playing, as taking on a character from the outside and playing it until it fits. In *Finnegans Wake*, too, the discreteness of identity (the handful of figures one can recognize on a fairly regular basis include Humphrey Chimpden Earwicker and Anna Livia Plurabelle, Shaun the Postman, and Shem the Penman, and their daughter, and sister Isabel) is almost completely dissolved in favor of children's games, nursery rhymes, riddles, puns, plays, closet dramas, jokes, jests, and so on. It is as though one's participation (with others) in these kinds of games is a more compelling way to describe the experience of being human; a way to leave identity open, flexible, and malleable.

This way of thinking about the individual, the attitude of hubris or self-abandonment that, for Nietzsche, characterizes the Dionysian impulse, bears a certain resemblance to role-playing, acting, performance, as if identity were gained from performance rather than from introspection.

One will remember, of course, that Nietzsche's discussion of the Dionysian suspension of the discreteness or separateness of individual identity comes within a larger discussion of the origins of tragedy; a dramatic, theatrical form, which calls for the renewal of identity through the taking on of another's. This is the kind of identity assumed by Buck Mulligan when the narrative, beginning with description, moves into his thoughts (and out again) in "Telemachus":

> And putting on his stiff collar and rebellious tie he spoke to them, chiding them, and to his dangling watchchain. His hands plunged and rummaged in his trunk while he called for a clean handkerchief. God, we'll simply have to dress the character. I want puce gloves and green boots. Contradiction. Do I contradict myself? Very well then, I contradict myself. Mercurial Malachi. A limp black missile flew out of his talking hands. (*U* 1.513–18)

Readers often approach Mulligan with wariness and extreme caution, and it is true that Joyce seems to take care to load his character with unsavory, even fiendish, associations. The first scene, for example, has overtones of both a black mass, celebrated by Mulligan and attended by Stephen, and the account of the temptation of Jesus in the desert, in which Stephen, of course, plays Jesus and Mulligan plays the role of Satan. However, notice how Mulligan, tries the role of Jesus on for size, although (of course) always from a satirical standpoint: "—Mulligan is stripped of his garments" (*U* 1.510). The point here, though, is that no human being is ever a self-identical, philosophical subject, consistent, rational, predictable, and nonselfcontradicting, but rather people are made up of a variety of roles, some of them perhaps mutually exclusive.

This is the idea behind the theme of the continual transformation of the individual into someone (or something) else that runs throughout *Ulysses*. Together with the idea of role-playing or character-acting, the idea of self-transformation has great implications for thinking about romanticism. As Bloom returns from Dlugacz's he brings Molly her mail, including her letter from Boylan, and Molly asks him a simple question about a word she has come across in her reading:

> —Here, she said. What does that mean?
> He leaned downward and read near her polished thumbnail.
> —Metempsychosis?
> —Yes. Who's he when he's at home? (*U* 4.337–40)

This simple question, to be sure, carries implications for everyone involved in the events that will transpire on this day. "—Metempsychosis, he said, frowning. It's Greek: from the Greek. That means the transmigration of souls" (*U* 4.341–42). This generates Molly's famous reply: "—O, rocks! she said. Tell us in plain words" (*U* 4.343). Here Joyce conjures up the spirit of Ovid's *Metamorphoses*. Everything changes; nothing stays the same. All characters become or tend toward something else over the course of time. The punning play on the first syllables of the word Bloom initially mishears: "—Met him what? he asked" (*U* 4.336), gives weight to the idea that identity is connected to the roles one plays; connected to one's ability for self-creation or self-fashioning; and to one's capacity to play or read a part. After chattering about the book Molly is reading, Bloom's eye catches the picture of *The Bath of the Nymph*, which hangs over the bed, and he comes round to this thought: "—Metempsychosis, he said, is what the ancient Greeks called it. They used to believe you could be changed into an animal or a tree, for instance. What they called nymphs, for example" (*U* 4.375–77).

In terms of the opposition between sympathetic wit and irony, Bloom moves back and forth between the two, not quite at home in either region, personality, ethos, or attitude. "Lestrygonians" begins with sympathy (Bloom feels for Farrell), moves to irony (Bloom leaves the first restaurant in disgust), back to sympathy (sees the blind stripling) and ends in ironic retreat from Boylan. Joyce even includes what appears to be a parody of romantic hermeneutics: the scene in which one learns about the hermeneutic significance (perhaps impact is a better word) of pigeon shit (*U* 8.401–03). What is most interesting is how Joyce reverses the priority of sympathy and irony; the ironist is most sympathetic of all, while the sympathetic man or woman gets trapped within the dominant narrative, a narrative which recognizes only itself and which renders the sympathizer unable to escape. For Bloom, however, the movement is through desublimation to understanding; understanding comes from the outside in.

It is perhaps "Scylla and Charybdis," however, in which the multiplicity of the subject receives its fullest and most dizzying treatment. Mulligan's entrance in the library, just as Stephen is foundering in his Shakespeare lecture, furthers this idea and also facilitates the being born (in Shandy-esque fashion) of Bloom, halfway through his own book, the book that bears his name as its title. Here Joyce demonstrates an under-appreciated feature of this scene, just that, despite Stephen's feelings of contempt for Mulligan, something has been direly missing in his thinking until Mulligan enters the room and injects a mocking levity into things. One thinks of the encounter in Plato's *Symposium* between Socrates and Alcibiades in which Socrates's legendary powers of self-control are put to the test by the passionate discourse and sheer physical presence of Alcibiades. In the early hours of the morning when almost everyone else has slipped off to sleep, Socrates must finally acknowledge that the really masterful dramatist must be at least two-sided; must have a facility for writing comedy as well as for writing tragedy, as if identity must be somehow double, dialogic, relational, as though an isolated or sealed off subject makes no sense (not even to itself).

Julia Kristeva remarks on how the doubleness of speech, its excessiveness with respect to meaning or intelligibility, leads to doubleness or division within the speaking subject itself: "The problem of the heterogeneous in meaning, of the unsymbolizable, the unsignifiable, which we confront in the analysand's discourse as an inhibition, a symptom, or an anxiety, characterizes the very condition of the speaking being, who is not only split but split into an irreconcilable heterogeneity."[19] Here, the subject resides on a rift or tension between two sides of language, the one side providing for the articulation of comprehensible meaning through the use of words as a means of communication, and the other side withdrawing into a region of unintelligibility, a morass of verbal chaos, loose ends, and grammatical and syntactical breakdowns and refusals, a side of language that is irreducible to significance. Kristeva famously describes this irreducible language as the semiotic *chora*, which exists prior to the production of rational or logical discourse, a side of language which exists on the other side of sense or meaning. In any case, for Kristeva, the subject resides in a region of conflict or site of contention between two linguistic forces, a serious, sense-making impulse and a scattering, disseminating impulse. And one must always negotiate a way through this conflict, needing to wager, again and again, the price to be paid for identity.

Stephen and Bloom (even more so) inhabit this realm of the in between and negotiate a way through the split subject in "Scylla Charybdis." As the episode begins, Stephen is conversing with Lyster, Eglinton, Best, and Russell in the National Library on the subject of literature, Goethe, and the possibility of writing an Irish national epic. The conversation pits Lyster, the Quaker librarian, and his friends, Eglinton, Russell, and Best, against Stephen's youthful determination, intelligence and wit; faculties Stephen employs repeatedly to hold out for the possibility of a less serious, more frivolous interpretation

of Shakespeare. As the scene opens, Stephen is outnumbered and seeks
a more flexible discursive space in which to operate. While the elders
hold to an unbearably ethereal notion of art and while the narrative
seems to uphold this seriousness, Stephen seeks a more ironic, laughing
or comic notion. The oracular Russell, for instance, insists that:

> Art has to reveal to us ideas, formless spiritual essences. The supreme
> question abut a work of art is out of how deep a life does it spring. . . .
> The deepest poetry of Shelley, the words of Hamlet bring our minds
> into contact with eternal wisdom, Plato's world of ideas. All the rest is
> the speculation of schoolboys for schoolboys. (*U* 9.48–53)

Stephen, however, strives to step back from this notion of art as the
revelation of formless spiritual essences and to cultivate a view of art as
something more trivial in its origins, something which holds to the ordinary world of temporality, serio-comic instability, laughter, irony
and humor. "Aristotle was once Plato's schoolboy," Stephen says (*U*
9.57). This is the principle that he will use to interpret Shakespeare,
that is, the idea that origins, rather than being foundational events of
supreme significance and moment, are rather trivial, silly, humorous,
serio-comical and, more often than not, deeply equivocal events containing an inextricable mixture of joy and sorrow. One could think of
this as the theory of the origin of the work of art as *"quintessential
triviality"* (*U* 9.287). Here at the outset, Stephen, already beginning to
wander, counsels himself away from the seriousness of traditional
thought: "Hold to the now, the here, through which all future plunges
to the past" (*U* 9.89) Any attempt to reach the past, Stephen appears
to say, must pass through the prism of the present.

Following this back and forth play between Stephen and the schoolmasters, Stephen begins (with perhaps surprising assertiveness) to acknowledge that the artist may be a less than entirely self-possessed
being, one more inclined than not to reside in a region of doubt or uncertainty, one who is made up of elements of both *sophrosyne* and *hubris*:

> —As we, or mother Dana, weave and unweave our bodies, Stephen said,
> from day to day, their molecules shuttled to and fro, so does the artist
> weave and unweave his image. And as the molecule on my right breast is
> where it was when I was born, though all my body has been woven of
> new stuff time after time, so through the ghost of the unquiet father the
> image of the unliving son looks forth. (*U* 9.376–81)

An interesting point to be made here is that, although Joyce commonly is taken to be a writer who privileges paternity over maternity, the artist Stephen describes exhibits a side of himself that is more than a little like Penelope, one who weaves and then unweaves an identity out of each new day, one whose identity undergoes constant permutation, re-vision, and alteration. Stephen lets go of the priestly image of the artist and sees such a one as more like a Penelope, who resides between weaving and unweaving, story and lyric, seriousness and play.

At first, Stephen has trouble articulating this theory, to the point of having to ask himself whether he really knows what he is talking about. All this changes, however, with the dramatic entrance of Buck Mulligan: "A ribald face, sullen as a dean's, Buck Mulligan came forward, then blithe in motley, towards the greeting of their smiles" (*U* 9.485–86). If Mulligan began by speaking "sternly" and so embodying the author of *Tristram Shandy* (*U* 1.19), now, his face sullen as a dean's, he is matched with the Dean of St. Patrick's, another of Joyce's favorite maladroit mockers, a fig-ure who is reincarnated in *Finnegans Wake* as "Mr O'Shem the Draper" (*FW* 421.25). It appears that Joyce's plans for Mulligan are close to the heart of what his later writings are about. Now again the scene begins to resemble the *Symposium*, in which Socrates lectures a group of friends on the subject of love and then is himself taught an embarrassing lesson by the boisterous and drunken Alcibiades, who enters the dinner party (to choruses of laughter) and turns things more or less upside down. Likewise, Stephen's lecture enters a more complex phase, as though Stephen's clarity of vision needs Buck's self-abandonment, humor, and mocking wit to be complete. With Mulligan's entry, Stephen's discourse is taken to another level. Mulligan's mockery grafts onto Stephen's Aristotelian insistence on particulars a Wildean sense of humor, recklessness, and playfulness, which turns the tables on the schoolmasters. Malachi Mulligan's cheerful irrever-ence for academic authority counteracts the encroaching gloom of the scene and adds an edge of contemporary life to the discussion:

> Buck Mulligan thought, puzzled.
> —Shakespeare? he said. I seem to know the name.
> A flying sunny smile rayed in his loose features.
> —To be sure, he said, remembering brightly. The chap that writes like Synge. (*U* 9.507–11)

What comes out of this odd marriage between Aristotle and Oscar Wilde is a revised conception of the artist as an ironist, a shape shifter, more of a wit and a comedian, a satirist, fool, and clown; a joker who is seemingly, as with the mocker, "never taken seriously when he is most serious" (*U* 9.543). That is, the ironist remains on the margins or the outside, agile, flexible, and instead of relying on a foundation of tradition for thought manipulates the humor of ordinary words. But this isn't to say the ironist is merely playing with words; on the contrary, it represents a certain way of thinking with words.

Perhaps instigated by Mulligan, the schoolmasters pick up this line of thought, Eglinton asking about prince Hamlet and whether anyone has made him out to be an Irishman. This is an interesting line of thought, Shakespeare as Irish wit, but what is perhaps even more provocative is Best's comment: "—The most brilliant [theorizing] of all is that story of Wilde's, Mr Best said, lifting his brilliant notebook. That Portrait of Mr. W. H. where he proves that the sonnets were written by a Willie Hughes, a man all hues" (*U* 9.522–24). Best, ending with a pun, is beginning to propose an interpretation of Shakespeare that takes the view of the lyrical poems as its starting point rather than the plays or even the longer narrative poems, as though, again, there is something about the sonnet that gets closer to wit, humor, and irony than narrative can.

The rest of the episode argues by means of the truthful humors of words and teaches, as with the many senses of jokes, puns, plays, and jests, one is always more than one thing at a time; simultaneously this and that at any given moment. The language of the narrative, rising to the challenge of this assertion of multiple identity, asserts an exuberantly ambiguous lyrical presence. When Shakespeare's will is mentioned, as if to keep up with the spirit of the wordplay (in fact, as if to best it), the narrative metamorphoses:

> He left her his
> Secondbest
> Bed.

Punkt.

> Leftherhis
> Secondbest
> Leftherhis
> Bestabed
> Secabest
> Leftabed.

Woa! (*U* 9.697–707)

This is the lilting side of language that turns narrative inside out. It will give Buck Mulligan his revenge and bring the book back down to earth. Shakespeare ceases to be the exemplary bard and becomes the rather ubiquitous "Rutlandbaconsouthamptonshakespeare or another poet of the same name" (*U* 9.866). As Mr Best has only just affirmed: "—A myriadminded man, Mr Best reminded. Coleridge called him myriadminded" (*U* 9.768–69). The ironist is also many things at once, and is never simply a one-sided subject or a one-dimensional being.

Bloom, too, resides in this region of the in-between, being born (in a sense) out of the interanimation of *sophrosyne* and *hubris* exhibited in the library, out of the interplay of Stephen Dedalus and Buck Mulligan. At the end of "Scylla and Charybdis," Bloom walks out between the two men, an ordinary and hardly noticeable act that nonetheless has some ludicrous consequences. This is a key moment: Bloom, the sympathetic fool, is born, somewhat like Tristram Shandy, in the middle of the book, out of the melancholy intelligence of Stephen Dedalus and the tripping and sunny wit of Buck Mulligan. The narrative, liberated from the constraint of meaningful or truthful representation, now begins to buckle and give itself over to the laughter of the word, laughter in which even Stephen, instigated by the Buck, for a time takes part: "He laughed to free his mind from his mind's bondage" (*U* 9.1016). One recalls Nietzsche's initial description of how the opposition between Apollo and Dionysus continually breaks apart and is then reconciled to itself. So here, Stephen and Buck have a temporary reconciliation, which gives birth to Leopold Bloom, holy fool.

It makes sense, then, that Joyce generally turns his narrative over to fools, clowns, ironists, and buffoons; those who, like Buck Mulligan and unlike the philosopher, won't be tempted to take words too seriously and will be quick to disown them if the need arises; why Stephen regularly goes unheeded or just tolerated (as mad bad black-clad poet). One's outsidedness with respect to words does not have to be thought of as an evasion of ethical responsibility, as Kierkegaard thought; rather, one can see it as an acknowledgement of the real limits of one's discourse or vocabulary and a venturing out to its boundaries; to the edge of what it can say, even into the realm of what it cannot say, into the realm of the unsayable or even the sacred. Schlegel describes romantic poetry as transcendental buffoonery and his poet engages in continuous self-parody, while Byron, one recalls, shows his narrator to be a fool; not only getting a bedpan dumped on his head but also going so far as to discuss with his readers the function of his liver, the lazaret of bile. And there is always Nietzsche's counsel of lightheartedness in the practice of a gay science, a nontheoretical mode of thinking which remains fragmentary, incomplete, sketchy, work in progress.

Lightheartedness is what Stephen noticeably lacks. He needs to learn to be more foolish, not to take everything to heart. (At least in this respect, Buck Mulligan seems to be right.) Stephen's attitude toward the past in "Nestor" clings to Nietzsche's forgetfulness but ignores Nietzsche's buffoonery. Enter Stephen as one-sided Nietzschean visionary: "History . . . is a nightmare . . ." (*U* 2.377). Stephen, filled with a brooding mood, remains bound by excessive seriousness until Buck Mulligan ("Puck Mulligan" *U* 9.1142) enters the library and turns laughter loose on Stephen, laughter that annoys him but, as it happens, enables him to make good on his promise of a wit's theory of *Hamlet*. Mulligan's "mocker's seriousness" (*U* 9.544) temporarily liberates Stephen from the oppressive seriousness of the Dublin schoolmasters and allows him to think through a particularly narrow passage. *Ulysses* takes leave of the poet as visionary and creates a serio-comic version, a transcendental buffoon of some resourcefulness, whose ordinary powers of arranging or inventing things (and not of having visions or dreams) count for originality. Joyce develops the artist to an extreme in Shem the Penman, the tragic jester. He turns out in the person (or I should say in the body) of Bloom a more comically human Zarathustra, a domesticated version of Nietzsche's holy fool: "I am a fool perhaps," Bloom thinks to himself on Sandymount Strand (*U* 13.1098) after he has reached a version of the romantic sublime watching Gerty McDowell.

However, as almost always with Joyce, this is not the whole story. Alasdair MacIntyre has famously argued that a viable ethical theory can be grounded on only one of two conceptual foundations: Aristotle or Nietzsche.[20] MacIntyre, given his particular priorities and commitments, would like for us to choose Aristotle. Those who have abandoned all hope can choose Nietzsche if they like. But in *Ulysses* (and, in ways that have only recently come to light, *Finnegans Wake*) Joyce boldly offers us a third way. Between the bone-dry Aristotelianism of Stephen Dedalus and the lurid Nietzscheanism of Buck Mulligan there comes the unlikely figure of Leopold Bloom, an unremarkable Dublin Jew. And it is on his emergence as a representative of a comparatively weak ethic of care based partly on Hebrew, and not just Greek, tradition that the rest of the novel arguably turns.

From the Work's Worklessness to Words' Wakefulness

While roughly the first third of *Ulysses* is governed by a state of the art narrative design, a narrative technique informed by what Hugh Kenner has dubbed the "Uncle Charles Principle," that is, the idea that "the narrative idiom need not be the narrator's" (18), the middle third of the novel, as if to renounce the ambitions of this revolutionary narrative, takes an extravagantly digressive turn. It becomes, among other things, a study of all the sorts of endless forms and wayward ways digression can take. One has only to think of the "Cyclops" episode, in which lengthy lyrical and often vulgar, obscenely funny digressions spring spontaneously out of the heads of words or phrases or sentences within the narrative per se as though every word of the first narrator's story, in this case the tale told by the dun and full of sound and fury, touches tangentially on an endless number of parallel language views, narratives, worlds, and universes; as though each sentence, phrase, or word has at least two sides, a serious or straightforward one and a ludicrous, transgressive, unacceptable, or mocking one. Here in "Cyclops," the dun's narrative takes a digressive, somewhat obscene lyrical turn:

> And then he [Bloom] starts with his jawbreakers about phenomenon and science and this phenomenon and the other phenomenon.
>
> The distinguished scientist Herr Professor Luitpold Blumenduft tendered medical evidence to the effect that the instantaneous fracture of the cervical vertebrae and consequent scission of the spinal cord would, according to the best approved tradition of medical science, be calculated to inevitably produce in the human subject a violent ganglionic stimulus of the nerve centres of the genital apparatus, thereby causing the elastic pores of the *corpora cavernosa* to rapidly dilate in such a way as to instantaneously facilitate the flow of blood to that part of the human anatomy known as the penis or male organ resulting in the phenomenon which has been denominated by the faculty a morbid upwards and outwards philoprogenitive erection *in articulo mortis per diminutionem capitis*. (*U* 12.466–78)

It as though every word in the book could spring, without warning, into its own full-blown narrative; as though (turning the thought inside out) a narrative is, in the end, only a digression from the standpoint of a lyrical fragment. From this point of view, narrative is a function of the more primordial condition of language; as spontaneous lyrical outburst or even a scream; from this standpoint, the narrative is lyricism subdued or brought under rational control.

While he describes language as a system of signs, Nietzsche also thinks of language as something on the order of primitive music or song; a language without words; a more visceral use, or non-use of language that is as inclined as not to retreat back into itself and keep a strictly laughing silence. One can begin to speculate about this Nietzschean description of language by returning to *The Birth of Tragedy*. In this essay, Nietzsche comes close to saying that dialogue, or literary narrative generally, is an offshoot, a special case, or specific feature of a primordial language, in which the primary function is not communication of information or ideas but a return to a state of identification with a primal oneness. However, this oneness is nothing like Eden or a prereflective identity but rather a mixture of pain and joy, which gives rise to itself in rapturous song.

> For this reason it is impossible for language to exhaust the meaning of music's world-symbolism, because music refers symbolically to the original contradiction and original pain at the hearty of the primordial unity, and thus symbolizes a sphere which lies above and beyond all appearance. In relation to that primal being every phenomenon is merely a likeness, which is why language, as the organ and symbol of phenomena, can never, under any circumstances, externalize the innermost depths of music . . .. (*GT* 51; *BT* 36)

Nietzsche struggles here to describe a preverbal or presemantic level of expression. Preverbal language (if one can speak of it in that way) embodies a primal contradictoriness in human existence before speech has a chance to reduce it to unity and coherence. It is as though the act of speech were a falling away from a primal mode of being, as though it were a ludicrous halftruth or near miss which is always comical in its insufficiency. One way to think about Nietzsche's claim that "tragedy arose from the tragic chorus and was originally chorus and nothing but chorus" (*GT* 52; *BT* 37), then, is to think of it as a language without intelligibility, a language without reason or without logic, a pre-Socratic chorus or song where individual identity is dissolved. As though language now could be said to be speaking through a human collective and not grounded in the subjectivity of an individual or as though language had more than merely a subjective origin. For Nietzsche, an excess of intelligibility is, for all intents and purposes, what killed the power of ancient tragedy. Thus, the law of the new Socratic drama became: "'In order to be beautiful, everything must be reasonable [*verständig*: comprehensible or intelligible]'" (*GT* 85; *BT* 62).

And so the chorus was pushed further and further into the background of dialogue. Narrative suppressed the contradictory voices and presence of the lyric.

This suggests that Nietzsche, like Joyce, is concerned with a language already disposed to go elsewhere; words striving to come into their own, apart from human purposes or goals, intentions or desires. It is linguistic anarchy which turns words loose inside the system and confuses everything. Everyday talk is taken up in the excessive drive of language, becomes implicated in the movement toward incomprehensiblity. The second third of *Ulysses* starts to look as if (feeling gravity's pull) it is falling or straying into this realm of language, language that offers itself as digressive, laughing, maddening, song; what is excessive with respect to normal speech, and what is left over when the statement or idea has been extracted. "Calypso" is one of the first passages in *Ulysses* in which language makes an appearance like this, in its own right or out of its own mind. As Bloom makes his way to Dlugacz's to pick up a kidney for breakfast, he passes an open schoolroom window out of which tumble strains of a children's school lesson in the alphabet. Not so much of an uneasiness as just a lilt on the part of language, the alphabet catches the ear of Bloom (and the eye of the narrator) as he is walking past:

> He passed Saint Joseph's National school. Brats' clamour. Windows open. Fresh air helps memory. Or a lilt. Ahbeesee defeegee kelomen opeecue rustyouvee doubleyou. Boys are they? Yes. Inishturk. Inishark. Inishboffin. At their joggerfry. Mine. Slieve. Bloom. (*U* 4.135–39)

A relatively unremarkable passage in itself, it nevertheless intimates the eagerness of words to have their say about things, an eagerness which will come to dominate the book, reaching a crescendo in "Circe." One thing to note here is Bloom's outsidedness, an exteriority which (by chance) makes another truth, another perspective, and a more material perspective on language available. Bloom's exteriority with respect to language makes possible an alternative view of it, which takes into account its unpredictable materiality, and takes into account the fact that language is more than a product of the differences within a system of signifiers. The lyrical impulse of language has a mind of its own.

This thought is amplified significantly in the "Aeolus" episode, in which Bloom and Stephen can be found in the *Freeman's Journal* and *National Press* offices at noontime. For the first time, the language of the book speaks forcefully and independently of a speaking subject, asserting itself against the rational and ordering impulse of a more editorial consciousness, in this case Bloom's:

> The machines clanked in threefour time. Thump, thump, thump. Now if he got paralysed there and no-one knew how to stop them they'd clank on and on the same, print it over and over and up and back. Monkeydoodle the whole thing. Want a cool head. (*U* 7.101–04)

Bloom's reminder to himself, for restraint or for an attitude of detached coolness, recalls a similar moment of lyrical outburst in "Hades." It is also the tension in the opening episode between Stephen's principled but misguided self-possession and Buck's protean and perhaps overbearing self-abandonment, and between dispositions of sophrosyne and hubris, the individual embodiments of the Apollonian and Dionysian aesthetic impulses at work in Nietzsche's account of the origins of tragedy. Now the work done by each of these impulses is dispensed by Joyce again, this time between the relatively self-controlled or control seeking consciousness of the first narrator (a somewhat Bloom-like or Bloom-liking figure, Bloom being the prudent member one will recall [*U* 12.211]) and the more out of control, exuberant, mocking, caustic lyrical consciousness of the second narrator, who is less a narrator than an anarchic force or impulse of language. He is the one who turns the story counterclockwise, against Bloom, against itself, against its telling, and against what one would think of as the narrative portion.

> Sllt. The nethermost deck of the first machine jogged forward its flyboard with sllt the first batch of quirefolded papers. Sllt. Almost human the way it sllt to call attention. Doing its level best to speak. That door too sllt creaking, asking to be shut. Everything speaks in its own way. Sllt. (*U* 7.174–77)

Normally, one thinks of narration as being under the control of a speaker, a storyteller, someone who takes care of words and their meanings and takes care to get them right. The lyrical word, on the other hand, as Joyce works with it or, better, appears to let it go, tends toward exactly the opposite; toward a prankish dispossession of narrative consciousness and persistent digression. Ironic consciousness has no real control over words but rather suffers the consequences of various maddening appearances and wayward wanderings.

One can see this at work in "Lestrygonians." At one point Bloom's inner monologue is made up of words and phrases stolen from other people, words that are not his own: "Please tell me what is the meaning. Please tell me what perfume does your wife. Tell me who made the world. The way they spring those questions on you" (*U* 8.328–30). Here three voices—those of Molly, Martha, and Milly—speak (again) through Bloom, their fragmentary questions remaining with(in) him throughout the day. As if to suggest that the private realm, Bloom's private realm, is always made up of the echoes of other people's talk. It is always a multiple or dialogic arena resonant with the tones of other people's voices, a kind of echo chamber in the head. This means that Joyce's notion of ironic consciousness, far from being a realm of privacy or sanctuary where in the individual exercises self-creative freedom, is more a relational self in an intimate relationship or friendship. It is always composite, multiple, and many-sided; a chain or a garland of fragments, a loose collection of bits of roles that never fit into a self-identical whole. While roles can be maintained for various periods of time, within the realm of intimacy or friendship the self is exposed as a jumble of broken fragments, other people's sayings, half-truths, and ill-fitting masks; bits and pieces of language which by themselves are never enough to constitute a self-contained subject. Rather, they remain a collection of questions that are always directed toward other people, calling for a response, as if the self can never exist by itself but needs the answering stress of another voice to be complete or to begin to be itself.

The passage in "Lestrygonians" raises the question of language and its relation to consciousness: to whom (if anyone) does the language of these sentence fragments belong? It is hard to say. What becomes questionable is whether consciousness is more than a place, scene, or a stage, where other people's words (and others before them) strut and fret their hour. A room or a chamber is always ringing with the inevitable echoes of words that sound almost like other words. In this way, one's freedom of action is not predicated on originality or genius, but on invention and arrangement, quotation and repetition, parody and wit; on making a beginning, however tentative. This is why *Ulysses* is a book in which language asserts itself against the control of the speaking subject. One can play with language but never quite own it or completely control it. Rather, one picks up the echo in one's ear. Increasingly, the book becomes a dialogue between language and the speaking subject. To put it another way, the book begins to embody a struggle between the initially straightforward narrative and an outrageous linguistic consciousness that continually calls into

question the primacy of the narrative (the story of what certain
Dubliners did on June 16, 1904). The self is never entirely effaced. It
asserts itself by entering into the play of quotation and by inflecting
those quotations so as to make something new. This is partly the way
parody works: by means of inflection. As Schlegel makes clear, romantic poetry is primarily an antigeneric genre based on the freedom
of the poetic word, its outsidedness with respect to narrative. The linguistic fragments of the text (the disembodied language which exists
outside the narrative but inside the text) issue a laughing protest
against narrative; these fragments undercut narrative, calling it to give
an account of itself.

The "Sirens" episode is, of course, famous as a linguistic imitation of
the structure of music or (if you'd rather) a liberation of the musical
possibilities of words, anyhow a generous estimation and display of the
song-like quality of language. One of the most notable (even alarming)
qualities of "Sirens" is the way in which the language of the episode
embarks on a many sided mimicry of the one-sided narrative voice, as
though the narrator loses control and the bottom of language falls out
(in a vaguely Nietzschean way), while individual words, phrases, scraps
of songs, and fragments begin to display the buried life they secretly
tender beneath the flattening effect of narrative. This mocking rebellion sounds as though it could be behind the attitude of disdain for
character and action displayed by the language in "Sirens." At the outset of the chapter, Misses Kennedy and Douce, nearly indistinguishable
barmaids in the lounge of the Ormond Hotel, and perhaps also echoes
(in their own way) of the Scylla and Charybdis (and of each other),
begin flirtations with someone ("the honourable Gerald Ward A. D.
C." [*U* 10.1179]) in one of the carriages of the cavalcade of William
Humble, earl of Dudley, which passes in front of the hotel on its way
through Dublin. Their flirtations produce an infectious laughter which
proves contagious.

> —Look at that fellow in the tall silk.
> —Who? Where? gold asked more eagerly.
> —In the second carriage, miss Douce's wet lips said, laughing in the sun.
> He's looking. Mind till I see. (*U* 11.70–73)

The laughter spreads from the Misses Kennedy and Douce to the language of the narrative, as though the contagion of laughter is repeated
not only on the level of narrative, that is, not only by other characters

within the narrative, but on the level of language itself. So language soon begins to imitate the barmaids' flirtatious (spectacular) giggling:

> Douce gave full vent to a splendid yell, a full yell of full woman, delight, joy, indignation.
> —Married to the greasy nose! she yelled.
> Shrill, with deep laughter, after, gold after bronze, they urged each other to peal after peal, ringing in changes, bronzegold, goldbronze, shrilldeep, to laughter after laughter. And then they laughed more. Greasy I knows. (*U* 11.171–77)

The development of a full-scale linguistic mimicry of the narrative, although intimated for some time in other chapters, most notably in "Aeolus," emerges full-blown for the first time here in the "Sirens" episode. Although it may appear as a surprise to a first-time reader of *Ulysses,* Joyce has carefully laid the groundwork for this rebellion of words against the narrative desires of the speaking subject. Several themes converge in the passage marked above: an exuberance of character gives rise to an exuberance of language, which, figured as laughter, begins to perpetuate itself by means of a complex series of internal verbal echoes.

The sentence at the middle of the passage nicely illustrates this laughing echo effect: "Shrill, with deep laughter, after, gold after bronze, they urged each to peal after peal, ringing in changes, bronzegold, goldbronze, shrilldeep, to laughter after laughter." The seemingly innocuous echo of "laughter" with "after" starts a chain reaction. Various words respond to the soundings of other (echoing or even ringing) words. As if there were a secret language spoken by language to itself alone (as if language were not necessarily anything human). Here one thinks of Schlegel's insight into the strangeness or otherness of language, the thought entertained in the essay "On Incomprehensibility" that there could well be "a connection of some secret brotherhood among philosophical words that, like a host of spirits too soon aroused, bring everything into confusion" (*KA* 2: 364; *LF* 260). Now it is not even philosophical words that are subject to dissembling but ordinary speech that gets taken up into the play. One of the interesting points to note here is how the speakers, the Misses Douce and Kennedy, act less to speak language as to facilitate it or encourage it (and each other); that is, part of the effect of this laughing language is a peculiar dissolution of hard and fast boundaries between individual speakers and an absorption into a language game. As with Buck Mulligan in the opening episode, there is little concern here with respecting the outlines of the individual but stress falls on the way language circulates among individuals and how it may even carry them along with it, should they be willing.

One can further develop this thought—that roughly with "Sirens" *Ulysses* begins to surrender its rationally governed state of the art narrative to a more aimless, mocking, laughing lyrical impulse which comes to it (the narrative) from the outside—by returning to Nietzsche's distinction between Apollonian and Dionysian art. In a telling juxtaposition, Nietzsche introduces the exemplary figures of Homer and Archilochus, often depicted together on Greek cameos and other works of art, to elucidate the Apollonian-Dionysian opposition. "Compared with Homer, this Archilochus frankly terrifies us with his cries of hatred and scorn, with the drunken outbursts of his desire" (*GT* 43; *BT* 29). For Nietzsche, Archilochus represents the Dionysian artist who, unlike the Apollonian artist (who remains firmly in control of reality by means of a dream image), lets go of himself and is caught up in what he represents, "become[s] entirely at one with the primordial unity, with its pain and contradiction, and . . . produces a copy of this primordial unity as music . . ." (*GT* 43–44; *BT* 30). Just as the Misses Douce and Kennedy act as vehicles for the joyous music of words, so here Archilochus acts as something like a human vessel through which there appears the revelry of this originary state of contradiction:

> When Archilochus, the first lyric poet of the Greeks, simultaneously proclaims his crazed love and scorn for the daughters of Lycambes, it is not his passion that dances before us in orgiastic frenzy: we see Dionysos and the maenads, we see the intoxicated enthusiast Archilochus sunk in sleep . . . and now Apollo approaches and touches him with a laurel. The Dionysiac-musical enchantment of the sleeper now pours forth sparks of imagery, as it were, lyric poems which, unfolded to their fullest extent, are called tragedies and dramatic dithyrambs. (*GT* 44; *BT* 30)

As Nietzsche insists, "the ecstasy of the Dionysiac state, in which the usual barriers and limits of existence are destroyed contains, for as long as it lasts, a lethargic element in which all personal experiences from the past are submerged" (*GT* 56; *BT* 40). For Archilochus, the poem does not begin with an idea or a story, but by means of elusive sparks emitted by the music of language. The work of art (if this thought can be maintained) begins with language itself. *Finnegans Wake* appears to be just such a work, a work inspired by language, a work held together by the sheer power of its lyricism, its music, and its laughter. A joyous, yet sorrowful music grounded in a language that is already there, like the words of a nursery rhyme, song, or a children's game; a language in which one participates. *Ulysses* is a work in which the principle of *principium individuationis*, which safeguards the law of the discreteness of entities, is shattered. All things become near or distant echoes of all other things, as though all things are slightly similar to (and also slightly different from) all other things. More importantly, this principle appears to apply to words. Take, for example, the opening section: "Hush! Caution! Echoland!" (*FW* 13.5). This is a warning to the speaking subject to set aside its desire for mastery and self-control and to listen now, momentarily, for the echoes of words. Joyce repeatedly makes this invitation to his reader, an invitation to step back from the desire to read the text in the sense of getting its narrative aspects, deep structure, or story under control, and to take up a more indolent attitude toward the text:

> So?
> Who do you no tonigh, lazy and gentleman?
> The echo is where in the back of the wodes; callhim forth! (*FW* 126.1–3)

As well as being "in the back of the wodes [woods]," the echo also issues from "in the back of the wodes [words]," the thought being that the object of *Finnegan's Wake* is to cultivate these echoes from out of the dark side of words. In an early review of *Finnegans Wake*, Joyce's friend Oliver Gogarty writes that "Joyce's language is more than a revolt against classicism, it is more than a return to the freedom of slang and thieves' punning talk. It is an attempt to get at words before they clarify in the mind."[21] Gogarty's description of the language of the book is not far off the mark: Joyce's efforts throughout *Finnegan's Wake* are an effort to get at words which haven't yet stabilized into terms or concepts; a presemantic side of language that has withdrawn from intelligibility. Take for example this well-known exhortation:

> Clap your lingua to your pallet, drop your jowl with a jolt, tambourine until your breath slides, pet a pout and it's out. Have you got me, Allysloper? (*FW* 248.8–10)

Here is a description of speaking which views it as something more than finding the right words for ideas already in place, which sees it as facilitating language in making its presence felt or known, in helping it emerge in its own way. There is something serendipitous about this way of thinking about language, as though the most truthful part of language is the unsystematic part, the part that exceeds theories and explanations, the side of language that, like nature, loves to hide.

Harry Levin captures this accidental spirit of the book when he says, "it is lavish with small rewards, unexpected confidences, and delightful souvenirs, which it scatters among the most casual passers-by. In spite of its proclaimed privacy, there is something for everybody in *Finnegans Wake*. It is, in Joyce's apt coinage, a funferal."[22] This agrees with the ironist's assessment of what calls for interpretation: it is the trivial or obvious truth that Schlegel finds important enough to cultivate. The romantic is in love with details, with the singular and the accidental. The romantic is in love with what seems to elude explanation. More to the point: within the context of the tension between narrative and lyric in Nietzsche and Joyce, Levin says "[t]he appropriate mood for reading *Finnegans Wake* is that elicited by the five books of Rabelais, or—to come nearer home with an Anglo-Irish parallel—Tristram Shandy." And, Sterne's other half, Jonathan Swift. The reason for this, Levin says, is that Joyce, like Sterne and sometimes Swift, lost interest in the narrative component of art:

> . . . the reader must expect digression instead of narration. The broad outline will be always before him and the crowded texture will be full of interesting details. But in the middle distance, ordinarily the center of the reader's interest, the action will be shadowy and capricious. . . . The real source of continuity . . . is the flow of language. Once we have realized this, we have granted words a new importance. We realize that for Joyce they are matter and not manner.[23]

So instead of following the dictates of the syllogism, the more skeptical (and less self-possessed) ironist follows the path of the laughter of words, their "echolalias, intonations, irrecuperable ellipses, asyntactical and alogical constructions" and just tries to stay with them, tries to keep up with them, so to speak, rather than retrieve statements from them or get them under control.[24]

All this linguistic tomfoolery, however, isn't simply a substitution of playfulness for seriousness. Rather, it is a duplicitous and laughing truth, the serious side of language, an unstable countersublime, which brings things back to earth and brings one back to oneself, back to life, back from the sublime to everyday reality, however mixed and sordid that may be. In *Finnegans Wake* everything comes down to irreducible pairs or couples: "And his two little jiminies, cousins of ourn, Tristopher and Hilary, were kickaheeling their dummy on the oil cloth flure of his homerigh, castle and earthenhouse" (*FW* 21.11–13). Here "Tristopher and Hilary" or, from the words out of which they spring, triste or tristis, and hilarity or hilaros, sorrow and laughter, sadness and joy, somberness and prankishness, come together, come into their own as a pair, two who are as inseparable in *Finnegan's Wake* as the two senses of the title itself; *Finnegans Wake*, death and life, end and beginning. Joyce's laughing degradations of one-sided representation are not just deconstructions that send one spiralling down into the void, but are always bound up with the possibility of making another beginning. At one point in "Aeolus," for example, a voice speaks from out of the pages of the newspaper (perhaps the author's voice) and says: "I have often thought since on looking back over that strange time that it was that small act, trivial in itself, that striking of that match, that determined the whole aftercourse of both our lives" (*U* 7.763–65). This is a good example of how the poetic word expends itself on making trivial beginnings rather than designing projects. But by the same token, one remembers how the laughter of "Hilary" is always set over against the sadness of "Tristopher," a somber note which never completely dies out, a "Longindying call" (*U* 11.12) the most exuberant hilarity can never completely overcome. And so, although the Joyce's laughing words have an uplifting, rollicking, mocking effect, they also acknowledge an unearthly humor, a humor so dark and strange as to take up within it or just uncover the deepest and most unforgettable sorrows. This is the celebrated doublin existents of *Finnegan's Wake* that provokes a most scandalous petition: "Loud, heap miseries upon us yet entwine our arts with laughters low" (*FW* 259.7–8).

It is as though (to take only one example) Boylan's sing-along with Molly on the afternoon of June 16, 1904 is precisely what "by a commodious vicus of recirculation" (*FW* 3.2) leads to a reunion (of sorts) of Molly and Bloom. One might even call it, using Joyce's idiom, an accident of providence. Perhaps Nietzsche would call it the elusive untruth or error on which the truth of things ultimately rests. According to this upside-down logic, it is Boylan's violation of Molly's (and Bloom's) bed that recalls to (him) Bloom his own violation(s) and calls him (Bloom) back to his senses (of Molly), to a (somewhat comical) sense of Molly (literally? "He kissed the plump mellow yellow smellow melons of her [Molly's] rump" [*U* 17.2241]). Here it makes perfect sense to start off at the bottom at the day's inglorious end. Regardless, Joyce's refusal of one-sided seriousness represents an effort to get away from a purely instrumental view of language and make room for a more fecund language that is always beside itself with laughter; a language always willing to call off thoughts awhile and leave reality root-room. One could say that Joyce, as well as liberating narrative from mythic seriousness and restoring to it an intimacy with the unfinished present, turns the word loose on narrative and exposes it to the threat of the wayward, conceptually unmanageable lyrical fragment.

For this reason, it is not clear whether Joyce's poetics has much to do with meaning as it is conventionally understood. The aim of Joyce's text is not the communication of meaning or the discovery of truth so much as a demonstration of what an exclusive concern with deep meaning forces one to overlook: "the now, the here" of reality. With *Ulysses,* Joyce demystifies the ideality of interpretation and restores the tremendous complexity involved in understanding everyday life, to (nearly) quote Nietzsche again.

The suggestion here is that for Joyce this task of holding to reality is best accomplished via the laughing, joking word, the silly or humble pun; the moment when language fails (or refuses) its speaker, fails (or refuses) to represent accurately (or narrowly or exactly) the world of discrete physical objects and turns in comically on itself, on its own pretension and folly. It is only another way of saying that the truth makes its appearance when language breaks down, stutters, or stumbles; when one is at a loss for words. The task is not only to hold to reality but to let it be just as it is. Letting go of words, the participation in their potential for mockery, foolery, laughter, and ultimately regeneration, is linked with the letting go of reality (into its ownmost being). An authentic, radical or just obvious kind of freedom (a freedom which is more [or less] than a liberation of the subject) exists with which romantic poetry is concerned.

Toward the end of Shaun's first watch in *Finnegans Wake*, Shem is described as one who "[w]as down with the whooping laugh at the age of the loss of reason," an outcast who is unquestionably weird and "middayevil down to his vegetable soul" (*FW* 423.25–28). In so locating Shem outside the limits of the rational, one who breaks down (or out) into the whooping laugh at the loss of reason and enters a region of middayevil darkness, Joyce figures Shem as a skeptic, who simultaneously loses his mind (so to speak) and looks laughingly back at those unfortunates with minds (of a certain kind) still left to lose. Shem abandons the idea of thinking according to the procedures of progressive scientific narrative and enters a less stable, more nomadic region of thought. He becomes an outcast or an exile, a pariah or a wanderer, an itinerant thinker who reflects less according to the dictates of reason than according to the winding and digressive path set out by the lyrical humors of words.

In contrast to a more strategic thinking, whose conclusions are almost always announced in the particulars of its method, this skeptical, experimental, provisional, and unreasonable mode of thinking abandons agendas, projects, and programs in favor of the winding, wayward, and contradictory path(s) of language; irrational way(s) which seek to maintain an uneasy intimacy with the outside or the exterior, the borders of what counts as rational, a no-one's-land of thinking which, by virtue of its proximity to outsidedness, comes into contact with freedom and so, as Gilles Deleuze notes (in connection with Nietzsche), gives birth to Dionysian laughter.[25] In this respect, Joyce looks back to Nietzsche's nomadic digressions into skeptical, uncertain, strangely humorous (ludicrous) territory for thinking; territory marked by aphoristic, litterish, fragmentary writing(s) following the duplicitous leads of language and often lingering near a threshold which separates and joins the systematic narrative and the potentially dangerous openness beyond.

If one thinks of romantic poetry as writing caught up within a conflict between narrative and lyrical impulses and a thoughtful wandering between the narrative and the lyrical fragment inspired by both Homer and Archilochus, one can understand the later writings of Joyce as attempts (following Nietzsche) to refuse the transparent language of narrative and rehabilitate the truth value of the singular, material, or lyrical side of language. This is the more conceptually unmanageable side of words ordinarily effaced in the attempt to gain control of things, and so reach a more ludicrous or laughing (and unstable) understanding of what is at issue.

That is, one can see Joyce as continuing Nietzsche's efforts to shake thinking loose from its metaphysical pretensions and turn it into (or out toward) a more foolish kind of thinking, fragmentary thinking which maintains contact with the exterior or the outside, makeshift thinking which follows the crooked path of language and so resembles the nomad's traveling or the skeptic's wandering in the dark.

This darkly humorous, ludicrous, fragmentary rationality, abandons Kantian efforts to establish conditions under which knowledge might advance with that undeviating certitude which characterizes the progress of science, and turns instead to an aimless wandering governed by the humor of words. It turns reading away from analysis or critique and toward reading-as-rumination, as Nietzsche (following Schlegel) has it. This more mindless (skeptical) thinking remains forever work in progress, moving back and forth between wisdom and experience, knowledge and becoming, the inside and the outside, the serious and the ludicrous, finding its way as best as it can, at the limits of the system or the project. Adorno has famously remarked that Penelope weaving and then unraveling her tapestry each day as she awaits her husband's return might be taken as an allegory of art. Adorno's observation might well serve as a description of *Ulysses*, a book which weaves and then unweaves its narrative in the space of a single day, its last words given over to the thoughts of Penelope who turns away (puts to sleep) all her various suitors' attempts to possess or control her; and *Finnegans Wake* might be taken as a sophisticated elaboration of the second half of the idea which pushes hermeneutics to the limit, a book in which narrative has apparently been removed altogether to reveal a laughing, contradictory, material side of language, a chorus of dispossessed words which maintain a dizzying intimacy with their origins in the human body.

One might think of this as the serio-comical, parodic, or material otherness of words. The work that embodies such thinking emerges within a characteristic strife between narrative and lyrical impulses. That is, in the fragmentary work there exists a more or less novelistic tension between two kinds of language, the transparent and obedient language of narrative and the more unruly language of the lyric, song or fragment, an uncontrollable language born out of the laughter of Dionysus before that laughter was suppressed by the rationalism of Socrates. The model for this work (celebrated by Schlegel) is the dialogue of fragments, the conversation which erupts without warning (without justification) and consists of a back and forth movement between the horizon of truth generated by the expectation of a whole and the revisionary and even deconstructive work done by each part as it enters more fully into the play. The work thought of as a dialogue of fragments now becomes the exemplary, model work, opening itself into the full clarity and insight provided by a coherent narrative, and then just as quickly withdrawing from this clarity into itself, dissembling, retreating into a laughing, mocking, unsettling darkness. The romantic work, by virtue of this event-character of its being, allows thought to remain incomplete, unfinished, fragmentary, always moving toward the more ludic region of outsidedness or unintelligibility, where the work of reading (which is more than the retrieval of statements) becomes crucial. If *Ulysses* works to maintain a balance between these two impulses, narrative and lyric, *Finnegans Wake* gives in (almost) completely to lyrical laughter, gives itself over to what cannot be said in ordinary daylight language or, as Joyce said in a famous locution, what "cannot be rendered sensible by the use of wideawake language, cutandry grammar and goahead plot."[26] So the words of *Finnegans Wake* declare their resistance to appropriation: "this is nat language in any sinse of the world" (*FW* 83.12). The withdrawal of the book's language(s) into a less controlled space (or silence) closely resembles what Kristeva has described as an eroticization of speech, a borderline discourse "completely different from the communication of dialogue . . . the domain of equivocation and Witz" in which meaning or semantic content is no longer so important as the more primary material existence of the word itself.[27]

This movement toward the outside of the seriousness of the system can be thought of as a movement toward freedom; a movement away from one-sided understandings toward an acknowledgement of the provisionality of understanding. This freedom, however, is less a liberation of the subject than a recovery of the instability of the ordinary. Rather than freeing oneself from the ties that bind, this freedom is a movement outside the bounds of custom, habit, or official codes of conduct; away from the dictionary of received ideas; an attempt to recover something of the heterogeneity of life before it congeals into stereotypes or formulas. Words, as well as human beings, are always many things at once.

Strangers in the Night

Earlier I reflected on how de Man's conception of the allegorical structure of literary rhetoric might be contrasted with Bakhtin's conception of the dialogic structure of novelistic discourse. While de Man traces the slippage of language and consciousness into a state of inevitably inauthentic being, Bakhtin underscores the dialogic property of novelistic discourse, the novel's propensity for foregrounding the tension between unifying and dispersing or scattering forces at work in

any given utterance. Bakhtin emphasizes the novel's linguistic consciousness as a liberating movement that leads beyond one-sided understandings, a movement through the desublimation of authoritative
representation and back down to the earth, toward the regenerating possibilities contained within ordinary life. Zarathutra's admonition to his
followers to remain faithful to the earth thus provokes two influential
and perhaps antithetical interpretations of language. One can acknowledge that romanticism is always caught between these two alternatives,
between, shall we say, deconstruction and dialogue. Kierkegaard, one
will remember, describes the contours of German romanticism as "a
teeter-totter, the ends of which are irony and humor [and whose] oscillation[s] [are] extremely varied, all the way from the most heaven-
storming humor to the most desperate bowing down in irony" (430).
Surely this description contains both de Man's and Bakhtin's perspectives, as though poetry cannot be defined but only experienced in terms
of its movement between the sublime and the ridiculous.

From this standpoint, wisdom concerning romantic poetry leads not
to conclusive assertions of its sublime or ridiculous nature but only to
the folly of another attempt at getting close to it, another setting out,
another beginning. Molly's "[y]es" (*U* 18.1) echoes Bloom's "[y]es" (*U*
4.138), but also says something new or (in)different, her own yes, an inflection of that heard word. Transcendental buffoonery is reduced to
provisional truth (more like a working model of the provisional truth).
In Hannah Arendt's words, quotation becomes a form of self-insertion
into a world, a nativity. Think here of the myth of Antaeus wrestling
Hercules (retold by Kierkegaard [277]) in which Antaeus, by being
thrown to the ground and so returning to the earth, gains enough
strength to begin again. It is only later, when Hercules holds Antaeus
high in the air, preventing him from regaining his groundedness, that
Hercules can overcome him.

Joyce's book can be thought of as a gloss of this story, how people,
narratives, and language, gain wisdom through folly, misunderstanding,
and defeat, by turning their gaze away from the sky and (re)turning to
the earth. Individuals maintain strength in spite of repeated defeat,
learn something, gain something, and eventually make a beginning out
of an end. It is the complicated and certainly politically problematical
story of Ireland's submission to England. In any case, Joyce exploits the
foolishness behind wisdom, the error or falsity behind truth, cultivates
the dark or unruly side of understanding as well as its rational side,

examines the truth of mis(sed)understanding, much as Schlegel advocates a kind of reading which passes through incomprehensibility to get at the trivial (but more vital) truth(s) of things. It is only by means of such ironic indirection that one gets anywhere near the truth.

Throughout *Finnegans Wake*, Joyce reinforces this thought: "Here we'll dwell on homiest powers, love at the latch with novices nig and nag" (*FW* 266.14–15). The "homiest" realm for Joyce is always the most elusive and unstable of all, the realm of the human body and the physical comedy of words, which makes Richard Rorty's distinction between public and private, with irony always belonging to the isolated realm of the private, seem too serious and isolated to bear. With no audience for the performance, what's the point? This is something Buck and Stephen know well.

Joyce's poetic genius comes into play at moments when it is apparent that there isn't simply one all-encompassing story to be told but that "every telling has a taling and that's the he and the she of it" (*FW* 213.12). Every narrative, sentence, or word has a laughing, dark, strange, unruly, nonsensical double, a side turned away from clarity or meaning or truth. A side which resists the speaking subject's control and recedes into what the truth often overlooks, namely the human body or the material existence of words. This is the upshot of what Kenner calls the duet of the two narrators in *Ulysses*; what can be taken as a continual, laughing protest against serious, one-sided representation, a struggle between sense and nonsense, fixed system and flexible fragment, narrative point and lyrical titter, ideal order and real existence. The dark, strange laughter of romantic poetry calls us back to an intimacy with clumsiness and incompleteness, messiness and disorder, and takes us to the threshold of a beginning. It is here that one begins to experience the force of the incompleteness, fragmentation or outsidedness of being and finds that one's capacity for making only sense (and abiding there) is severely tested by the lunacy of ordinary life.

In this sense, Joyce's book embodies a fulfillment of Schlegel's idea of romantic poetry as transcendental buffoonery which subsists on a diet of self-parody and wit, laughing self-consciousness, a kind of poetry "whose essence lies in the relation between ideal and real. . . . In all its descriptions," Schlegel insists, "this poetry should describe itself, and always be simultaneously poetry and the poetry of poetry" (*KA* 2:204; *LF* 195). The linguistic consciousness of *Ulysses* critiques narrative in a way that marks the book as what Schlegel calls "transcendental poetry"

(*KA* 2:204; *LF* 195). That is, it seems always to be ringing (singing) with the echo of its own self-interpretation. Of course, one thinks also of Nietzsche's characterization of himself as one having an aversion to resting for too long in any one point of view or frame of mind and his need for multiple aspects or perspectives. This is what Joyce's text does: it provides the stimulus of the enigmatic for his reader in the form of thousands of fragments and endless shifts in point of view, compelling her to become a more active coworker in the production of what one could (loosely) call meaning.

One of the most important consequences of this two-sided work, the work that is forever becoming, is that it throws added weight onto the activity of reading or interpretation. Here one has only to remember Schlegel's description of the classic as a work that continually motivates or calls for reading: "A classical text must never be entirely comprehensible. But those who are cultivated and who cultivate themselves must always want to learn more from it" (*KA* 2:168; *LF* 144–45). Schlegel insists that analytical interpretation can never uncover the secret of the fragmentary work and only a divinatory criticism could begin to cope with its protean transformations of meaning. In this sense, the work is a refusal of moralistic, programmatic, one-sided interpretation, a protest which amounts to a refusal on the part of the work to allow itself to be construed as a simple illustration or demonstration of an ideology or a thesis; rather, the work demands that its readers cultivate a more down-to-earth, linguistically conscious, and makeshift mode of interpretation which, in its own back and forth play between narrative and lyric, tries to capture the event of the work's world and maintain an intimacy with it.

From such a vantage point, one never has the last word because there is always another side of words to be considered; something that enters at the last moment to render one's interpretation fallible, incomplete, or just comically clumsy. The romantic in this sense remains an amateur, an incompetent, a fool or a wanderer, someone who never presumes to be in possession of the sole pathway to the truth. Nietzsche, like Joyce, doesn't see this sort of incompetence as a lamentable failure (a situation to be rectified or transcended) but rather as the course of ordinary life. Life frequently (if not always) calls for further interpretation, reading, and reflection on things that matter.

This down-to-earth mode of reading may be thought of as a hermeneutic of freedom that resists dogmatism, moralistic thinking, and absolutist claims in favor of an endless circling, traveling, or wandering. For this reason, the romantic is often accused of being an aimless, shiftless spendthrift or a ne'er-do-well; he flirts a little too much with chaos and anarchy, and counts some shady company among his friends. But these unlikely friends are the unpredictable detours that take one outside the system and over some of the most fruitful ground for thinking. Thinking is eminently a way that cannot be foreseen or anticipated, but only undergone or followed. Having avoided one another throughout the day, for instance, Leopold Bloom finally discovers Stephen Dedalus in Bella Cohen's brothel in Nighttown, extricates him from a swindle in progress and directs him to the safety of a cab shelter and from thence, finally, home to Eccles Street.

One can think of the fragmentary work as an embodiment of Nietzsche's suspicion that the truth may well be unstable, without bounds, and (one's worst fear) it may depend on accident, chance, untruth, or error. The thought of questioning the priority of truth over error suggests that error is woven into the fabric of everyday life. That is, everyday life is error-prone. This thought certainly squares with a reading of *Ulysses*, a book in which error, misunderstanding, doubt, and confusion abound. For example, Bantam Lyons misconstrues Bloom's throwaway remark to him in the morning as a tip on the probable winner of the Gold Cup race. Bloom is about to dispose of his newspaper:

> —I was just going to throw it away, Mr Bloom said.
> Bantam Lyons raised his eyes suddenly and leered weakly.
> —What's that? his sharp voice said.
> —I say you can keep it, Mr Bloom answered. I was going to throw it away that moment.
> Bantam Lyons doubted an instant, leering: then thrust the outspread sheets back on Mr Bloom's arms.
> —I'll risk it, he said. Here, thanks. (*U* 5.534–41).

Later at Barney Kiernan's, Lyons' misunderstanding fuels a whole constellation of (mis)interpretations of Bloom as tightfisted Jew. In the long run, however, Joyce makes error the loophole through which people move unthinkingly to avoid a deterministic kind of existence; error provides a space of freedom for people to move (clumsily, foolishly, awkwardly) back to other people. Truth, it would seem, rests (all too often) on the possibilities made possible by the untruth of error or accident. So Molly's (mis)interpretation of what Bloom mumbles (to her) as he falls asleep, "roc's auk's egg" (*U* 17.2328–29) opens a space (just a tiny crack perhaps) for a beginning. And in *Finnegans Wake*, Shem the Penman writes by means of a "transaccidentat[ion]" of words, turns leftover words into works of art, as though "the sibspeeches of all mankind have foliated (earth seizing them!) from the root of some funner's stotter" (*FW* 96.30–31). One can think of it as Joyce's ludic(rous) ethics, an ethics that moves clumsily toward relations with others, by means of accidents.

From the Fragmentary Work to the Fragmentary Imperative: Blanchot and the Quest for Passage to the Outside

(Friedrich Schlegel's fragmentary will is the very will to the Work . . . But what Blanchot calls the fragmentary exigency exceeds the work, because that exigency exceeds the will.)
—Philippe Lacoue-Labarthe and Jean-Luc Nancy

Granted, Socrates does not write; but, beneath the voice, it is nevertheless through writing that he gives himself to others as the perpetual subject perpetually destined to die. He does not speak; he questions. Questioning, he interrupts and interrupts himself without cease, giving form to the fragmentary; through his death, he cause speech to be haunted by writing . . .
—Maurice Blanchot

If the writings of Byron and Joyce are the apotheosis of romantic poetry's fragmentary work, Blanchot articulates a further distinction between the fragmentary work and the fragmentary imperative.[1] In an essay on the German romantics, Blanchot registers his dissatisfaction with Schlegel's tendency to pull up short when confronted with the most exacting demands of writing. In Schlegel's case, says Blanchot, "the fragment often seems a means for complacently abandoning oneself to the self rather than an attempt to elaborate a more rigorous mode of writing" (*EI* 526; *IC* 359). Blanchot seems to be thinking of the literary vertigo that consumed, for example, Coleridge, a great thinker and as Mill rightly recognized one of the spirits of the age. But he was also unable to finish works once they were begun; finding himself almost pathologically unable to achieve the kind of completion he sought, he all but abandoned poetry. He littered his life with bits and pieces of unfinished business, scraps of lectures, outlines of essays, long dreamed-of (but never executed) master works.[2] In Blanchot's eyes, a poet like Coleridge tells a cautionary tale (as does Byron), having wasted an opportunity to explore the outer limits of discursive reason and the interstices of the universe. More generally, for Blanchot the romantics think of the fragment too narrowly, in terms of the broken or dilapidated classical artifact or the exotic textual fragment rather than as a much more essential component of a more radical kind of writing, thinking, and living.

Let me explore this idea further by returning to a work mentioned previously, Fontenelle's *Conversations on the Plurality of Worlds*. Fontenelle published this little book in the seventeenth century amidst great scientific and religious unrest. When it first appeared, the Roman Catholic Church found itself increasingly on the defensive: Protestant religious leaders were seeking to displace it theologically, while a new experimental and empirical science was displacing it epistemologically. The world, it seemed, was breaking away from its traditional foundations. As Nina Rattner Gelbart points out in her Introduction to the English translation, Fontenelle

> courted danger when he wrote his pioneering work in 1686. Less than a century earlier, in 1600, Giordano Bruno had been burned at the stake for, among other offences, desacrilizing the Earth by suggesting the possibility of multiple inhabited worlds in the universe. Only fifty years before Fontenelle wrote, Galileo had lost his freedom and had been placed under permanent house arrest for writing on daring astronomical theories.[3]

What specifically were the ideas that made this book so dangerous? Well, among other things, following Copernicus, Tycho, Kepler, and Galileo, Fontenelle offered a radically new picture of the universe and, what is more, of what it means to learn, think, and acquire knowledge of it.[4] Fontenelle's universe is a universe of pluralities, a universe of many different worlds, each filled with stars and moons in the face of which, to rephrase a line from Blake, almost anything is possible to be believed. Our only apparent limitation as seekers of knowledge, as one of the characters in the *Conversations* puts it, is our eyesight.[5] One imagines Bakhtin nodding in agreement.

The book, structured around a series of conversations that take place between a Marquise and her older male companion over the course of five evenings, begins less like a quasi-scientific treatise on astronomy or cosmology and more like the prelude to a kiss. "The First Evening" begins with the older gentleman describing the scene:

> One evening after supper we went to walk in the garden. There was a delicious breeze, which made up for the extremely hot day we had had to bear. The Moon had risen about an hour before, and shining through the trees it made a pleasant mixture of bright white against the dark greenery that appeared black. There was no cloud to hide even the smallest star; they were all pure and shining gold and stood out clearly against their blue background. The spectacle set me to musing, and I might have gone on like that for some time if it had not been for the Marquise, but in the company of such a lovely woman I could hardly give myself up to the Moon and stars.[6]

The Marquise and her mentor spend the next five nights gazing at the nighttime sky, talking about philosophy and cosmology, gently teasing one another, and wondering about the perennial questions that confront humankind. Over the course of these conversations, they discuss everything from Descartes' theory of vortices to the probability that we will someday travel to the moon to the possibility of extraterrestrial life. Most important: reversing the trajectory of Descartes' subject-object model of knowledge, they wonder if beings from distant worlds are straining to gain knowledge of the earth and its inhabitants with the same fervor and passion that the two of them are straining to see the stars that fill their nighttime sky.

It is certainly a memorable text and one with which Blanchot was, as a French schoolboy, undoubtedly familiar. In fact, one way to approach Blanchot's late writing, especially *The Infinite Conversation* (1969), is to read it as a repetition, albeit with important differences, of Fontenelle's *Conversations*. That is, Blanchot's work might profitably be read as serving the same function for the late twentieth century that Fontenelle's text served during his own time: facilitating a revolution in how we understand the physical universe as well as the place of the human in relation to it.

Although never mentioned by name, Fontenelle's legacy clearly registers throughout the opening pages of Kevin Hart's book on Blanchot, *The Dark Gaze*.[7] Hart begins by underscoring the importance of Blanchot's cosmology, without which much of his *oeuvre* makes only a fitful kind of sense. Viewing Blanchot from the standpoint of the philosophy of science (and in the tradition of Fontenelle), Hart shakes loose a side of him that allows his writing to fall into a more accessible design than is usually available. Hart recounts how almost as an afterthought in "Ars Nova," a review of Georges Poulet's book, *The Metamorphoses of the Circle* (1961) and a French translation of Adorno's *Philosophie der neuen Musik* (1949), Blanchot reflects on the possibility of there being another dimension to the universe. Blanchot writes:

> It is nearly understood that the Universe is curved, and it has often been supposed that this curvature has to be positive: hence the image of a finite and limited sphere. But nothing permits one to exclude the hypothesis of an unfigurable Universe (a term henceforth deceptive); a Universe escaping every optical exigency and also escaping consideration of the whole world—essentially non-finite, disunited, discontinuous. What about such a Universe? (*EI* 513-14; *IC* 350)

Playing the part of a latter day Fontenelle, Blanchot wonders whether or not our relation to the stars is inflected in ways that we can fully understand and begin to fathom. He talks about a curvature of the universe that we cannot measure but that alters our every breath, and movement, and act of being. Blanchot is in effect announcing a second Copernican Revolution; he is situating the stars not only out of the empirical reach of our senses but also on the other side of a negative curvature—an inflection—of the known universe.

He is here invoking the figure of the disaster or the outside, the impossible or the neutral. "The disaster," Blanchot says at the start of *The Writing of the Disaster* (1980), "ruins everything, all the while leaving everything intact" (*ED* 7; *WD* 1). The disaster as such does not belong to the world of subjects and objects nor to the history of science and technology, at least not as these things have been so far understood. If Fontenelle acknowledged the ruined integrity of Ptolemy's cosmos, which posited the stars as fixed points in the watery firmament, then Blanchot intuits the ruin of Copernicus's, which assumed that the stars are other worlds analogous to our own that might be known empirically by trekking through physical space. The age of exploration in that sense, implies Blanchot, of course goes on; but thinking of ourselves as subjects traveling over the face of the earth-as-an-aggregate-of-objects no longer suffices as a model of investigation.

What exactly, though, does this mean? Is the disaster a watershed event that distinguishes what comes after it from what went before? Is it like the discovery of a new planet that, as in Keats' sonnet, suddenly swims into view? Well, in some cases (and for many the Holocaust or Shoah is just such a case) this is so, but for Blanchot the disaster is apparently more like an extra dimension of the universe in which time stands still and space is subject to a negative curvature. On its own terms, the disaster refuses the grasp of the knowing intellect and hides itself within its own irregular laws. Blanchot affirms this again and again: "The disaster is separate; that which is most separate" (*ED* 7; *WD* 1). Just so: it is beyond our reach. This is consistent with what he says in his review of the two books. "But will he ever be ready to receive such a thought," Blanchot wonders:

> a thought that, freeing him from the fascination with unity, for the first time risks summoning him to take the measure of an exteriority that is not divine, of a space entirely in question, and even excluding the possibility of an answer, since every response would necessarily fall anew under the jurisdiction of the figure of figures? This amounts perhaps to asking ourselves: is man capable of a radical interrogation? (*EI* 514; *IC* 350)

Blanchot then shifts abruptly from the history of science to the question of literature. However, for Blanchot this is perhaps the most serious question one can ask, and he presses it to its tipping point: "That is, finally, *is he capable of literature*, if literature *turns aside and toward the absence of* a book?" (*EI* 514; *IC* 350, emphases mine). This question seems to have been lurking behind Blanchot's review all along and it is not an easy question to address. Blanchot embarks on a quest for a kind of writing that would exceed the book as a limit concept, in both its sacred and secular senses, much in the way one might rethink the world without access to the stars as its cosmological condition. The exigency of fragmentary writing is an imperative that risks asking us to take the measure of an exteriority that is not divine or metaphysical, of a space entirely in question, and even excluding the possibility of an answer. It remains true to the object of its investigation only by giving space for the negative curvature of the universe to leave its mark.

In order to explore this further, let me return to Blanchot's criticism of German romanticism. Although Blanchot certainly has affinities with the romantics, and may even be said to belong to their tradition of fragmentary reflection, finally he sees himself as moving beyond their practice of composing fragmentary works and engaging in something quite different.[8] What is this difference? "In truth," Blanchot writes, "and particularly in the case of Friedrich Schlegel, the fragment often seems a means for complacently abandoning oneself to the self rather than an attempt to elaborate a more rigorous mode of writing." We have encountered these words before. But let us continue a little further down this path. "Then to write fragmentarily," Blanchot says, "is simply to welcome one's own disorder, to close up upon one's self in a contented isolation, and thus to refuse the opening [*l'ouverture*] that the fragmentary exigency represents; an exigency that does not exclude totality, but goes beyond it" (*EI* 527; *IC* 359).

Two things must be noted here. First, Blanchot complains that Schlegel too often indulges in a fragmentary *style* rather than delving into what the fragmentary imperative demands. Blanchot associates this indulgence with a certain kind of intellectual complacence or lack of discipline. Schlegel, in other words, turns to the fragment in order not to finish what he has started to think; in order not to think through completely and precisely what it is that he is actually saying. Blanchot, by contrast, understands fragmentary writing as more rigorous mode of writing; a more disciplined and severe kind of writing, a tireless vigilance in which what is most essential to writing comes to the fore and the idle chatter of the self-seeking or self-aggrandizing subject is patiently burned off or pared away. Much like Heidegger's reformulation of freedom so that it functions outside the ego as the letting-go of the world of objects in order that the things of the world might be themselves, fragmentary writing in Blanchot's special sense is radically non-subjective and non-transitive, opposed both to the daylight of rational inquiry and the nighttime of Hegelian negation.[9]

Second, the fragmentary exigency is opposed to the relative autonomy of the romantic fragment (think of the hedgehog). Instead of affording seclusion or refuge, the peace and solitude of the ruined landscape or the bucolic garden, the fragmentary exigency represents an unsettling opening [*ouverture*] onto something new and unpredictable, a space of risk or trauma, *within* the ordinary world. The word Blanchot uses here, *ouverture*, derives from the French word "*ouvert*" which means "to open" and has as its English cognate the word *overture*, which can mean both an opening and a beginning. Also, and this is the sense to underline here, an initiative or a tendency, perhaps especially an invitation to respond. Indeed, Blanchot often speaks as one invited to entertain the claim—the overture—of a certain kind of appeal. But what could be the force of such an appeal?

One might say that the force of Blanchot's fragmentary imperative lies equally in its break with Kant's emphasis on subjectivity, and with Heidegger's emphasis on ontology, or being; in short, in its increasingly thoughtful engagement with the writings of Bataille and Levinas. Starting from subjectivity and ontology respectively, both Kant and Heidegger open up new paths for thinking about the question of freedom. Still, for Blanchot, each remains bound to a certain way of doing philosophy, and so to a certain way of avoiding the thought of what philosophy must exclude in order to begin: the singularity or strangeness of the other—its irreducibility to categories of understanding or appropriation, and its being grounded upon the nothingness of Being. Blanchot declines these avenues partly because of the violence they do to what they purport to grasp. Instead, he writes or opens the fragment toward a peculiar and often frustrating lack of will, and, at the same time, a quasi-ethical dimension that nevertheless does not quite constitute an ethics. Rather than asserting itself over the world of objects by way of affirmation or negation, or accepting or rejecting outright the claim of an other, this wrecked work, now understood as workless [dé-soeuvré], this ruin enjoins one to practice a barely noticeable (and controversial) form of passivity [passivité] or, as I prefer, to embark upon the quest for passage. But passage in this sense contains a pun on the not or the pas of the way, rendering it as much a pas-sage as a passage. One might see it as a difficult dialogic passage in which one's traversal of the earth is marked by the radical neutrality, torture, suffering, and trauma of the way.[10]

Interruption

Blanchot thinks of the summons that invites us to take the measure of the outside as an interruption that disrupts the narrative of everyday life. Recall once again the opening scene of *Tristram Shandy* in which Mrs. Shandy interrupts her husband's conjugal efforts with a simple request or, more precisely, a question: "*Pray, my dear* [she asks] *have you not forgot to wind up the clock?*" (*TS* 6). In response to this, Walter explodes:

——— *Good G—!* Cried my father, making an exclamation, but taking care to moderate his voice at the same time, ——— *Did ever woman, since the creation of the world, interrupt a man with such a silly question?* Pray, what was your father saying? ——— Nothing. (*TS* 6)

Whereupon chapter 1 ends, and is immediately followed by this paragraph from the beginning of chapter 2:

> ——— Then, positively, there is nothing in the question, that I can see, either good or bad. ——— Then let me tell you, Sir, it was a very unseasonable question at least, ——— because it scattered and dispersed the animal spirits, whose business it was to have escorted and gone hand-in-hand with the *HOMUNCULOUS*, and conducted him safe to the place destined for his reception. (*TS* 6)

Sterne's tale begins with Tristram's mother interrupting his father in the midst of their connubial congress with a question concerning a household duty toward maintaining the time. This interruption sets in motion a potentially infinite conversation between the two brothers, Walter and Toby, and many others. The book opens both with and as a fragmentary work, in the sense that Mrs. Shandy's question tears open the temporarily reunified beast with two backs to expose the unsettling space of the in-between. One might call this the unsettling ambiguity of the fragment.

Blanchot would find a lot to think about in Walter's predicament, which is, of course, the predicament of thinking and writing after Plato—or, more exactly, after Socrates. In the *Symposium*, the arch-philosopher Socrates finds himself interrupted by his amorous shadow, Alcibiades. In Schlegel's *Lucinde*, too, Julius describes how, as he is writing to his beloved Lucinde, he is "interrupted in the middle of [his] profound feelings and tender ideas about the wonderful and wonderfully complicated dramatic interrelation of [their] embraces by a rude and unkind chance" (*KA* 5:8; *LF* 44–45). For his part, Blanchot often returns to this theme: "Questioning, [Socrates] interrupts and interrupts himself without cease," he writes, "giving form to the fragmentary; through his death, he causes speech to be haunted by writing" (*ED* 107; *WD* 65). Similarly, the predicament of the Jena romantics is whether to read the Socratic dialogue as a coherent whole or as a collection of shattered pieces; whether to try to re-assemble the dialogue or to allow it to fall (to assist in tearing it) further apart.

The way Blanchot sees it, however, life—interrupted—nonetheless goes on. Interruption in this sense appears to change nothing. In a cryptic essay on "Interruption" from *The Infinite Conversation*, which could have been inspired by Sterne's novel, or Schlegel's, Blanchot addresses this question of interrupted conversation, but in a more rigorous and specific sense. The essay centers on a more precise activity that Blanchot describes as

> the necessity of the interval. The power of speaking interrupts itself, and this interruption plays a role that appears to be minor—precisely the role of a subordinated alternation [*alternance*]. This role, nonetheless, is so enigmatic that it can be interpreted as bearing the very enigma of language: pause between sentences, pause from one interlocutor to another, and pause of attention, the hearing that doubles the force of locution. (*EI* 106; *IC* 75)

Here Blanchot invokes a poetics of the pause; a theory of conversation or dialogue whereby its most crucial moment is the moment before it begins. The moment of silence that awaits each act of speech or writing is such that its echo rings out in the shadow of speech or writing. These silent interstices bear, Blanchot observes, the enigma of language. It is as though the silent act of listening somehow amplified language or allowed language to speak a second time. And it would be this additional speech—fragmentary speech—that would come between the other partners in a conversation, holding them together but also keeping them apart.

This way of looking at *entretien*, or conversation, completely transforms it. "What is now in play, and demands relation," Blanchot continues:

> is everything that separates me from the other, that is to say the other insofar as I am infinitely separated from him—a separation, fissure, or interval that leaves him infinitely outside me, but also requires that I found my relation with him upon this very interruption that is *an interruption of being*. This alterity [*altérité*], it must be repeated, makes him neither another self for me, nor another existence, neither a modality or a moment of universal existence, nor a superexistence, a god or a non-god, but rather the unknown in its infinite distance. (*EI* 109; *IC* 77, my emphasis)

Blanchot focuses on the moment of the pause, the open space (that spaces the relation) between myself and another that brings the other near to me and at the same time holds her at a distance; it is, as it happens, an infinite distance. My being-in-relation to another is no longer a matter of some shared essence or being but rather the unknown in its infinite distance, an other as other without appropriation or interference. As Blanchot notes, it is "[a]n alterity that holds in the name of the neutral" (*EI* 109; *IC* 77). This alterity is thus an intermittent space of neutrality where power relations suddenly have the potential to reverse without warning; where master and slave experience a suspension of their roles in the old opposition. Things somehow appear differently. And yet they are the same.

Blanchot attempts to clarify a space in which nothing holds sway on behalf of the outside or the neutral by appealing to a conceptual scheme taken from the discipline of geometry:

> To simplify, let us say that through the presence of the other understood in the neutral there is in the field of relations a distortion preventing any direct communication and any relation of unity; or again, there is a fundamental anomaly that it falls to speech not to reduce but to convey, even if it does so without saying it or signifying it. Now it is to this hiatus—to the strangeness, to the infinity between us—that the interruption in language itself responds, the interruption that introduces waiting. But let us understand that the arrest here is not necessarily or simply marked by silence, by a blank or a gap (this would be too crude), but by a change in the form or the structure of language (when speaking is first of all writing)—a change metaphorically comparable to that which made Euclid's geometry into that of Riemann. . . . A change such that to speak (to write) is to cease thinking solely with a view to unity, and to make the relations of words an essentially dissymetrical field governed by discontinuity; as though, having renounced the interrupted force of a coherent discourse, it were a matter of drawing out a level of language where one might gain the power not only to express oneself in an intermittent manner, but also to allow intermittence itself to speak: a speech that, non-unifying, is no longer content with being a passage or a bridge—a non-pontificating speech capable of clearing the two shores separated by the abyss, but without filling in the abyss or reuniting its shores: a speech without reference to unity. (*EI* 109-10; *IC* 77-78)

Such a space is perhaps little more than a ripple passing through the relations that appear on the surface of things to unify the world and its inhabitants. In a remarkable locution, however, Blanchot imagines a sea-change in our conceptual scheme comparable to the shift from Euclidean to non-Euclidean geometry. Such a shift calls for a "non-pontificating" speech that bridges—but nevertheless holds apart—the two participants in any given relation, refusing to reduce either the abyss or its shores to a function of unity or synthesis.

Elsewhere, in "A Plural Speech," Blanchot explains:

> Dialogue is a plane geometry wherein relations are direct and remain ideally symmetrical. But let us suppose that the field of relations rests upon some anomaly analogous to what physicists would call a curvature of the universe; that is, a distortion preventing any possibility of symmetry and introducing between things, and particularly between [one human being] and [another], a relation of infinity. (*EI* 115; *IC* 81)

This is how Blanchot reimagines Socratic dialogue: as a dialogue stretched or broken open, inflected with an anomalous (or even ominous) curvature such that it is no longer symmetrical with itself, no longer constituted by two relatively equal interlocutors or languages but always slightly offset in its quirky (or perhaps ruined) diameter. However, one might say that at this point it is no longer dialogue but rather more along the lines of what Blanchot calls a conversation distorted or bent by a relation of infinity. At any rate, it is a poetics of the pause, whereby poetry allows an interruption of philosophy's consolation and so mediates or facilitates the touch of (the being touched by) what Blanchot calls the outside.

Nietzsche's Style

Like many of his contemporaries on the French intellectual scene during the middle third of the twentieth century, Blanchot's later writings display evidence of a sustained intellectual struggle with Nietzsche. This Nietzsche is a many-sided, self-contradictory and spurious Nietzsche, a relentless practitioner of fragmentary writing but not necessarily a particularly self-consistent thinker.[11] Blanchot's practice of fragmentary writing is informed by an effort to mediate between the romantic conception of the fragment and the post-romantic conception that sees it as coming both before and after Hegel. Such a concern with the fragmentary addresses some of the critical objections of Levinas, especially his critique of Heideggerian ontology from the standpoint of the ethical relation—that is, by an effort to read the fragmentary as opening onto the hybrid space of the ontological-ethical, a region Blanchot calls the outside or the neutral.

To oversimplify things greatly, "Nietzsche and Fragmentary Writing" picks up where "The Athenaeum" leaves off. In this essay, Blanchot takes pains to dislodge Nietzsche from the grip of what in the first half of the twentieth century had become a common interpretation of him: as the giant behind the philosophical masterpiece, *The Will to Power*.[12] This is Heidegger's interpretation of Nietzsche as the last metaphysician. However, dissatisfied with this caricature, and with how popular interpreters had begun to regard the work—as Nietzsche's masterpiece, the systematic work holding all of the contradictory strands of his thought together—Blanchot turns to fragmentary writing as Nietzsche's characteristic mode.[13]

The fragmentary mode would seem to be the perfect mode for Nietzsche because, according to Blanchot:

> there is nothing [in Nietzsche's work] that might be called a center . . .
> But since what he conceives that is essential manifests itself also in what
> is apparently accidental, none of it can be neglected or scornfully rejected,
> including the posthumous writings, on the pretext that they would
> merely give another form to thoughts already expressed. (*EI* 210; *IC* 140)

Here the fragment—the fragmentary—is no longer dialectically opposed to the system. The strength of Nietzsche's thought resides in an inexorable going-beyond the opposition between system and fragment into a more disjointed, partly chaotic and even anarchic, region of thinking:

> The incomparably instructive force of Nietzsche's thought is precisely in
> alerting us to a non-systematic coherence, such that all that relates to it
> seems to press in from all sides in order to resemble a coherent system,
> all the while differing from one. (*EI* 210-11; *IC* 140)

Nietzsche strains thinking toward the outside, a region where thinking no longer has recourse to the power of will or the judgments of affirmation or negation. Its features often appear to initiate a coherent system, but in the end it does not cohere. Something remains.

Developing this thought, Blanchot distinguishes between two kinds of speech in Nietzsche. In the second fragment, which begins—as each fragment does—with a sign borrowed from mathematical notation (±), he writes:

> ± ± There are two kinds of speech in Nietzsche. One belongs to philosophical discourse, the coherent discourse he sometimes wished to bring to term by composing a work of great scope, analogous to the great works of the tradition. Commentators strive to reconstitute this. His broken texts can be considered sad elements of this ensemble or whole. . . .
>
> Let us admit this. Let us admit as well that such a continuous discourse may be behind these divided works. It remains nonetheless true

that Nietzsche does not content himself with such a continuity. And even if a part of these fragments can be brought back to this kind of integral discourse, it is manifest that such a discourse—philosophy itself— is always surpassed by Nietzsche; that he presupposes it rather than gives it exposition, in order, further on, to speak according to a very different language: no longer the language of the whole but of the fragment, of plurality, of separation. (*EI* 27-28; *IC* 151-52)

Blanchot reads Nietzsche as applying pressure to the dialectical opposition between system and fragment, of whole and part, in order to redefine the fragment as fragmentary. According to this logic, the fragmentary is no longer understood simply by appealing to the whole from which it is torn away or broken off but rather it is itself originary. With Nietzsche, the fragmentary work begins to give way to the fragmentary imperative.

In a useful discussion of Blanchot's text in *Very Little . . . Almost Nothing*, Simon Critchley notes that the double plus-minus mathematical notation ($\pm$ $\pm$) perhaps signifies the essential ambiguity of fragmentary writing: "My hypothesis here," Critchley writes:

> is that the above sign—the simultaneity of the positive and the negative— provides a formula for the linguistic ambiguity expressed in and as literature. The power of literature is located in the irreducibility of ambiguity and the maintenance of this ambiguity is literature's right. Literature always has the right to mean something other than what one thought it meant; this is, for Blanchot, both literature's treachery and its cunning version of the truth ('*sa vérité retorse*'). (49)

Critchley is one of Blanchot's most searching and incisive readers, and his account of the plus-and-minus sign ($\pm$) is helpful. Recalling Bakhtin and novelistic discourse, one can see how Blanchot is inviting us into another dimension altogether. For if Bakhtin demonstrates how words appear one-sided when used as serious instruments for viewing objects or ideas, but then appear doubled over with laughter when viewed from the margins of a discourse or at the crossroads between two discourses; then Blanchot opens another dimension completely by assigning an essential ambiguity—and thus the potential for a more radical negativity—to fragmentary writing. Fragmentary writing does not need the external pressure of dialogue or historical context in order for its ambiguity to show itself; rather, that ambiguity is internal to it from the start.

With this in mind, it might be easier to see why Blanchot insists that Nietzsche moves beyond the fragment (or the "aphorism") and on to something else he calls "fragmentary writing." Whereas the fragment is all too often closed in on itself, solitary in its wandering, fragmentary writing establishes a field of infinite relations and is exposed to the outside in a radical manner. Blanchot observes:

> there is no doubt also that this form is linked to the mobility of research, to the thought that travels (to the thought of a man who thinks while walking and according to the truth of the march). It is also true that it seems to be close to aphorism, since it is agreed that the aphoristic form is the form in which Nietzsche excels . . . But is this truly his ambition?; and does the term aphorism meet the real measure of what he is seeking? . . . The aphorism works as a force that limits, encloses. A form that takes the form of a horizon: its own. . . . the aphorism is as unsociable as a stone . . . (*EI* 228-29; *IC* 152)

By contrast, what Blanchot calls "fragmentary writing [*écriture fragmentaire*]" strives to be inherently un-self-identical and plural. Its working unsettles unities and wholes and searches for another kind of order. Unlike the aphorism, which remains isolated and static, fragmentary writing is characterized by mobility and exposure to what it does not yet or cannot contain.

Blanchot's sense that the use of the fragment enables a mobility of research, a thought that travels, puts one in mind of Byron the wandering outlaw. Blanchot thinks of this, however, as a speech that remains infinitely responsive to the overture of the fragmentary imperative. He writes:

> ± ± Fragmentary speech does not know self-sufficiency; it does not suffice, does not speak in view of itself, does not have its content as meaning. But neither does it combine with other fragments to form a more complete thought, a general knowledge. The fragmentary does not precede the whole, but says itself outside the whole, after it. (*EC* 229; *IC* 152)

Here Blanchot alludes to the fact that, as suggested earlier, fragmentary speech comes both before and after Hegel. The exigency of fragmentary writing—distinct from the fragmentary work of romantic poetry—does not represent a stage on the way to dialectical overcoming but remains incomplete by virtue of an exigency of language and thought. At the same time, it is excessive with respect to the system in which knowledge comes to know itself absolutely. Fragmentary writing is governed by the literary *ab*-solute, a slight tweaking of the gears of the machinery of the dialectic. The exigency of fragmentary writing occupies this marginal site of discourse: it is what is inspired by all that has been said, when nothing remains unsaid. Just a slight raising of one's eyebrows. So, Blanchot says:

> ± ± This speech that reveals the exigency of the fragmentary—a non-sufficient speech, but not through insufficiency, unfinished, but because foreign to the category of completion—does not contradict the whole. On the one hand, the whole must be respected. . . . But there is another thought and a very different wish that in truth is not one. It is as though everything were now already accomplished: the universe is our lot, time has ended, we have left history through history. What, then, is there still to say, what is there still to do? (*EC* 229-30; *IC* 153)

This is the strange region in which the exigency of fragmentary writing obtains.

What, then, of the law of non-contradiction? Scholars of romanticism have long remained wary of Schlegel's flouting of this principle. In the "Telemachus" episode of *Ulysses*, Malachi Mulligan appears to channel an unwavering refusal to subscribe to it: "Contradiction. Do I contradict myself? Very well, then, I contradict myself. Mercurial Malachi" (*U* 1.517–18). Enter Nietzsche. Blanchot writes:

> ± ± The fragmentary speech that is Nietzsche's does not know contradiction. . . . The contradictory affirmations are a moment of this critical work: Nietzsche attacks the adversary from several points of view at the same time, for plurality of viewpoint is precisely the principle that the adverse thought fails to recognize. . . . These oppositions say a certain multiple truth and the necessity of thinking the multiple if one wants to say what is true in accordance with value—but this multiplicity is still in relation with the one, still a multiple affirmation of the One. (*EC* 230; *IC* 153)

Or again:

> ± ± Fragmentary speech does not know contradiction, even when it contradicts. . . . The fact of being always posed at the limit [of logic or sense] gives to the fragment two different traits: it is first a speech of affirmation, affirming nothing but this plus, this surplus of affirmation that is foreign to possibility; and yet it is nonetheless in no way categorical, neither fixed as a certainty nor posited in a relative or an absolute positivity, still less saying being in a privileged manner, or saying itself

on the basis of being but rather already effacing itself, slipping outside itself by a sliding that leads it back toward itself in the neutral murmur of contestation. (*EC* 231; *IC* 153-54)

This is the double imperative of the fragmentary imperative. It is

thought as the affirmation of chance, the affirmation wherein thought relates itself necessarily, infinitely, by way of that which is aleatory (not fortuitous); a relation wherein thought gives itself as a thought that is plural. (*EI* 232; *IC* 154)

This is no longer Fontenelle's liberal pluralism, a pluralism of worlds, a fecund and copious pluralism, but rather a pluralism inhering within the thought of the world itself, a pluralism of speech. This pluralism is

a pluralism neither of plurality nor of unity that the speech of the fragment bears in itself as the provocation of language—a language still speaking when all has been said. (*EI* 232; *IC* 155)

This follows directly from Blanchot's re-conceptualization of the fragment as fragmentary speech, as workless work, the imperative of fragmentary writing. The scattering force of the fragmentary imperative unsettles the linguistic or (if one prefers) representational link between subject and object, jarring the world loose from the grasp of philosophical discourse and at the same time dissolving the subject behind such discourse. The fragment, in unsettling itself, unsettles the world of objects and the subject of philosophy.

± ± The plurality of plural speech: a speech that is intermittent, discontinuous; a speech that, without being insignificant, does not speak by reason of its power to represent, or even to signify. What speaks in this speech is not signification, not the possibility of either giving meaning or withdrawing meaning, even a meaning that is multiple. From which we are led to claim, perhaps with too much haste, that this plurality designates itself on the basis of the between [*l'entre-deux*], that it stands a sort of sentry duty around a site of divergence, a space of dis-location that it seeks to close in on, but that always dis-closes it, separating it from itself and identifying it with this margin or separation, this imperceptible divergence where it always returns to itself: identical, non-identical. (*EI* 234-35; *IC* 156)

Blanchot insists that such a thought remains outside the dialectic of identity and difference, continuity and discontinuity. This discontinuity does not define itself in relation to a whole:

Discontinuity, the arrest of intermittence, does not arrest becoming; on the contrary, it provokes becoming, calls it up in the enigma that is proper to it. This is the great turning in thought that comes about with Nietzsche: becoming is not the fluidity of an infinite (Bergsonian) duré, nor the mobility of an interminable movement. The first knowledge is knowledge of the tearing apart—the breaking up—of Dionysus, that obscure experience wherein becoming is disclosed in relation with the discontinuous and as its play. The fragmentation of the god is not the rash renunciation of unity, nor a unity that remains one by becoming plural. Fragmentation is this god himself, that which has no relation whatsoever with a center and cannot be referred to an origin: what thought, as a consequence—the thought of the same and of the one, the thought of theology and that of all the modes of human (or dialectic) knowledge—could never entertain without falsifying it. (*EI* 235; *IC* 157)

Reversing the order of wholes and parts that romantics like Byron and Coleridge seem to take for granted, Blanchot claims that the greatest challenge for thought is to think this origin without unity. The challenge is to think this other origin without doing violence to it by appropriating it for a predetermined unity.

How does fragmentary speech approach such a region? Blanchot is careful to note that fragmentary speech is not simply a form of dialogue or even ordinary conversation but rather "the moving tear of time that maintains, one infinitely distant from the other, these two figures wherein knowledge turns" (*EI* 237; *IC* 158). Blanchot says that even the eternal return does not circumscribe this sort of speech:

Its role is still more strange. It is as though, each time the extreme has been said, it called thought outside (not beyond), designating to thought by its fissure that thought has already left itself, that it is already outside: in relation–without relation–with an outside from which it is excluded and, each time, necessarily, does not truly make the inclusion by which it encloses itself. (*EI* 237-38; *IC* 158)

This is crucial to understanding Blanchot. The speech of the fragment is turned not toward the beyond as the next best category of existence or being or truth or authenticity but toward an acknowledgement of the outside [*le dehors*] in which thought *always already* dwells. The outside is less a new space or frontier beyond where we are now than a negative curvature within what already exists.

± ± Fragmentary speech is barely speech—speech only at the limit. This does not mean that it speaks only at the end, but that in all times it accompanies and traverses all knowledge and all discourse with another language that interrupts speech by drawing it, in the turn of a redoubling, toward the outside where the uninterrupted speaks, the end that is never done with. (*EI* 239; *IC* 159)

Thus far these reflections have circled around Nietzsche's style and its alleged nihilism. But Blanchot suggests that Nietzsche's text holds out the possibility of moving through nihilism toward something else. He writes: "That this speech may seem to play the game of nihilism and lend to nihilism, in its unseemliness, a suitable form—this it will never deny. And yet how far it leaves [*laisse*] this power of negation behind" (*EI* 239; *IC* 160). Perhaps this is what Kristeva calls the fourth term of Hegel's dialectic, intermittently disclosed in Byron's verses, but on full display in Nietzsche's writings. "It is not that in playing [*jouant*] with it negation undoes [*déjoue*] it. To the contrary, it leaves [*laisse*] this power of negation a free field" (*EI* 239; *IC* 160). Nietzsche critiques ontology's degeneration into metaphysics and proceeds to draw attention to a force of thought that requires a thorough examination. Of this elusive force Blanchot writes:

> Force says difference. To think force is to think it by way of difference. This is first to be understood in a quasi-analytical fashion: whoever says force says it always as multiple; if there were a unity of force there would be no force at all. . . . Thus the distance that separates forces is also their correlation—and, more characteristically, is not only what distinguishes them from without, but what from within constitutes the essence of their distinction. In other words, what holds them at a distance, the outside, constitutes their sole intimacy; it is that by which they act and are subject, "the differential element" that is the whole of their reality, they being real only inasmuch as they have no reality in and of themselves, but only relations: a relation without terms. . . .
>
> The intimacy of force resides in its exteriority. . . . Exteriority— time and space—is always exterior to itself. It is not correlative, a center of correlations, but instead institutes relation on the basis of an interruption that does not bring together or unify. Difference is the outside's reserve; the outside is the exposition of difference; difference and outside designate the originary disjunction—the origin that is this very disjunction itself, always disjoined from itself. (*EI* 241; *IC* 161)

Influenced by Bataille and Levinas, Blanchot acknowledges Nietzsche's contribution but at the same time looks beyond Being as a foundation and speculates about the possibility of a thinking that is not predicated on being or nothing. Blanchot follows Levinas in making relation, not being, foundational. In another context Blanchot writes: "What Bataille and Levinas have in common, or what is similar in one and the other, is the gift as the inexhaustible (the infinite) demand [*exigence*] of the other and of others [*de l'autre et d'autrui*], a demand that calls for nothing less than impossible loss: the gift of interiority" (*ED* 170; *WD* 110). Blanchot now describes the gift as an exigency that demands a response: "The I that is responsible for others, the I bereft of selfhood [*moi sans moi*], is sheer fragility, through and through on trial" (*ED* 183; *WD* 119). In nominating a "relation without terms," Blanchot imagines a thought that could respond to "the multiple as multiple" (*ED* 197; *WD* 129) without reducing it to unity.

The fragmentary imperative threatens the dissolution of the subject; the unsettling dialogue Blanchot understands as *l'entretien infini* calls one away from stable self-identity toward the experience of consciousness without subjectivity. Such a work has no subject; no object: it is no longer productive work but speech lured into (exposed to) the "outside." The fragmentary transforms interpretation. Here again is Blanchot:

> Nietzsche expresses himself in still another way: *"The world: the infinite of interpretation (the unfolding of a designating, infinitely)."* . . . [In this aphorism] Nietzsche dismisses the "who?," authorizes no interpreting subject, and recognizes interpretation only as the neutral becoming—without subject and without complement—of interpreting itself, which is not an act but a passion and, by this fact, holds in itself "Dasein"—a *Dasein* without *Sein*, Nietzsche immediately adds. Interpreting, the movement of interpretation in its neutrality—this is what must not be taken as a means of knowing, an instrument thought would have at its disposal in order to think the world. The world is not an object of interpretation, any more than it is proper for interpretation to give itself an object, even an unlimited object, from which it would distinguish itself. The world: the infinite of interpretation; or again, to interpret: the infinite: the world. (*EI* 245-46; *IC* 164)

In this fragment Blanchot declares the end of the world as modernity has known it. The world is no longer to be construed as a world of objects that can be known by a subject; rather, our relation to the world is now understood in terms of an infinite responsibility. This has some rather bizarre consequences. It is not distant beings who may be watching us from afar that strikes Blanchot as interesing but something far more unsettling: "Something wakes: something keeps watch without lying in wait or spying. The disaster watches. . . . Who watches? The question is obviated by the neutrality of the watch that no one watches.

Watching is not the power to keep watch—in the first person; it is not a power, but the touch of the powerless infinite, exposure to the other of the night. . . ." (*ED* 82; *WD* 48–49). This is the other of the night that falls outside the system precisely when the system works as it should. Being exposed to this other night means being touched by a weakness that does not congeal into a defect but that falls outside into a relation with what Blanchot calls the neutral. This is the double imperative that Blanchot calls the fragmentary imperative:

> ± ± Marks of breakage [*brisées*], fragments, chance, enigma: Nietzsche thinks these words together, especially in *Zarathustra*. His effort is thus double. First, wandering among men, he feels a kind of pain at seeing them only in the form of debris, always in pieces, broken, scattered, and thus as though on a field of carnage or slaughter; he therefore proposes, through the effort of a poetic act, to carry together and even bring to unity—the unity of the future—these chaotic pieces, shards, and accidents that are men. This will be the work of the whole, a work that will accomplish the integral. . . . But his *Dichten*, his poetic decision, takes as well a very different direction. Redeemer of chance is the name he claims for himself. What does this mean? Saving chance does not mean returning it to a series of conditions; this would be not to save it, but to lose it. To save chance is to safeguard it from everything that would keep it from being affirmed as dreadful chance: what the throw of the dice could never abolish. (*EI* 250-51; *IC* 167)

The fragmentary imperative is a double imperative: an exigency to name what can be named under the rule of discursive reason—the logic of the narrative or the system—while at the same time responding to what escapes the system and falls outside. It is as if for Blanchot the language of the fragmentary persists along two separate but parallel lines: one turned inside and governed by the opposition of day and night, the other turned outside toward the endless watchfulness of the neutral.

Toward the end of the essay, Blanchot returns to the idea of romantic poetry as work predicated on the reciprocal interplay between wit and irony. At the same time, he is clearly impatient with the limitations of such an opposition. The fragmentary imperative of plural speech, as he sees it, opens beyond this opposition toward the possibility of a reconfiguration of thought itself. He writes:

> The [value of fragmentary words] is not one of representation. They figure forth nothing, except the void they animate without declaring it. . . .
> On the one hand, their role is to give an impetus; on the other (and it is the same), to suspend. But the pause they institute has the remarkable

character of not posing the terms whose passage they both ensure and arrest, and neither does it set them aside; it is as though the alternative of positive and negative, the obligation to begin by affirming being when one wants to deny it, were here, at last, enigmatically broken. (*EI* 253; *IC* 169)

Once again, Critchley is a useful guide:

> it is once again perhaps helpful to place Blanchot's work in the wake of Jena Romanticism, which would have as its central project *the production of literature as its own theory*, and whose genre of expression is the *fragment*. Form and content somehow conspire in Blanchot's work to produce, beyond the criticism/fiction divide, a fragmentary writing, an *Aufhebung* of the *Aufhebung* of the fragment.... writing produces itself *ironically* and *wittily* as a refusal of comprehension, an enactment of a field of fragmentation that produces an alterity irreducible to presentation or cognition, an alterity that can variously be named with the words absence, exteriority, the night, the outside, dying, and, as we will see, the *il y a*. (34-35)

Critchley usefully locates both Blanchot's proximity to Jena romanticism and, at the same time, his profound distance from it. While Blanchot follows the romantics in disturbing the divide between theory and practice and in making the fragment central to his theory of literature, he also takes a step beyond them to facilitate fragmentary writing. No longer merely the aesthetic value of an isolated, fragmented *objet d'art*, the fragmentary imperative of fragmentary writing enacts a field of fragmentation that produces an alterity which remains other as its very own way of being faithful to the system of the same.

Thinking with Pain

Written from the hither side of a long fascination with Nietzsche and fragmentary writing, Blanchot's *The Writing of the Disaster* points one in two important directions. First, it challenges one to consider more carefully the difference that Nietzsche's writing makes in the conception of the fragmentary (its critique of the romantic fragment); and, second, it puts into play an exigency or imperative often only hinted at in previous collections of aphorisms or fragments. In this sense, Blanchot continues to respond to Levinas's critique of Heideggerian ontology from the standpoint of the question of post-metaphysical ethical relation. Blanchot chooses to figure the infinity of this relation in the most disturbing manner possible, by invoking the Holocaust or Shoah, the ultimate moral failure of our time and a stumbling-block to progressive thinking.[14]

The Writing of the Disaster has little to offer in the way of traditional expository writing, nor does it move forward with any apparent logic from one significant point of emphasis to another. Rather, the text organizes itself around small clusters of fragments related to a topic or a closely related series of topics and builds gradually upon the resonances generated therein. Its gradually rising and yet faintly echoing voices generate an accumulated sense of intense and concentrated meditation on sacred ruins or ashes. Of course, Blanchot is no Byron. Nonetheless, there is a sense of close proximity between the sacred and the profane that would perhaps have appealed to Byron.

In any case, *The Disaster* begins with a series of related fragments on the subject of the disaster itself. The first sentence does not hold out much hope to the curious reader: "The disaster ruins everything, all the while leaving everything intact" (*ED* 7; *WD* 1). What is one to make of this? It becomes almost immediately clear that by "disaster," Blanchot means something far more (or other) than simply the origin of the work of art or the space of literature; it is these things and much more. The "disaster" is, first, the disaster of Auschwitz: the moral disaster of the concentration camps and the intellectual disaster that, as Adorno argues, ruins efforts at making adequate sense of them. The "disaster" is also the disaster of time and history—the human inability to reach the disaster of temporality and historicity that awaits us behind time and history. Finally, it is also that which simply irreducible or unassimilable: "There is no reaching the disaster," Blanchot says.[15] Here Blanchot patiently inflects the thought of the work's fragmentary origin with an ethical or, better, relational edge: "The disaster is separate; that which is most separate" (*ED* 7; *WD* 1). It is a spacing that spaces nothing in particular:

> It does not touch anyone in particular; "I" am not threatened by it, but spared, left aside. It is in this way that I am threatened; it is in this way that the disaster threatens in me that which is exterior to me—an other than I who passively becomes other. There is no reaching the disaster. (*ED* 7; *WD* 1)

Crudely, one might begin to think of the "disaster" as a kind of "spacing" or "drift" introduced into the world from outside the world (or even generated within its own interstices) by what supports it—the wear and tear of the universe, long past, continuing on. Blanchot writes:

> The disaster is not somber, it would liberate us from everything if it could just have a relation with someone; we would know it in light of language and at the twilight of a language with a *gai savoir*. But the

disaster is unknown; it is the unknown name for that in thought itself which dissuades is from thinking of it, leaving us, but [for] its proximity alone. Alone, and thus exposed to the thought of the disaster which disrupts solitude and overflows every variety of thought, as the intense, silent and disastrous affirmation of the outside. (*ED* 14; *WD* 5)

In a fragment on romanticism and Sade, Blanchot rehearses the theme of "the relation between the word of art and the encounter with death: in both cases, we approach a perilous threshold, a crucial point where we are abruptly *turned back*" (*ED* 18; *WD* 7). It is as if Blanchot were thinking of Shakespeare's great tragedy and pondering the question of how to confront death and then go beyond it—not simply by witnessing death or—perish the thought—by dying oneself but rather by thinking through with even greater rigor what death projects before itself and what it leaves behind. For Blanchot, however, the character of Hamlet has his origins in an even more ancient character: the poet Orpheus who traverses the borderlands between the living and the dead.

By trying simply to negate the disaster, one only feeds the disaster. One must proceed rather by way of what Blanchot calls refusal: "To write: to refuse to write—to write by way of this refusal [*refuser d'écrire—d'écrire par refus*]" (*ED* 22; *WD* 10). As if one were to push through to the other side of writing so that writing comes not from the will to write, nor from the inclination to write, nor from the capacity to write: writing that is a refusal to write, and a writing that is supported precisely by this refusal. Or, as Blanchot (this locution becomes more and more problematic) himself writes: "To want to write: what an absurdity. Writing is the decay [*déchéance*] of the will, just as it is the loss of power, and the fall of the regular fall of the beat, the disaster again" (*ED* 24; *WD* 11). This last sentence hints at the Nietzschean pedigree of the disaster, as one endeavors to inhabit "the regular fall of the beat" in a piece of music without anticipation or resistance. To will that it fall where it falls; to cease to will that anything be any different than it is already. To will that things be exactly as they are.

The fragment's persistent opposition to system threatens to absorb it within the very system it opposes; the fragment, as Lacoue-Labarthe and Nancy insist, is in fact the romantic-era re-formulation or re-figuration of the system. But, unlike the romantic-era writing of fragments, it is the continual openness of the fragmentary to the "possibility of failure," rather than the pursuit of an impossible perfection by way of becoming, that for Blanchot characterizes "fragmentary writing" and its movement away from the system, its positioning of itself not so much against anything as just elsewhere.

Blanchot uses the example of Bartleby the Scrivener, from Melville's short story of the same name, to make precisely this point about the writing of the disaster:

> Refusal is said to be the first degree of passivity [*la passivité*]. But if refusal is deliberate and voluntary, if it expresses a decision–though this be a negative one–it does not yet allow separation from the power of consciousness, and comes no closer to passivity than this act, of refusal, on the part of a self. And yet refusal does tend toward the absolute, independent of any determination whatsoever. This is the core of refusal which Bartleby the scrivener's inexorable "I would prefer not to" expresses: an abstention which has never had to be decided upon, which precedes all decisions and which is not so much a denial as, more than that, an abdication. Bartleby gives up (not that he ever pronounced, or clarifies this renunciation) ever saying anything; he gives up the authority to speak. This is abnegation understood as the abandonment of the self, a relinquishment of identity, refusal which does not cleave to refusal but opens to failure, to the loss of being, to thought. "I will not do it" would still have signified an energetic determination, calling forth an equally energetic contradiction. "I would prefer not to . . ." belongs to the infiniteness of patience; no dialectical intervention can take hold of such passivity. We have fallen out of being [*hors de l'être*], outside [*dans le champ du dehors*] where, immobile, proceeding with a slow and even step, destroyed men come and go. (*ED* 33-34; *WD* 17)

In a wonderful but terrifying locution, Blanchot calls it "*le champ du dehors*" or, literally, "the field of the outside." Nowhere: but not the nowhere of the thinker who insists on objectivity or a standpoint somehow free of prejudice. Gadamer, among others, has shown how this idea of objectivity is seriously flawed.[16] This region is rather the place of places where one can let go of the desire to decide either for or against, to take one's place on either left or the right, to intervene on behalf of one's best thinking. This is an unsettled and unsettling region of fascination where initiative comes not from within oneself—from one's thinking and willing—but from elsewhere. Exposure to this kind of neutrality makes one responsive rather than decisive or original.

Blanchot goes on to meditate on the non-concept of passivity in a more precise and rigorous way:

> Passivity, passion, past, pas (both negation and step—the trace of movement or advance) [*Passivité, passion, passé, pas (à la fois négation et*

trace ou mouvement de la marche)]: this semantic play provides us with a slippage of meaning, but not with anything to which we could entrust ourselves, not with anything like an answer that would satisfy us. (*ED* 33; *WD* 16-17)

Like the mystical *via negativa* in which obstacles eventually serve as openings to heightened religious experience, Blanchot's sense of the "not" in the "step" along the way attends to a discursive motion—it is hardly a movement—that allows speech to risk the approach of the neutral or the outside, the impossible or the night. In an orthodox religious context, this would be perhaps the darkest night of the soul imaginable. For Blanchot, it marks the possibility of a register of experience ultimately irreducible to the usual narratives of experience—comic or tragic—that we appropriate in order to structure or lives.

> Passivity neither consents nor refuses: neither yes nor no, without preference, it alone suits the limitlessness of the neutral, the unmastered patience which endures time without resisting. The passive condition is no condition: it is an unconditional which no protection shelters, which no destruction touches, which is as remote from submission as it is bereft of initiative; with it, nothing begins. (*ED* 52; *WD* 29-30)

One can think of this as an exposure to the outside such that only by keeping silent and remaining absolutely still could one escape the endless violence of the constant opposition between affirmation and negation.

> What is it that rings false in the system? What makes it limp? The question itself is immediately unsteady and does not amount to a question. What exceeds the system is the impossibility of its failure, and likewise the impossibility of its success. Ultimately nothing can be said of it, and there is a way of keeping still (the lacunary silence of writing) that halts the system, leaving it idle [*le laissant désoeuvré*], delivered to the seriousness of irony. (*ED* 79-80; *WD* 47)

This would seem to be the aim of the fragmentary imperative in Blanchot's sense: to let the "system-work" fall outside the economy of means and ends, such that its worklessness is revealed. For the worklessness of the work now no longer constitutes simply a style or a fashion but rather a demand or an imperative, the fragmentary imperative, in which the (infinite) possibility of a relation with another may make its appearance.[17] The responsibility of literature is to hold open space for just this possibility.

Notes

Chapter 1. Setting Out: Toward Irony, the Fragment, and the Fragmentary Work

1. Although Marjorie Levinson insists "[w]e should no longer elucidate English practice by German aesthetics" (*The Romantic Fragment Poem: A Critique of a Form* [Chapel Hill and London: The University of North Carolina Press, 1986]. p. 11), one can nevertheless observe that German romantic theory is informed from the start by writers like Boccaccio, Cervantes, Dante, Shakespeare, Swift, Sterne, and Goethe. On these matters, see Stuart Barnett's Critical Introduction to his translation of Friedrich Schlegel's *On the Study of Greek Poetry*, trans., ed. Stuart Barnett (Albany: State University of New York Press, 2001). Barnett's response to critics who object to invoking Schlegel's name in discussions of English romanticism is compelling and worth citing at some length:

> It is this large-scale, historical perspective that characterizes Schlegel's approach to questions of literature from his "classicist" phase to his Romantic phase and on through his so-called Catholic-Conservative phase. It would be easy to conclude from the secondary literature in English that Schlegel, when he was not thinking obsessively about irony, only considered literature in a vacuum. Yet, despite what critics have implied, Schlegel did not think of literature in purely abstract terms. . . . Schlegel's conception of literature was, from beginning to end, profoundly historical. Whatever pronouncements Schlegel did make about literature as such were always based upon detailed and rigorous historical study. Hence it is not just that the literature of antiquity consistently played a role in Schlegel's thought. Rather, it is that Schlegel's notion of Romanticism was from the outset predicated upon a broad, historical study of literature. Romanticism, accordingly, was not seen simply as a moment within which literature became conscious of itself; it was also seen as the fruition of the history of Western literature itself. Indeed, the very impetus for the conceptualization of the Romantic . . . was the search for a resolution to a cultural dilemma of massive historical proportions between classical and postclassical literature. (6)

For Schlegel's original text, see *Über das Studium der griechischen Poesie*, ed. Ernst Behler (1979), Vol. 1 of *Kritische Friedrich-Schlegel-Ausgabe*, ed. Ernst Behler, Jean-Jacques Anstett, Hans Eichner, et. al., 35 vols. to date (München: Ferdinand Schöningh; Zurich: Thomas, 1958-).

2. *Kritische Friedrich-Schlegel-Ausgabe*, Vol. 2: *Charakteristiken und Kritiken I (1796-1801)*, ed. Hans Eichner (1967), p. 182; *Friedrich Schlegel's Lucinda and the Fragments*, trans. Peter Firchow (Minneapolis: University of Minnesota Press, 1971), p. 175. Hereafter abbreviated *KA* and *LF*, respectively. In an assessment of Firchow's translations, Hans Eichner points to several passages where different readings may be preferred. See his review of *Friedrich Schlegel's Lucinde and the Fragments* in *The German Quarterly*, Vol. 6, No. 3 (May, 1973): 478-81. For the most part, I follow Firchow's translations of Schlegel's writings. Where I have made alterations, or where I have followed the translation but feel that no English word or phrase can adequately render Schlegel's German, I have supplied the German between brackets in the text.

3. Laurence Sterne, *The Life and Opinions of Tristram Shandy, Gentleman*, ed. Melvyn New and Joan New (Harmondsworth: Penguin, 1997). Hereafter abbreviated *TS*. In his essay "The Novel as Parody: Sterne's *Tristram Shandy*," Viktor Shklovsky proclaims, "Tristram Shandy is the most typical novel in world literature." See *Theory of Prose*, trans. Benjamin Sher (Elmwood Park, IL: Dalkey Archive Press, 1991), p. 70. To the extent that novelistic discourse parodies philosophy's dream of a realist epistemology predicated on essentially transparent speech (that is, the idea of a philosophical character), this is of course right. My argument in this book, however, is that what Schlegel calls *romantische Poesie* internalizes this parody—inscribes the quarrel between philosophy and poetry into the working of the romantic work of art—and thus helps give birth to what we call literature or the literary absolute.

Simon Critchley's *On Humor* (London and New York: Routledge, 2002) includes a brief discussion of *Tristram Shandy* that sheds light on both its literary and philosophical stakes. Critchley writes: "What Sterne calls 'the Shandian system' is entirely made up of digressions." This will surprise no one who has opened the book. Yet where do these digressions lead? What truth do they reveal? Critchley muses:

> Perhaps this: that through the meandering circumlocutions of *Tristram Shandy* . . . we progressively approach the things themselves, the various *pragmata* that make up the stuff of what we call ordinary life. That is to say, the *infinitely digressive movement of Sterne's prose actually contains a contrary motion within it, which is progressive*. We might think of this as a cosmic phenomenology which is animated by a concern for the things themselves, the *things which show themselves when we get rid of our troubling opinions*. (21, emphases mine)

So the narrative structure of *Tristram Shandy* consists of a constant interplay between "two contrary motions—progressive and digressive—that is at the heart of humour" (22). I would only add that this is also true of words themselves, that there is a back and forth movement in the way of words that allows things to reveal themselves. Words, in others words, are not so much names or signs as agents of revelation.

4. Richard A. Lanham, *Tristram Shandy: The Games of Pleasure* (Berkeley, CA: University of California Press, 1973), p. 1. See also Peter Conrad, *Shandyism: The Character of Romantic Irony* (Oxford: Blackwell, 1978). Conrad writes:

> Shandyism refers to a character and a form: to an inspirationally erratic individual and the chaotic structure he inhabits. This book begins by deriving both the character of Tristram and his collapsed, wayward form from a romantic recomposition of Shakespeare. Romanticism discovers its source in Shakespeare, and Sterne's romantic originality consists in his rearrangement of the vexed Shakespearean relation of tragedy and comedy, which for him are no longer literary forms but reflexes of moods, paradoxically interchangeable. From this similitude between tragedy and comedy comes irony, the visionary composite expounded by Sterne's German critics. (vii)

For a sense of where *Tristram Shandy* may well lead, see Hugh Kenner, *The Stoic Comedians: Flaubert, Joyce, and Beckett* (1962; Berkeley, CA: University of California Press, 1974) and Gerald L. Bruns, *Modern Poetry and the Idea of Language: A Critical and Historical Study* (New Haven and London: Yale University Press, 1974).

5. Philippe Lacoue-Labarthe and Jean-Luc Nancy, *The Literary Absolute: The Theory of Literature in German Romanticism*, trans. Philip Barnard and Cheryl Lester (Albany: State University of New York Press, 1988), p. 85. Hereafter abbreviated *LA*. The book originally appeared in French as *L'absolu littéraire* (Paris: Éditions du Seuil, 1978) but invited a second, more intense and controversial, reading when it appeared in English translation. For a reading of *The Literary Absolute* that attempts to clear up much of the confusion that has surrounded it since its first publication, see Daniel J. Hoolsema, "The Echo of an Impossible Future in *The Literary Absolute*," in *Modern Language Notes* Vol. 119, No. 4 (2004): 845-868. Hoolsema's essay also usefully engages Lacoue-Labarthe's essay, "The Echo of the Subject," in *Typography: Mimesis, Philosophy, Politics*, ed. Christopher Fynsk, pp. 139-207 (Stanford, CA: Stanford University Press, 1998).

For a view that focuses more specifically on the philosophical stakes of the German romantic *conception* of the fragment, see Rodolphe Gasché's "Ideality in Fragmentation," in Friedrich Schlegel's *Philosophical Fragments*, trans. Peter Firchow (1971; Minneapolis: University of Minnesota Press, 1991), pp. vii-xxxii:

> Whether the very concept of the fragment, as well as its history, is indeed sufficient to describe the form of the more significant literary experiments from the

late nineteenth century up to the present, as well as to conceptualize the intrinsic difference(s), heterogeneity, plurality, and so forth, of the text, has to my knowledge never been attended to explicitly. What should be obvious is that if the fragment, or rather its notion, is to bring out the radical notion of a totality of writing, or the text, it must be a notion of fragment thoroughly distinct from its (historically) prevailing notion(s). A concept of the fragment that merely emphasizes incompletion, residualness, detachment, or brokenness will not serve here. (vii)

Stephen Watson's "The Rationality of the Fragment" also examines the philosophical stakes of the fragment. See Stephen H. Watson, *Extensions: Essays on Interpretation, Rationality, and the Closure of Modernism*, pp. 245-59 (Albany: State University of New York Press, 1992).

6. See György Lukács, *The Theory of the Novel : A Historico-philosophical Essay on the Forms of Great Epic Literature*, trans. Anna Bostock (Cambridge, MA: MIT Press, 1971); M. M. Bakhtin, *The Dialogic Imagination: Four Essays*, ed. Michael Holquist, trans. Caryl Emerson and Michael Holquist (Austin, TX: University of Texas Press, 1981); and Julia Kristeva, *Desire in Language: A Semiotic Approach to Literature and Art*, trans. Alice A. Jardine (New York: Columbia University Press, 1980).

7. This is a theme that has received increased attention in recent years in scholarly discussions of Plato. See, e.g. Martha Nussbaum, *Love's Knowledge: Essays on Philosophy and Literature*, esp. pp. 3-53 (New York and Oxford: Oxford University Press, 1990); Andrea Wilson Nightingale, *Genres in Dialogue: Plato and the Construct of Philosophy* (Cambridge: Cambridge University Press, 1996); and Diskin Clay, *Platonic Questions: Dialogues with the Silent Philosopher* (University Park, PA: The Pennsylvania State University Press, 2000).

8. See Maurice Blanchot, *L'écriture du désastre* (Paris: Éditions Gallimard, 1980), pp. 30-34; *The Writing of the Disaster*, trans. Ann Smock (Lincoln: University of Nebraska Press, 1986), pp. 14-17. Hereafter abbreviated *ED* and *WD*, respectively. Discussing this movement without progress, Blanchot notes: "Passivity, passion, past, *pas* (both negation and step—the trace or movement of an advance): this semantic play provides us with a slippage of meaning, but not with anything to which we could entrust ourselves, not with anything like an answer that would satisfy us" (*ED* 33; *WD* 16-17).

9. For an important discussion of this pre-Socratic or rhetorical ideal of life, see Eric A. Havelock, *Preface to Plato* (Cambridge, MA and London: Belknap Press, 1963). See also Richard A. Lanham's *The Motives of Eloquence: Literary Rhetoric in the Renaissance*, esp. pp. 1-35 (New Haven and London: Yale University Press, 1976).

10. Robert Langbaum, *The Poetry of Experience: The Dramatic Monologue in Modern Literary Tradition* (1957; New York: Norton, 1963), p. 210, emphasis mine.

11. Martin Heidegger, "Der Ursprung des Kunstwerkes," in *Gesamtausgabe* (Frankfurt: Vittorio Klostermann, 1977), Vol. 5, p. 35; "The Origin of the Work of Art," in *Poetry, Language, Thought*, trans. Albert Hofstadter (New York: Harper and Row, 1975), p. 49.

12. Of course, nothing comes from nothing. According to Melvyn New, the text's interpretive community includes:

> all the authors and books summoned by Sterne, all the documents and cultures and artefacts from which he erects his edifice, in short all that illustrates to us what it means to live in a world written by God, and hence always approximated—but never finalized—by the same human endeavor. (xxxv)

That is, insofar as there is dialogue in which the characters participate and out of which the novel's drama is born, there is also dialogue among various voices of tradition, the source materials out of which the concrete verbal textures of the book are conceived. See the Editor's Introduction, pp. xxvii-xli of *Tristram Shandy*. As I read him, New wants to insert Sterne back into his own time, to situate him once again within the context of his own day and age. He is particularly interested in recovering Sterne the clergyman from the diabolical postmodernists who have remade Sterne in their own foot-loose and fancy-free image. Thus, New writes, "a good reader of *Tristram Shandy* must confront Sterne's twenty-two year career as a village vicar" (xxxiii); and, more generally, the "'new' wisdom [sic] argues [for] the traditional nature of Sterne's enterprise, his embeddedness in his own time and place" (xxxvii). There is much to admire in such a reading.

13. Maurice Blanchot, *L'entretien infini* (Paris: Éditions Gallimard, 1969), p. 183; *The Infinite Conversation*, trans. Susan Hanson (Minneapolis and London: University Minnesota Press, 1993), p. 125. Hereafter abbreviated *EI* and *IC*, respectively.

14. Paul de Man, "The Rhetoric of Temporality," in *Blindness and Insight: Essays in the Rhetoric of Contemporary Criticism*, 2nd ed., rev., pp. 187-228 (Minneapolis: University of Minnesota Press, 1983). For another side of de Man's thinking about irony, see "The Concept of Irony," in Paul de Man, *Aesthetic Ideology*, pp. 163-84 (Minneapolis: University of Minnesota Press, 1996). Also consider Ernst Behler's assertion that "When Friedrich Schlegel decided to extend the restricted use of irony, as encountered in the rhetorical tradition of Europe, to works of Boccaccio, Cervantes, Sterne, and Goethe . . . he gave irony a completely new scope and effected a fundamental change in the concept in Western literary theory." See Behler, *German Romantic Literary Theory* (Cambridge: Cambridge University Press, 1993), p. 146.

15. Anne K. Mellor, *English Romantic Irony* (Cambridge, MA and London: Harvard University Press, 1980).

16. See Jerome J. McGann, *The Romantic Ideology: A Critical Investigation* (Chicago and London: University of Chicago Press, 1983).

17. See Hans-George Gadamer, *Truth and Method*, 2nd rev. ed., trans. Joel Weinsheimer and Donald G. Marshall (New York: Crossroad, 1991), p. xv. Hereafter abbreviated *TM*. Originally published as *Warheit und Methode* (Tübingen: J. C. B. Mohr [Paul Siebeck], 1960), this translation is based on the revised and expanded 5th German ed., *Gesammelte Werke*, Vol. 1 (Tübingen: J. C. B. Mohr [Paul Siebeck], 1986).

18. Marjorie Levinson, *The Romantic Fragment Poem*, p. 216. In spite of the unquestionable erudition of her account, I think Levinson is a little too cavalier in her dismissal of the impact of poetic form, a vital feature of poetry that working poets have historically used in ingeniously meaningful ways. For a corrective to such a view, see Susan J. Wolfson's *Formal Charges: The Shaping of Poetry in British Romanticism* (Stanford, CA: Stanford University Press, 1997).

19. Thomas McFarland, *Romanticism and the Forms of Ruin: Wordsworth, Coleridge, and Modalities of Fragmentation* (Princeton, NJ: Princeton University Press, 1981), p. 5. Other studies of fragmentary poetics I have found useful include Balachandra Rajan, *The Form of the Unfinished: English Poetics from Spenser to Pound* (Princeton, NJ: Princeton University Press. 1985) and Anne Janowitz, *England's Ruins: Poetic Purpose and the National Landscape* (Cambridge: Blackwell, 1990). See also John Beer, "Fragmentations and Ironies," in *Questioning Romanticism*, ed. Beer, pp. 234–64 (Baltimore and London: Johns Hopkins Press, 1995).

20. Martin Heidegger, *Sein und Zeit*, 7th ed. (1927; Tübingen: Max Verlag, 1953); *Being and Time*, trans. by John Macquarrie and William Richardson (New York: Harper, 1962); *Being and Time: A Translation of Sein und Zeit*, trans. by Joan Stambaugh (Albany: State University Press of New York, 1996). Hereafter abbreviated *SZ*, *BT*, and *JS*, respectively.

21. In another context (a discussion of Paul de Man's essay, "The Rhetoric of Temporality"), Jochen Schulte-Sasse notes how "de Man systematically reduces the ambiguity of [Peter] Szondi (and the Romantics) through translation." See Schulte-Sasse, Gen. ed., Haynes Horne, Andreas Michel, Elizabeth Mittman, Assenka Oksiloff, Lisa C. Roetzel, Mary R. Strand, coeds., trans., *Theory as Practice: A Critical Anthology of Early German Romantic Writings* (Minneapolis and London: University of Minnesota Press, 1996), p. 7.

22. Walter Benjamin, *The Origin of German Tragic Drama*, trans. John Osborne (1977; London and New York: Verso, 1998), p. 176. The original German

text appeared as *Ursprung des deutschen Trauerspiels* (Frankfurt am Main: Suhrkamp Verlag, 1963).

23. Walter Benjamin, *Illuminations*, trans. Harry Zohn (New York: Schocken, 1969), p. 261. The selections translated and included in *Illuminations* are taken from *Schriften*, 2 Vols., ed. Theodor W. Adorno (Frankfurt am Main: Suhrkamp Verlag, 1955).

24. Geoffrey H. Hartman, *A Critic's Journey: Literary Reflections, 1958–1998* (New Haven: Yale University Press, 1999), p. 197.

25. Jerome J. McGann, "History, Herstory, Theirstory, Ourstory," in David Perkins, ed., *Theoretical Issues in Literary History*, pp. 196–205 (Cambridge, MA: Harvard University Press, 1991).

26. See Emmanuel Levinas, "Ethics as First Philosophy," in Seán Hand, ed., *The Levinas Reader*, pp. 75–87 (Oxford, UK and Cambridge, MA: Black-well, 1989). For a defense of deconstruction that is grounded on the claim that such criticism is often more attuned to the question of the Other than plain-style criticism, see G. Douglas Atkins, "Dehellenizing Literary Criticism," in *College English*, Vol. 41, No. 7 (March, 1980): 769–779. For an assessment of the increasingly central place of the Other in contemporary literary study, see Derek Attridge, "Innovation, Literature, Ethics: Relating to the Other," in *Publications of the Modern Language Association*, Vol. 114, No. 1, Special Topics: Ethics and Literary Study (January, 1999): 20–31.

27. See Paul de Man, *Allegories of Reading: Figural Language in Rousseau, Nietzsche, Rilke, and Proust*, pp. 3–19 (New Haven and London: Yale University Press, 1979).

28. For a discussion of these matters, see Andrew Bowie, "'Non-Identity': The German Romantics, Schelling, and Adorno," in Tilottama Rajan and David L. Clark, eds., *Intersections: Nineteenth-Century Philosophy and Contemporary Theory*, pp. 243–60 (Albany: State University of New York Press, 1995).

29. Jean-Luc Nancy, *The Birth to Presence*. Translated by Brian Holmes, et. al. (Stanford, CA: Stanford University Press, 1993), p. 254.

30. Stanley Cavell is one of the few philosophers to have been moved by Lacoue-Labarthe and Nancy's insights into the romantic work's *désoeuvrement* or worklessness. See Cavell's *This New Yet Unapproachable America: Lectures After Emerson After Wittgenstein* (Albuquerque, NM: Living Batch Press, 1989). In addition, Simon Critchley is one of the few philosophers to appreciate Cavell's attunement to Blanchot's—and Lacoue-Labarthe and Nancy's— reading of the fragmentary work. See Critchley, *Very Little . . . Almost Nothing: Death, Philosophy, Literature* (London and New York: Routledge, 1997). In *The*

Rhetoric of Failure: Deconstruction of Skepticism, Reinvention of Modernism (Albany: State University of New York Press, 1996), Ewa Płonowska Ziarek juxtaposes Cavell's account of skepticism with Derrida's critique of structuralism in order to foreground the relations between these movements and literary modernism.

31. Astradur Eysteinsson, *The Concept of Modernism* (Ithaca and London: Cornell University Press, 1990), p. 202.

32. See David K. O'Connor, ed., *The Symposium of Plato: The Shelley Translation*, (South Bend, IN: St. Augustine's Press, 2002), pp. xi–xliv. Closely related to O'Connor's remarks about the *Symposium*, Alven M. Neiman's reflections on Socrates as an exemplary teacher are extremely lucid. See "Socrates and the Ironic Teacher of Virtue," James W. Garrison and Anthony G. Rud, Jr., eds., *The Educational Conversation: Closing the Gap* (Albany: State University of New York Press, 1995), pp. 61–83 and "Self-Examination, Philosophical Education and Spirituality," *Journal of the Philosophy of Education*, Vol. 34 (4 November 2000): 571–91.

33. In an unpublished MS., "Romantic Fragments: *Lyrical Ballads* and *Guesses at Truth*," Stephen Prickett considers the English fragment—exemplified by *Lyrical Ballads* and *Guess at Truth* by A. W. and J. C. Hare—against the background of German romanticism. Prickett's reading raises many useful questions about the application of German romantic literary theory to English romanticism. See also his discussions of the fragment in *Origins of Narrative: The Romantic Appropriation of the Bible*, pp. 205–214 (Cambridge: Cambridge University Press, 1996) and *Narrative, Religion and Science: Fundamentalism versus Irony, 1700–1999*, pp. 114–21 (Cambridge: Cambridge University Press, 2002).

Prickett's thoughts concerning the fragment are intriguing, particularly the idea that it embodies a revolutionary new way of looking at the world. Prickett writes:

> I want to suggest that behind those twin conceptions of the 'fragment' and the 'experiment' is another word for which neither Wordsworth nor Coleridge yet have a word. Indeed, if I am right, the word eventually chosen still had some way to go after its coinage in the early nineteenth century before it acquired the meaning for which the *Lyrical Ballads* were striving. That word is 'pluralism.' What makes this collection of lyrics unique, it seems to me, is not their reference to the economic distress of the poor so beloved by social historians, but their sense of the sheer diversity and complexity of the society they portray. (5)

Prickett is surely right about the diversity and complexity portrayed. However, I would also maintain that such a way of looking at the world predates romanticism; as Bakhtin suggests, it probably has its origins in Greek and Latin antiquity. See M. M. Bakhtin, "From the Prehistory of Novelistic Discourse," in *The Dialogic Imagination*, pp. 41-83. See also Margaret Anne Doody's important study, *The True Story of the Novel* (New Brunswick, NJ: Rutgers University Press, 1996), which unsettles the old distinction between the novel and romance, arguing instead that the novel's diversity originates in antiquity and profoundly influences all of western civilization. In a sense, Doody is reading a version of Bakhtin's idea of novelistic discourse back into the very foundations of English literary tradition.

Chapter 2. Rethinking Romantic Poetry: Schlegel, the Genre of Dialogue, and the Poetics of the Fragment

1. The most important work on this subject is Ernst Robert Curtius, *European Literature and the Latin Middle Ages*, trans. Willard R. Trask (Princeton, NJ: Princeton University Press, 1953). Curtius emphasizes how the comparative uniformity of Latin literary culture gradually dissolved into a plurality of vernacular cultures:

> The flowering of the vernacular literatures from the twelfth and thirteenth centuries onward in no sense signifies a defeat or retreat of Latin literature. Indeed, the twelfth and thirteenth centuries are a culminating point of Latin poetry and learning. . . . For centuries longer, Latin remained alive as the language of education, of science, of government, of law, of diplomacy. In France it was not abolished as the language of law until 1539, at the instigation of Francis I. But as a literary language too, Latin long survived the end of the Middle Ages. . . . In France, England, Holland, and Germany it also had brilliant representatives in the sixteenth and seventeenth centuries. (26)

2. In a review of *The Literary Absolute*, Thomas Pfau draws attention to the central role played by subject-formation within German Idealism and German romanticism and the opportunity Lacoue-Labarthe and Nancy miss for applying it to British romanticism:

> It may be the consistent avoidance of any contextualization which renders Lacoue-Labarthe's and Nancy's exposition of Schlegel somewhat too air-tight and hermetic. . . . The reader is left wondering why the *Bildung* of "auto-constitution of the subject" is nowhere set in relation to the romantic concept of the "imagination" (which the authors do not even mention in their all too brief discussion of Kant's "schematism," where they had convincingly located the origins of the "philosophical crisis" that produced romanticism and literature). Furthermore, it is a surprisingly reductive understanding of, for example, English romanticism ("Romantic—especially in its English provenance—is the landscape before which one feels the sentiment of nature"[4]), which causes the authors to overlook some concrete instances (e.g., the imaginative or ironic formation of character in Wordsworth's *Prelude* and Byron's *Don Juan*, respectively) of the very Work that, in the theoretical idiom of Schlegel, remains forever absent or incomplete. (312)

Thomas Pfau, rev. of Philippe Lacoue-Labarthe and Jean-Luc Nancy, *The Literary Absolute*, in *Studies in Romanticism* 29 (Summer 1990): 309–13. See also

Piotr Parlej, *The Romantic Theory of the Novel: Genre and Reflection in Cervantes, Melville, Flaubert, Joyce, and Kafka* (Baton Rouge and London: Louisiana State University Press, 1997). Parlej provides a rigorous account of the philosophical stakes of Schlegel's theory of literature.

3. The German romantics acknowledge a rhetorical dimension to Socrates that has more in common with Odysseus than with the single-mindedness of the philosopher. This would be a Socrates still answerable to the truth of poetry. For an account of Plato's banishment of the poets, see Eric Havelock, *A Preface to Plato*. See also Hans-Georg Gadamer, "Plato and the Poets," in *Dialogue and Dialectic: Eight Hermeneutical Studies on Plato*, trans. P. Christopher Smith, pp. 39–72 (New Haven and London: Yale University Press, 1980) and *Literature and Philosophy in Dialogue: Essays in German Literary Theory*, trans. Robert H. Paslick (Albany: State University of New York Press, 1994).

4. Friedrich Schleiermacher, *Hermeneutik*, 2nd ed., ed. Heinz Kimmerle (1959; Heidelberg: Winter, 1974), p. 83; *Hermeneutics and Criticism and Other Writings*, trans. Andrew Bowie (Cambridge: Cambridge University Press, 1998), p. 23. Hereafter abbreviated *H* and *HC*, respectively.

5. Ernst Behler calls the idea "an old and humorous dictum of philological, editorial practice, relating to the emendation of texts," which the romantics raised to the level of a principle. See *German Romantic Literary Theory*, p. 275.

6. Studies of Schlegel that I have found particularly useful include Josef Körner, *Romantiker und Klassiker* (1924; Darmstadt: Wissenschaftliche Buchgesellschaft, 1971); Heinrich Nüsse, *Die Sprachtheorie Friedrich Schlegels* (Heidelberg: Winter, 1962); Hermann Patsch, "Friedrich Schlegels 'Philosophie der Philologie' und Schleiermachers frühe Entwürfe," in *Zeitschrift für Theologie und Kirche* 63 (1966): 434–72; and Hans Eichner, *Friedrich Schlegel*, (New York: Twayne, 1970). On the issue of the relationship between dialogue and deconstruction, see Ernst Behler, "Friedrich Schlegels Theorie des Verstehen: Hermeneutik oder Dekonstruktion?," pp. 141–60, and Hans-Georg Gadamer, "Frühromantik, Hermeneutik, Dekonstruktivismus," pp. 251–60, in *Die Aktualität der Frühromantik*, ed. Behler and Jochen Hörisch (Paderborn [et. al.]: Ferdinand Schöningh, 1987).

7. Richard Palmer, *Hermeneutics: Interpretation Theory in Schleiermacher, Dilthey, Heidegger, and Gadamer* (Evanston, IL: Northwestern University Press, 1969), p. 86.

8. Wilhelm Dilthey, *Selected Writings*, trans. ed. H. P. Rickman, pp. 247–263 (Cambridge: Cambridge University Press, 1976); "Die Entstehung der Hermeneutik," *Gesammelte Schriften*, Vol. 5, pp. 317–331 (Stuttgart: B. G. Teubner; Göttingen: Vandenhoeck und Ruprecht, 1964).

9. More recently, Dilthey's—and as a result Gadamer's—reading of Schleiermacher has been called into question, so that, among other things, Schleiermacher's views on language and history, and the kinship of these views to structuralism and post-structuralism, now appear as more central matters. See Manfred Frank, "The Text and its Styles: Schleiermacher's Hermeneutic Theory of Language," *boundary 2*, Vol. 11, No. 3 (Spring 1983): 11-28; Jean Grondin, *Introduction to Philosophical Hermeneutics*, esp. pp. 63-75 (New Haven and London: Yale University Press, 1994); and Andrew Bowie, *From Romanticism to Critical Theory: The Philosophy of German Literary Theory* (London: 1997).

10. One could say that Gadamer is trying to understand what Schleiermacher means here, namely whether misunderstanding is really "to be prevented in advance": this prevention of misunderstanding is the prophylactic task of method. Gadamer argues against method as prophylaxis—against trying to make understanding reproduce a prior self-understanding. Understanding is productive when it is brought out from under the instrumental control of interpretive method. In this sense, "loose" hermeneutics means: letting understanding happen—it is an event in which one is taken up rather than a product or an effect of consciousness, something to live through, to suffer, to undergo. It may be that Schlegel helps us to understand this looser side of hermeneutics, where what happens to the one who understands is open and unpredictable.

11. Behler suggests that Schlegel was actually the first to formulate a theory of understanding, only to have it rendered obsolete by Schleiermacher's revisions. See *Confrontations: Derrida/Heidegger/Nietzsche*, trans. Stephen Taubeneck, pp. 148–49 (Stanford, CA: Stanford University Press, 1991).

12. Wilhelm Dilthey, *Selected Writings*, p. 258.

13. See E. D. Hirsch, *Validity in Interpretation* (New York: Yale University Press, 1967).

14. Behler notes that Schlegel and Novalis understood the relationship between philosophy and poetry as a reciprocal interaction [*Wechselwirkung*] not based on subjugation of one to the other but rather on "a full maintenance of the mutual tension between the two poles." See *German Romantic Literary Theory*, p. 193.

15. Richard A. Lanham, *The Motives of Eloquence*, p. 3.

16. *Kritische Friedrich-Schlegel-Ausgabe*, Vol. 2: *Charakteristiken und Kritiken I (1796–1801)*, ed. Hans Eichner (1967), p. 285; "Friedrich Schlegel: Dialogue on Poesy (1799)," in Jochen Schulte-Sasse, *Theory as Practice*, p. 181.

17. M. M. Bakhtin, *The Dialogic Imagination*, p. 25. Hereafter abbreviated *DI*.

18. This form of interpretation can be thought of, in the words of Geoffrey Hartman, as "a labor that aims not to overcome the negative or indeterminate but to stay within it as long as necessary." See *Criticism in the Wilderness: The Study of Literature Today* (New Haven: Yale University Press, 1980), p. 270.

19. At times Behler's assessment appears to muffle Schlegel's intuitive Shandyism. In *German Romantic Literary Theory*, he argues that Schlegel's hermeneutics seeks a progressive clarification of the author's meaning, seeks "the correction of confusion" followed by the "comprehension of the principles of confusion . . . the last and most complex act [of understanding]" (279). However, I see (or want to see) Schlegel's deliberate recovery (acknowledgement) of chaos in the *Fragments* as more philosophically aimless, digressive, even arguably opposed to "clarification" as the aim or point of hermeneutics.

20. *Kritische Friedrich-Schlegel-Ausgabe*, Vol. 2: *Charakteristiken und Kritiken I (1796–1801)*, ed. Hans Eichner (1967), pp. 363–72; *Friedrich Schlegel's Lucinda and the Fragments*, pp. 259–71. Useful discussions of the essay include Cathy Comstock, "'Transcendental Buffoonery': Irony as Process in Schlegel's '*Über die Unverständlichkeit*,'" in *Studies in Romanticism* 26 (Fall 1987): 445–64; Georgia Albert, "Understanding Irony: Three Essais on Friedrich Schlegel," *Modern Language Notes*, Vol. 108, No. 5, Comparative Literature (December, 1993): 825–848; and Michel Chaouli, *The Laboratory of Poetry: Chemistry and Poetics in the Works of Friedrich Schlegel*, pp. 18-36 (Baltimore and London: Johns Hopkins University Press, 2002).

21. M. M. Bakhtin, *Speech Genres and Other Late Essays*, trans. Vern W. McGee (Austin: University of Texas Press, 1986), p. 141.

22. In *The First Hundred Years of Mikhail Bakhtin* (Princeton, NJ: Princeton University Press, 1997), Caryl Emerson reinforces the assumption that in addition to the well-known ideas of carnival and dialogue, the outside or outsideness constitutes a major idea in Bakhtin's thinking about aesthetics, ethics, and the novel. Emerson reads Bakhtin as insisting on an ethical dimension in art, a reading that moves Bakhtin closer to the company of thinkers like Blanchot and Levinas in recent debates concerning the ethical constitution, or appeal, of the work of art. Although it must be noted that Bakhtin's outside remains within a more or less modern and pluralistic conceptual framework, while for Blanchot and Levinas the outside or the neutral haunts, and represents a threat to, such a framework: it is elsewhere entirely. For a discussion of these matters, see Alain Toumayan, *Encountering the Other: The Artwork and the Problem of Difference in Blanchot and Levinas* (Pittsburgh, PA: Duquesne University Press, 2004). As Emerson notes, "Russian scholars who have worked on this idea . . . properly see it as the common denominator between Bakhtin's ethics and his aesthetics . . ." (207). This is a key point. I would argue that for Bakhtin the work of art teaches ethics, though perhaps not in the sense of a coherent moral or ethical set or rules or prescriptions, but rather in the sense

that works of art, like ethical dilemmas, expose one to the outside, where no rule or proscription will suffice to tell one how to act. See also Donald G. Marshall's response to the legendary Gadamer-Derrida encounter: "Dialogue and Écriture," in *Dialogue and Deconstruction*, ed. Diane P. Michelfelder and Richard E. Palmer, pp. 206–14 (Albany: State University of New York Press, 1989). In a provocative commentary, Marshall explores the elusive confrontation between hermeneutics and deconstruction through the lenses of the writings of Bakhtin and Blanchot, locating a fascinating nexus of dialogic cross-fertilization.

23. Gadamer tries to get at just this internally comprehensible (self-intelligible) dimension of language when he writes:

> But there is another dialectic of the word, which accords to every word an inner dimension of multiplication: every word breaks forth as if from a center and is related to a whole, through which alone it is a word. Every word causes the whole of the language to which it belongs to resonate and the whole world-view that underlies it to appear. Thus every word, as the event of a moment, carries with it the unsaid, to which it is related by responding and summoning. (TM 458)

Here is language as a secret society in which every word echoes every other word or carries within it a slight resemblance to every word it is possible to speak or hear, so that when one word sounds, every other word resounds, answering the initial sounding of the first word (itself perhaps an echo). One could call or think of this ongoing riot of sounding words the infinite conversation of language, a language poem that is constantly going on, constantly ringing, only the human desire for sense or intelligibility prevents us from lending it an ear.

24. Schlegel's notion of language is inextricably tied to the notion, or rather the work, of fragmentation. Blanchot describes Nietzsche's fragmentary writing in a way that illuminates Schlegel's fragmentary practice. "The first knowledge," writes Blanchot, "is knowledge of the tearing apart—the breaking up— of Dionysus, that obscure experience wherein becoming is disclosed in relation with the discontinuous and as its play. The fragmentation of the god is not the rash renunciation of unity, nor a unity that remains one by becoming plural. Fragmentation is this god himself . . ." (*EI* 235; *IC* 157).

25. Søren Kierkegaard, *The Concept of Irony: With Continual Reference to Socrates, together with Notes of Schelling's Berlin Lectures*, trans. Howard V. Hong and Edna H. Hong (Princeton, NJ: Princeton University Press, 1989), p. 324.

Chapter 3. Nothing so Difficult as a Beginning: Byron's Pilgrimage to the Origin of the Work of Art and the Inspiration of Exile

1. Henry Taylor, "Preface to *Philip Van Artevelde* (1834)," in *Byron: The Critical Heritage*, ed. Andrew Rutherford, pp. 325–29 (London: Routledge and Kegan Paul, 1970), p. 327.

2. Eliot famously wrote: "Of Byron one can say, as of no other English poet of his eminence, that he added nothing to the language, that he discovered nothing in the sounds, and developed nothing in the meaning, of individual words." T. S. Eliot, *On Poetry and Poets* (London: Faber and Faber, 1957), pp. 200–01. One of my aims in this chapter is to trace Byron's attentiveness to a poetic experience of nothingness that Eliot was, for whatever reasons, unable to fathom. On this issue, see Peter J. Manning's essay, "*Don Juan* and Byron's Imperceptiveness to the English Word," in *Reading Romantics: Texts and Contexts*, pp. 115–44 (New York: Oxford University Press, 1990). On the shortcomings of New Critical readings of romantic poetry generally, with some discussion of T. S. Eliot, see Richard H. Fogle, "Romantic Bards and Metaphysical Reviewers," *English Literary History* 12 (1945): 221–50. This essay is reprinted in Robert F. Gleckner and Gerald E. Enscoe, eds., *Romanticism: Points of View*, pp. 151–67 (Englewood Cliffs, NJ: Prentice-Hall, 1962).

3. See George M. Ridenour, *The Style of Don Juan* (New Haven, CT: Yale University Press, 1960); Edward E. Bostetter, *The Romantic Ventriloquists: Wordsworth, Coleridge, Keats, Shelley, Byron* (1963; Seattle, WA and London: University of Washington Press, 1976); Brian Wilkie, *Romantic Poets and Epic Tradition* (Madison, WI: University of Wisconsin Press, 1965); Robert F. Gleckner, *Byron and the Ruins of Paradise* (Baltimore, MD: Johns Hopkins University Press, 1967); Jerome J. McGann, *Fiery Dust: Byron's Poetic Development* (Chicago and London: University of Chicago Press, 1968); and Michael G. Cooke, *The Blind Man Traces the Circle: On the Patterns and Philosophy of Byron's Poetry* (Princeton, NJ: Princeton University Press, 1969).

4. On the myth of the Fall, see Ridenour, *The Style of Don Juan*, pp. 19–50. For studies more systematically concerned with history, see Jerome J. McGann, "The Book of Byron and the Book of the World," in *The Beauty of Inflections: Literary Investigations in Historical Method and Theory*, pp. 255–93 (Oxford: Clarendon Press, 1988) and Jerome Christensen, *Lord Byron's Strength: Romantic Writing and Commercial Society* (Baltimore and London: Johns Hopkins University Press, 1992). More recently, Jane Stabler has navigated a way between poetics and historicism in *Byron, Poetics and History* (Cambridge: Cambridge University Press, 2002).

5. My starting point for such a reading is Anne K. Mellor's *English Romantic Irony*. See also Hermione de Almeida, *Byron and Joyce through Homer: Don Juan and Ulysses* (London and Basingstoke: Macmillan, 1981) and Frederick Garber, *Self, Text, and Romantic Irony: The Example of Byron* (Princeton, NJ: Princeton University Press, 1988). Although some criticize Mellor—particularly Jerome J. McGann in *The Romantic Ideology*—her book nonetheless repays repeated readings. See Mellor's subsequent review of *The Romantic Ideology* in *Studies in Romanticism* 25 (Summer 1986): 182-86, in which she counters McGann's critique of the romantic ideology by appealing to Bakhtin. The

force of Mellor's response registers in McGann's subsequent work as, for example, in *Black Riders: The Visible Language of Modernism* (Princeton, NJ: Princeton University Press, 1993). Following Mellor, other critics have confirmed the value of Bakhtin's thought for reading Byron. See Michael Makovski, "Byron, Bakhtin, and the Translation of History," in *Rereading Byron: Essays Selected From Hofstra University's Byron Bicentennial Conference*, ed. Alice Levine and Robert N. Keane, pp. 21–42 (New York and London: Garland, 1993). In the same volume, Suzanne Ferriss employs Bakhtin and Kristeva to argue that Byron rejected "both Juvenal and Horace as models in favor of the competing tradition of Menippean satire" on his way to becoming the Byron of *Don Juan* (133). See "Romantic Carnivalesque: Byron's *The Tale of Calil, Beppo*, and *Don Juan*," pp. 133–49. See also Philip W. Martin, "Reading *Don Juan* with Bakhtin," in Nigel Wood, ed., *Don Juan*, Theory and Practice Series, pp. 92-118 (Buckingham: Open University Press, 1993).

6. Elizabeth French Boyd, *Byron's* Don Juan*: A Critical Study* (New Brunswick, NJ: Rutgers University Press, 1945), p. vi.

7. For a detailed exploration of this dimension of Bakhtin, see Ken Hirschkop, *Mikhail Bakhtin: An Aesthetic for Democracy* (Oxford: Oxford University Press, 2000).

8. Cf. Margaret Anne Doody's *The True Story of the Novel* for an erudite and lively revisionist discussion that locates the novel's origins in Greek and Latin antiquity. Challenging conventional wisdom that identifies the novel's origins in a turn from romance toward realism during the 17th and 18th centuries, Doody argues for a longer, more multicultural, and more continuous, tradition than has previously been available.

9. See Bernard le Bovier de Fontenelle, *Conversations on the Plurality of Worlds*, trans. H. A. Hargreaves (Berkeley, CA: University of California Press, 1990). Hargreaves bases this translation on the first French edition: *Entretiens sue la pluralité des mondes* (Paris: C. Blagart, 1686). See also Hargreaves, Translator's Preface, in *Conversations on the Plurality of Worlds*, pp. xxxiii-xlix, especially Choice of the Edition, pp. xlii–xliv.

10. Lord Byron, *The Complete Poetical Works*, ed. Jerome J. McGann, 7 vols. (Oxford: The Clarendon Press, 1980–86), Vol. 5, p. 69. Subsequent citations from *Childe Harold's Pilgrimage* and *Don Juan* refer to canto and stanza number(s). Citations from *The Giaour* refer to page numbers, while citations from *Manfred* refer to act, scene, and line number(s). All other citations from the poetry refer to *CPW* volume and page number(s). *Byron's Letters and Journals*, 12 vols., ed. Leslie A. Marchand (Cambridge, MA: Belknap Press, 1973–82) are abbreviated *BLJ* followed by volume and page number(s).

11. Edward Said, "Intellectual Exile: Expatriates and Marginals," in *The Edward Said Reader*, ed. Moustafa Bayoumi and Andrew Rubin, pp. 368–81 (New York: Vintage, 2000), p. 373.

12. Martin Heidegger, *Sein und Zeit*, p. 236; *Being and Time: A Translation of* Sein und Zeit, pp. 219-20. In this particular passage Stambaugh does not translate Heidegger's neologism describing historically situated concrete human existence, literally "There-being," but leaves it in the original German.

13. Julia Kristeva, *Desire in Language*, p. 65.

14. Julia Kristeva, *Revolution in Poetic Language*, trans. Margaret Waller (New York: Columbia University Press, 1984), p. 109.

15. Jane Stabler, *Byron, Poetics and History*, p. 2.

16. John Watkins, "Byron and the Phenomenology of Negation," in *Studies in Romanticism* 29 (Fall 1990): 395-411. For a fuller discussion of "*Negativität*," see Julia Kristeva, *Revolution in Poetic Language*, pp. 107-64. Note Kristeva's care in discriminating among negation [*Negation*], nothingness [*Nichts*] and negativity [*Negativität*], pp. 109-13. See also Sanford Budick and Wolfgang Iser, eds., *Languages of the Unsayable: The Play of Negativity in Literature and Literary Theory* (New York: Columbia University Press, 1989).

17. See Frederick L. Shilstone, *Byron and the Myth of Tradition*, pp. 1–41 (Lincoln and London: University of Nebraska Press, 1988).

18. As Jerome Christensen points out in *Lord Byron's Strength*, Jerome J. McGann, "Byron's best modern critic, revived the standard of sincerity and with it the genteel definition of Romantic poetry [in his 1989 essay "Lord Byron's Twin Opposites of Truth"]" (xiii). See McGann, "Lord Byron's Twin Opposites of Truth," in *Towards a Literature of Knowledge*, pp. 38–64 (Chicago: University of Chicago Press, 1989).

19. Jerome J. McGann, *Fiery Dust*, pp. 31–36.

20. M. K. Joseph, *Byron the Poet* (London: Victor Gollancz, 1964), p. 14.

21. Jerome J. McGann, "The Book of Byron and the Book of the World," p. 262.

22. Jane Austen, *Persuasion* (New York: Alfred A. Knopf, 1992), p. 98.

23. See, for example, Paul Elledge, *Lord Byron at Harrow School: Speaking Out, Talking Back, Acting Up, Bowing Out* (Baltimore, MD and London: Johns Hopkins University Press, 2000).

24. Byron's description of Manfred's insomnia anticipates in an uncanny way the thought of Emmanuel Levinas and Maurice Blanchot regarding the

solitude of existence. See Levinas, *Time and the Other; and additional essays*, trans. Richard A. Cohen, esp. pp. 42-57 (Pittsburgh, PA: Duquesne University Press, 1987) and Blanchot, *The Space of Literature*, trans. Ann Smock, esp. pp. 21–34 (Lincoln, NE: University of Nebraska Press, 1982). For the original texts, see Levinas, *Le Temps et l'autre* (1947; St. Clement, France: Fata Morgana, 1979) and Blanchot, *L'Espace litteraire* (Paris: Éditions Gallimard, 1955).

25. William Wordsworth, *Poetical Works; With Introduction and Notes*, ed. Thomas Hutchinson, A New Edition, rev. Ernest de Selincourt (1904; Oxford and New York: Oxford University Press, 1936), p. 377.

26. Stanley Cavell, *Must We Mean What We Say? A Book of Essays* (1969; Cambridge: Cambridge University Press, 2002), p. 324.

27. Moyra Haslett, *Byron's* Don Juan *and the Don Juan Legend* (Oxford: Oxford University Press, 1997).

28. In *Byron's* Don Juan *and the Don Juan Legend*, Haslett "question[s] the portrayal of Byron's Don Juan as the victim of seduction in considering the poem from an explicitly feminist perspective, a skeptical reading which has much in common with the suspicious interpretations typical of the poem's initial reception" (232).

29. See Thomas Carl Wall, *Radical Passivity: Levinas, Blanchot, and Agamben* (Albany: State University of New York Press, 1999).

30. McGann relies on Wittgenstein's notion of language-games in *Don Juan in Context* (Chicago and London: University of Chicago Press, 1976). My reading of Byron owes much to McGann's emphasis on the everyday and the ordinary, along with a similar emphasis in the writings of Wordsworth, Bakhtin, and Cavell. On the last of these, see especially "Epilogue: The *Investigations'* Everyday Aesthetics of Itself," in *The Cavell Reader*, ed. Stephen Mulhall, pp. 369–89 (Oxford: Blackwell, 1996). Cavell's juxtaposition of Wittgenstein and Schlegel is particularly suggestive.

31. This a feature of the poem explored in Jane Stabler's *Byron, Poetics and History*, esp. pp. 106-35. One should also consult Philip W. Martin, *Byron: A Poet Before His Public* (Cambridge: Cambridge University Press, 1982).

32. Geoffrey H. Hartman, *Criticism in the Wilderness: The Study of Literature Today* (New Haven and London: Yale University Press, 1980), p. 143.

33. *The Portable Hannah Arendt*, ed. Peter Baehr (New York: Penguin Books, 2000), pp. 457, 459.

34. Georges Bataille, *Visions of Excess: Selected Writings, 1927–1939*, ed. Allan Stoekl, trans. Stoekl, Carl R, Lovitt and Donald M. Leslie, Jr. (Minneapolis: University of Minnesota Press, 1985), p. 118.

Chapter 4. Narrative and Its Discontents; or, The Novel as Fragmentary Work: Joyce at the Limits of Romantic Poetry

1. References to Joyce are keyed to the following editions: *Ulysses: The Corrected Text*, ed. Hans Walter Gabler with Wolfhard Steppe and Claus Melchior (New York: Vintage Books, 1986), abbreviated *U* and cited by chapter and line number(s); *Finnegans Wake* (1939; Harmondsworth: Penguin Books, 1999), abbreviated *FW* and cited by page and line number(s); *A Portrait of the Artist as a Young Man*, ed. Seamus Deane (1916; Harmondsworth: Penguin Books, 1993), abbreviated *P* and cited by page number(s).

2. T. S. Eliot, "*Ulysses*, Order and Myth," *Dial* 75 (November 1923): 480–83.

3. Stuart Gilbert, *James Joyce's* Ulysses: *A Study* (1930; New York: Vintage, 1955). See especially the diagram of the narrative episodes included on p. 30. See also Frank Budgen, *James Joyce and the Making of* Ulysses (1934; Bloomington: Indiana University Press, 1960).

4. See Neil R. Davidson, *James Joyce,* Ulysses, *and the Construction of Jewish Identity: Culture, Biography, and 'the Jew' in Modernist Europe* (Cambridge: Cambridge University Press, 1998). For a pair of studies that further develop the issue of Otherness as it pertains in Joyce's works, see Vincent J. Cheng, *Joyce, Race, and Empire* (Cambridge: Cambridge University Press, 1995) and Joseph Valente, *James Joyce and the Problem of Justice: Negotiating Sexual and Colonial Difference* (Cambridge: Cambridge University Press, 1995). See also Brian W. Shaffer, "James Joyce and the Problem of Otherness," in *Modern Philology*, Vol. 95, No. 2 (November, 1997): 218–30.

5. For another, somewhat different, view of Joyce's indebtedness to romantic poetics, see Ginette Verstraete, *Fragments of the Feminine Sublime in Friedrich Schlegel and James Joyce* (Albany: State University Press of New York: 1998). Verstraete's book is perhaps especially interesting for the ways in which its exploration of the feminine sublime intersect with recent work on both Byron and Joyce that revolves around the issue of gender. While I agree with much of what Verstraete has to say, and find her book fascinating, my focus is not so much on the sublime *per se* as on the ordinary and the everyday, on the capacity of the non-dramatic negativity of the fragmentary work to disclose things as they are.

6. See "The Villanova Roundtable: A Conversation with Jacques Derrida," in *Deconstruction in a Nutshell: A Conversation with Jacques Derrida*, ed. and with a Commentary by John D. Caputo, pp. 3–28 (New York: Fordham University Press, 1997), esp. pp. 25–28. See also "Re-Joyce, Say "Yes," pp. 181–200.

7. Jacques Derrida, *L'écriture et la différence* (Paris: Éditions du Seuil, 1967), pp. 227–28; *Writing and Difference*, trans. Alan Bass (Chicago: University of Chicago Press, 1978), p. 153.

8. See Jacques Derrida, "Two Words for Joyce," trans. Geoff Bennington, in Derek Attridge and Daniel Ferrer, eds., *Post-Structuralist Joyce: Essays from the French*, pp. 145–59 (Cambridge: Cambridge University Press, 1984), p. 149. Originally read as a paper at the Centre Georges Pompidou in Paris in 1982, a French text later appeared as part of *Ulysse Gramophone. Deux mots pour Joyce* (Paris: Éditions Galilée, 1987). For a lucid discussion of Derrida's influence on Joyce's reception in France, see Geert Lernout, *The French Joyce* (Ann Arbor: University of Michigan Press, 1990). For some of the most penetrating thought on the confluence of the writings of Derrida and Joyce, see Derek Attridge, *Peculiar Language: Literature as Difference from the Renaissance to James Joyce* (Ithaca, NY: Cornell University Press, 1988) and *Joyce Effects: On Language, Theory, and History* (Cambridge: Cambridge University Press, 2000). See also *The Cambridge Companion to James Joyce*, ed. Derek Attridge (Cambridge: Cambridge University Press, 1990), especially the essays by Attridge, Seamus Deane, Klaus Reichert, and Jean-Michel Rabaté. Reichert's essay, "The European Background of Joyce's Writing," pp. 55–82, is especially interesting for its discussion of Joyce's early encounter with Nietzsche.

9. Hugh Kenner, *Joyce's Voices* (Berkeley, CA: University of California Press, 1978), pp. 41–42.

10. Stuart Gilbert, *James Joyce's* Ulysses, p. 76.

11. See Martin Heidegger, "Was ist Metaphysik?," in *Wegmarken*, pp. 1–19 (Frankfurt am Main: Vittorio Klostermann Verlag, 1967); "What Is Metaphysics?," in *Basic Writings: From* Being and Time *(1927) to* The Task of Thinking *(1964)*, ed. David Farrell Krell, pp. 89–110 (New York: HarperCollins, 1993).

12. Emmanuel Levinas, "La realité et son ombre," in *Les Tempes Moderne*, Vol. 38 (1948): 771–89, p. 774; "Reality and Its Shadow," in *The Levinas Reader*, ed. Seán Hand, pp. 129–43 (Oxford: Blackwell, 1989), p. 131.

13. See Hugh Kenner, *Ulysses*, rev. ed. (1980; Baltimore and London: Johns Hopkins University Press, 1987), p. 57.

14. Nietzsche, *Sämtliche Werke. Kritische Studienausgabe in 15 Bänden*, ed. G. Colli and M. Montinari (Berlin: de Gruyter, 1980), Vol. 4: *Also sprach Zarathustra*, p. 49. Hereafter abbreviated *ASZ*. *Thus Spoke Zarathustra: A Book for None and All*, trans. Walter Kaufmann (Harmondsworth: Penguin Books, 1978), pp. 40–41. Hereafter abbreviated *TSZ*.

15. Although it is impossible to say with certainty how much Nietzsche Joyce actually read, Richard Ellmann lists three volumes of Nietzsche's writings, including *The Birth of Tragedy*, that were part of the library Joyce left behind him in Trieste when he moved to Paris in 1920. See Ellmann, *The Consciousness of Joyce*, pp. 97–134 (Toronto and New York: Oxford University Press, 1977). See also Michael Patrick Gillespie, *Inverted Volumes Improperly Arranged: James Joyce and His Trieste Library* (Ann Arbor, MI: UMI Research Press, 1983) and Gillespie, with the assistance of Erik Bradford Stocker, *James Joyce's Trieste Library: A Catalogue of Materials at the Harry Ransom Humanities Center* (Austin, TX: HRC, 1986).

16. Friedrich Nietzsche, *Sämtliche Werke*, Vol. 1: *Die Geburt der Tragödie. Unzeitgemässe Betrachtungen* I-IV, p. 25, hereafter abbreviated *GT. The Birth of Tragedy and Other Writings*, trans. Ronald Speirs (Cambridge: Cambridge University Press, 1999), p. 14, hereafter abbreviated *BT*.

17. Friedrich Nietzsche, *Sämtliche Werke*, Vol. 1: *Die Geburt der Tragödie. Unzeitgemässe Betrachtungen* I-IV, p. 314. *Unfashionable Observations*, trans. Richard T. Gray (Stanford, CA: Stanford University Press, 1995), p. 148.

18. For an illuminating look at this tension between seriousness and play, see Robert H. Bell, *Jocoserious Joyce: The Fate of Folly in* Ulysses (1991; Gainesville, FL: University Press of Florida, 1996).

19. Julia Kristeva, "Within the Microcosm of the 'Talking Cure'," in Joseph H. Smith and William Kerrigan, eds., *Interpreting Lacan* (New Haven: Yale University Press, 1983), pp. 35–36.

20. See Alasdair MacIntyre, *After Virtue: A Study in Moral Theory*, 2nd ed. (1981; Notre Dame, IN: University of Notre Dame Press, 1984), esp. pp. 109–20.

21. Robert H. Deming, ed., *James Joyce: The Critical Heritage*, 2 vols. (New York: Barnes and Noble, 1970) 2: 673.

22. Robert H. Deming, ed., *James Joyce*, 2: 694.

23. Robert H. Deming, ed., *James Joyce*, 2: 700–01.

24. Julia Kristeva, "Within the Microcosm of the 'Talking Cure'," pp. 37–38.

25. See Gilles Deleuze, "Pensée nomade," in *Nietzsche aujourd'hui* (Paris: Union Générale d'Editions, 1973).

26. Stuart Gilbert, ed., *Letters of James Joyce* (New York: Viking Press, 1957), p. 318.

27. Julia Kristeva, "Within the Microcosm of the 'Talking Cure'," p. 42 and p. 34.

Chapter 5. From the Fragmentary Work to the Fragmentary Imperative: Blanchot and the Quest for Passage to the Outside

1. In referring to this opposition, I follow Kevin Hart's distinction between the fragment and the fragmentary in *Postmodernism: A Beginner's Guide* (Oxford: Oneworld, 2004), pp. 67–86. More specifically, one can frame the distinction as one between the fragmentary *work* [*oeuvre*] and the fragmentary *imperative* [*exigence*]. The fragmentary *work* is a discrete work that remains incomplete or unfinished, even by design, while the fragmentary *imperative* exceeds the opposition between the work and the absence of the work, whole and part, totality and infinity, narrative and lyric, and invites one to confront what remains unthought in thinking.

The opposition stems ultimately from Heidegger's transition in his later writings from thinking about poetry in terms of *Poesie* or literary work to thinking about poetry in terms of *Dichtung* or a thickening of speech in which the truth of things discloses itself as an uncontainable event. Blanchot develops this distinction in the essay "Literature and the Right to Death" when he refers to the "two slopes [*deux versants*] of literature." See *La part du feu* (Paris: Éditions Gallimard, 1949), p. 318; *The Work of Fire*, trans. Charlotte Mandell (Stanford, CA: Stanford University Press, 1995), p. 330. For a succinct discussion of this distinction as it applies to Derrida's conception of literature, see Gerald L. Bruns, rev. of *Derrida, Heidegger, Blanchot: Sources of Derrida's Notion and Practice of Literature* [Cambridge: Cambridge University Press, 1995], by Timothy Clark in *Modern Philology*, Vol. 92, No. 4 (May, 1995): 533–37. Bruns writes:

> Clark's achievement is to address just this extraordinarily difficult question of the relationship between *Dichtung* and *Poesie*, or between what Blanchot calls the "two slopes [*deux versants*] of literature." This relationship is best conceived as the space between literature as an event and literature as a text. Clark's insight, clarified incisively in each chapter, is that dialogue is the form for traversing this space. . . . Dialogue is radically nonsubjective, or heteronomic. However, dialogue should be thought of not in terms of the Platonic agon but rather along lines suggested by Blanchot's account of fascination, in which we are drawn out of the place of subjectivity by the alterity of the image. (536)

2. See Coleridge's account of his life in *Biographia Literaria: or, Biographical Sketches of My Literary Life and Opinions*, ed. James Engell and W. Jackson Bate (Princeton, NJ: Princeton University Press, 1984), as well as that of biographer Richard Holmes in *Coleridge: Early Visions, 1772–1804* (1989; New York: Pantheon, 1999) and *Coleridge: Darker Reflections, 1804–1834* (1998; New York: Pantheon, 1999). It is telling that one of Coleridge's most enduring legacies is his marginalia. See, for example, Coleridge, *A Book I Value: Selected Marginalia*, ed. H. J. Jackson (Princeton, NJ: Princeton University Press, 2003) and, for a unique and stimulating look at the persistence of marginalia throughout history, see H. J. Jackson, *Marginalia: Readers Writing in Books* (New Haven and London:

Yale University Press, 2001). Finally, it is John Beer's estimation that "[a]s [Coleridge] tried to satisfy his various intellectual and emotional needs, his thinking was not only caught into [sic] fragmentary modes but began to generate writing that was itself riven, particularly in its poetic expression. In his work the concept of the 'Romantic fragment' comes into its own." See Beer, "Fragmentations and Ironies," in *Questioning Romanticism*, p. 237.

3. Fontenelle, *Conversations on the Plurality of Worlds*, p. vii.

4. Two features of the thinking Fontenelle espouses that would certainly have drawn fire from his contemporaries are (1) the ease with which skepticism is woven into and is necessary for thinking; and (2) the role played by the female, the way she gets the upper hand on occasion, the flirtatious atmosphere sustained throughout.

5. Fontenelle, *Conversations on the Plurality of Worlds*, p. 11.

6. Fontenelle, *Conversations on the Plurality of Worlds*, p. 9.

7. Kevin Hart, *The Dark Gaze: Maurice Blanchot and the Sacred* (Chicago and London: University of Chicago, 2004). See also Gerald L. Bruns, *Maurice Blanchot: The Refusal of Philosophy* (Baltimore and London: Johns Hopkins University Press, 1997) and Marlène Zarader, *L'être et le neuter: À partir de Maurice Blanchot* (Lagrasse: Verdier, 2001).

8. See Timothy Clark, "Modern Transformations of German Romanticism: Blanchot and Derrida on the Fragment, the Aphorism and the Architectural," in *Paragraph* 15.3 (1992): 232–47. See also Clark, "Contradictory Passion: Inspiration in Blanchot's *The Space of Literature* (1955)," in *The Theory of Inspiration: Composition as a Crisis of Subjectivity in Romantic and Post-Romantic Writing*, pp. 238–58 (Manchester and New York: Manchester University Press, 1997).

9. See G. W. F. Hegel, *Phenomenology of Spirit*, trans. A. V. Miller (Oxford: Oxford University Press, 1977), pp. 50–51. See also Sandford Budick's Introduction to *Languages of the Unsayable*, which discusses the ubiquity of negativity in modern literature and literary theory. For insight into the debate concerning negativity and deconstruction and how negativity in the latter may or may not share family resemblances with negative theology, see Jacques Derrida, "How to Avoid Speaking: Denials," in *Languages of the Unsayable*, pp. 3–70. The essay originally appeared as "Comment ne pas parler: Dénégations," in *Psyché: Inventions de l'autre*, pp. 535–95 (Paris: Galilée, 1987). See also Kevin Hart's engagement with Derrida in his essay "The God Effect," in *The Trespass of the Sign: Deconstruction, Theology and Philosophy*, pp. 271–98 (1989; New York: Fordham University Press, 2000).

10. See Michael Newman, "The Trace of Trauma: Blindness, Testimony and the Gaze in Blanchot and Derrida," Carolyn Bailey Gill, ed., *Maurice*

Blanchot: The Demand of Writing, pp. 153–73 (London and New York: Routledge, 1996). See also a remarkable essay by Sanford Budick, "Of The Fragment," in *Common Knowledge*, Vol. 5, No. 3 (Winter 1996): 118–140. Budick reflects on the multiple layers of biblical phrases—fragments—cited on the tomb of the famous Rabbi Loew of Prague (associated in Jewish tradition with the legend of the golem) and subsequently inscribed on the tomb of his own fifteen-year-old son upon his untimely death.

11. For a survey of writings on the new Nietzsche, as well as a few select essays on the old one, see David B. Allison, ed., *The New Nietzsche: Contemporary Styles of Interpretation* (1977; Cambridge, MA and London: MIT Press, 1985). In *Confrontations*, Ernst Behler deals with the ways in which Derrida's new Nietzsche challenges Heidegger's old Nietzsche and with some of the consequences of this challenge. In *The Other Nietzsche* (Albany: State University of New York Press, 1994), Joan Stambaugh, not satisfied with either the old Nietzsche or the new, attempts to "explore . . . a Nietzsche relatively untouched by [either] of these interpretations." A third Nietzsche, if you will. "It is not the whole of Nietzsche by any means," Stambaugh admits; "but it is there. I shall call the other Nietzsche: *Nietzsche the poetic mystic*" (ix).

12. Ernst Behler provides an overview of Blanchot's reading of Nietzsche in *Confrontations*, pp. 13–15. Behler provides a nice summary of Blanchot's view: "Of course, Blanchot argued, we can reorganize Nietzsche's contradictions coherently, especially if we arrange them in a hierarchical, dialectical, or Hegelian manner to facilitate a coherent reading. But even if we assume such a continuous discourse as the background for Nietzsche's discontinuous writings, we sense Nietzsche's dissatisfaction with that. His discourse is always already a step ahead of itself. He shelters his philosophy by exhibiting and formulating it in a completely different language, a language no longer assured of the whole, but consisting of fragments, conflicting points, and division" (14).

13. For Blanchot's account of how Nietzsche's sister tried to create for her brother in death the great philosopher's reputation that he lacked during his life by arranging for the publication of *The Will to Power*, see *The Infinite Conversation*, pp. 136–38. Blanchot's criticism of Mme. Forster-Nietzsche's creation of *The Will to Power* is sharp. Blanchot insists in *The Infinite Conversation* that in view of Mme. Forster-Nietzsche's interference, "*The Will to Power* is therefore not Nietzsche's book. It is a work fabricated by its editors and it is a false work, in the sense that what Nietzsche had written at various moments over the course of years traversed by the most diverse intentions, without order or system, is represented to us as the material of a systematic work that he had prepared and intended as such. . . . It sets before us fortuitous notes from which no one had the right to create a whole" (*IC* 137–38). For a view of Blanchot's ambivalence about Heidegger's reading of Nietzsche, see Michael Holland,

"'A Wound to Thought'," pp. 174–89 in Carolyn Bailey Gill, ed., *Maurice Blanchot*.

14. See Frank Kermode's noteworthy but somewhat disappointing assessment of Blanchot in *History and Value: The Clarendon Lectures and the Northcliffe Lectures* (Oxford: Clarendon Press, 1988). The lecture dealing with Blanchot, "Fragments and Ruins," pp. 128-46, is disappointing mainly because it assumes that anarchy is an action taken by solitary human subjects, like terrorists, rather than a way for things to be what they are. For a different, non-subjective, view of anarchy, see Reiner Schürmann, *Heidegger on Being and Acting: From Principles to Anarchy*, trans. Christine-Marie Gros in Collaboration with the Author (Bloomington: Indiana University Press, 1986). For a reading of Blanchot that stresses his anarchism, see Gerald L. Bruns, "Anarchic Temporality: Writing, Friendship, and the Ontology of the Work of Art in Maurice Blanchot's Poetics," in Kevin Hart and Geoffrey H. Hartman, eds., *The Power of Contestation: Perspectives on Maurice Blanchot*, pp. 121–40 (Baltimore and London: The Johns Hopkins University Press, 2004).

15. For a good account of what Blanchot means by the "disaster," see Gerald L. Bruns, *Maurice Blanchot*, pp. 207–34. As Bruns memorably puts it, "The disaster is a concept [sic] of exteriority rather than of catastrophe" (210).

16. See Hans-George Gadamer, "The Problem of Historical Consciousness," in Paul Rabinow and William M. Sullivan, eds., *Interpretive Social Science: A Second Look*, pp. 82–140 (Berkeley and Los Angeles, CA: University of California Press, 1987).

17. See Paul Davies's essay on Blanchot's relationship with Levinas, "Difficult Friendship," in *Research in Phenomenology*, Vol. 18 (1988): 149–72. See also Anne-Lise Schulte Nordholt, *Maurice Blanchot: L'écriture comme expérience du dehors* (Genève: Droz, 1995), esp. pp. 337–65.

Index